ROLLING THE IRON DICE

Recent Titles in
Contributions in Military Studies

ROLLING THE IRON DICE

Historical Analogies and Decisions to Use Military Force in Regional Contingencies

Scot Macdonald

Contributions in Military Studies, Number 199

GREENWOOD PRESS
Westport, Connecticut • London

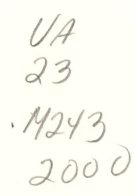

Library of Congress Cataloging-in-Publication Data

Macdonald, Scot, 1966-
   Rolling the iron dice : historical analogies and decisions to use military force in
regional contingencies / Scot Macdonald.
         p. cm—(Contributions in military studies, ISSN 0883-6884 ; no. 199)
      Includes bibliographical references and index.
      ISBN 0-313-31421-7 (alk. paper)
      1. United States—Military policy. 2. Great Britain—Military policy. 3. United
States—Foreign relations—1945-1989. 4. Great Britain—Foreign relations—1945–
I. Title. II.   Series.
   UA23.M243 2000   99-462359

British Library Cataloguing in Publication Data is available.

Library of Congress Catalog Card Number: 99–462359
ISBN: 0-313-31421-7
ISSN: 0883-6884

First published in 2000

Greenwood Press, 88 Post Road West, Westport, CT 06881
An imprint of Greenwood Publishing Group, Inc.
www.greenwood.com

Printed in the United States of America

The paper used in this book complies with the
Permanent Paper Standard issued by the National
Information Standards Organization (Z39.48–1984).

10 9 8 7 6 5 4 3 2 1

Dedicated to Aurora—we were together seven years, I'll remember you forever.

"If the iron dice must roll, may God help us."

—Theobold von Bethmann-Hollweg
German Chancellor, August 1, 1914

Contents

Preface

Leaders have long recognized the importance of history, both as a guide to the present and as a rhetorical device. The Greek historian Polybius wrote, "For it is history, and history alone, which, without involving us in actual danger, will mature our judgement and prepare us to take right views, whatever may be the crisis or the posture of affairs."[1] The Roman statesman Cicero wrote, "History is the witness that testifies to the passing of time; it illuminates reality, vitalizes memory, provides guidance in daily life, and brings us tidings of antiquity."[2]

When leaders face foreign policy crises, they often use historical analogies to draw lessons from the past to help them set a course in the uncertain and turbulent waters of international diplomacy. Even though history does not provide specific lessons for the present, historical analogies are a rational means of retrieving information from history, simplifying and organizing current information, and prescribing and justifying policy. Historical analogies also provide information about the stakes, adversaries, allies, time, risks, and policy options. Without historical analogies, every foreign policy crisis would appear to be unique.

This book analyzes the role of historical information, particularly historical analogies, compared to current information in British and American decision making during four foreign policy crises that involved the possible use of military force in regional contingencies. The central research questions are the following: by whom, when, and how are historical analogies used by foreign policy decision makers?

The introduction outlines the central theses of the book. First, that historical information, particularly lessons drawn from historical analogies, is commonly used in foreign policy decision making, especially involving the use of military force in regional contingencies. Second, that a range of individual and situational factors influence whether, and in what ways, historical and/or current information is used during a foreign policy crisis. Third, that the use of historical information can be rational and supports a model of multiple paths to rational decision making. Fourth, that, if historical information is used, such information can significantly influence foreign policy decisions.

The five chapters after the introduction analyze the individual and situational variables that influence the use of historical information. The chapter on leaders discusses the use of historical information and analogies by ten political leaders throughout their careers: their views about, and use of, historical information in their decision making and in their rhetoric. Personality, education, training, and foreign policy experience can influence the use of historical information.

Situational variables and the role of historical information compared to current information are then analyzed in the four case study chapters. Each case focuses on a crisis that involved Anglo-American decision making about a regional contingency involving the possible use of force by the United States and/or Britain. Each case chapter analyzes what, if any, historical information was used, by which policy makers, for what functions, and with what affect on policy. Although historical information is not a determining factor in all cases, it can shape how leaders frame a crisis, as well as their perceptions of adversaries, allies, time, stakes, risks, and policy options.

The first case is the British and American response to the North Korean invasion of South Korea in June 1950. Surprise, time pressures, and the personalities of President Harry S. Truman and Prime Minister Clement Attlee led to a reliance on historical information over current information. On the basis of the 1930's analogy, which was a cluster of analogies based on events, such as the 1938 Munich conference, and leaders, such as German Chancellor Adolf Hitler, from the 1930s, American policy makers went well beyond the information currently available and quickly decided to use military force. The British, also on the basis of the 1930's analogy, but significantly influenced by concerns about Anglo-American relations, also decided rapidly, although not as quickly as the Americans, to use force.

The second case is the 1951 nationalization of the Iranian oil industry. Unlike the Korean case, lack of time pressures or of surprise overrode the personal inclinations of Attlee and Truman to rely on historical information. Although there was a possible analogy to Mexico's nationalization of its oil industry, British and American decision makers did not rely on the Mexico analogy to make policy. British and American leaders focused on the current, Cold War situation to frame the crisis. Lack of a single, clear policy prescription derived from a historical analogy contributed to a succession of

British and American policies in response to the nationalization, which cul-
minated in an Anglo-American supported coup that overthrew Prime Minister Mohammed Mossadegh of Iran.

The third case is the 1956 Anglo-French intervention in Suez. Surprise,
perceptions of time pressures, and Prime Minister Anthony Eden's personal
experiences led the British to rely on lessons from the 1930s at the expense
of current information to frame their policy response. The British in the
Suez case offer evidence of the power of historical information to blind
leaders to current information that contradicts their historically based beliefs.
Eden accepted the 1930's analogy as valid for Suez and was determined to
apply its lessons, even as he ignored contradictory, current information. He
would use force to attempt to topple President Gamul Abdul Nasser of
Egypt, regardless of domestic and foreign opposition. The Americans perceived less time pressures. This, combined with the personal inclinations of
President Dwight D. Eisenhower and Secretary of State John F. Dulles not
to rely on historical information, led to the American reliance on current
information and a policy of negotiation instead of military intervention.

The 1958 American intervention in Lebanon and the British intervention
in Jordan the same year, the fourth case, provides evidence of the significant
influence of historical information on foreign policy decision making. The
British and the Americans relied on historical information, although both
balanced it with current information. Time pressures, surprise, and personal
differences in the beliefs of Prime Minister Harold Macmillan and Eisenhower about the use of history contribute to an explanation of their different
perceptions of the crisis. Macmillan, relying on lessons from Suez, ensured
U.S. support before intervening. In Washington, lessons based on historical
events in the late 1940s and early 1950s clustered around the concept of
indirect aggression significantly influenced policy making.

The conclusion presents an overview of the theses of the book on the
basis of the findings of the case studies. There is also a discussion of the role
of master analogies, such as the 1930s and the Vietnam War, and the use
of historical information in attempts to learn about foreign policy decision
making, specifically, and international relations, generally. The influence of
historical information in foreign policy decision making is an understudied
area. The book concludes with a discussion of where future research might
focus to travel some of the many paths not yet taken.

NOTES

1. Fuller, *The Conduct of War*, p. 151.
2. Bartlett, *Familiar Quotations*, p. 98.

Acknowledgments

In forty-six months of researching and writing this book I accumulated many debts. I would like to thank Michael G. Fry, who always pushed me to the edge of my intelligence, as well as Laurie Brand, Roger Dingman, and Eileen Crumm for their comments, which only improved the manuscript.

Like politics, money is the life's blood of research. I received research grants from the Harry S. Truman Library Institute, the Eisenhower World Affairs Institute, and, at the University of Southern California, the Center for International Studies and the School of International Relations. The personnel at the Eisenhower and Truman libraries were knowledgeable, friendly, and made doing research a pleasure. Dennis E. Bilger, Randy Sowell, and Elizabeth Safly at the Truman Library were especially kind to a graduate student on his first trip to an archive.

Without a publisher, a book is merely a manuscript gathering dust. My editor, Heather Staines, and Greenwood Press gave me the opportunity to publish a book and walked a first-time writer through the intricacies of the publishing world.

The KAM Institute supported me for years, both financially and emotionally, as did my mother, Lea, and father, Neil, the first Dr. Macdonald in the family. I would also like to offer an entirely different order of thanks to Ms. Aurora and Mr. MacDuff for always being there with an insightful comment when all looked black.

1

Introduction

Leaders often use historical information to diagnose and frame international crises, as well as to prescribe and legitimate policy. The most common means of retrieving information and lessons from history is by analogical reasoning. Although leaders often use historical analogies to frame diplomatic or economic crises,[1] historical analogies are most commonly used in national security crises, especially when such crises involve the possible use of military force. For example, since the Vietnam War, debates about U.S. military intervention, such as about Nicaragua in the 1980s, the Persian Gulf in 1990–91, and the former Yugoslavia in the 1990s, have often been argued from two antithetical positions, each based on a historical analogy: Vietnam (opposed to military intervention) and the 1930s (favoring military intervention). "It would not be a great exaggeration to say that the United States went to war [in the Persian Gulf] over an analogy."[2] Many other historical analogies have played prominent roles in debates in the United States and in Britain about regional contingencies and the possible use of military force. Analogies to the 1979–81 Iranian hostage crisis, the costly U.S. intervention in Beirut in 1983–84, and to Soviet-supported Nicaragua were used to support the October 1983 U.S. invasion of Grenada. During the 1982 Falklands War, British policy makers compared the Argentine junta to the Axis dictators of the 1930s. President Gerald Ford used the 1968 *Pueblo* incident as an analogy to the 1975 Cambodian seizure of the *Mayaguez*, while the Korean War and Munich analogies influenced the U.S. decision to escalate intervention in Vietnam in 1965. President John F. Kennedy used lessons from the outbreak of the First World War in 1914 and Pearl Harbor during the 1962 Cuban missile crisis. Even earlier, in the 1930s, the 1914 analogy was used to argue for a more conciliatory British policy toward Nazi Germany to avoid another potential world war. And, in 1917, British policy makers drew on the French revolution to frame the Russian Bolshevik Revolution.[3]

Although analogical reasoning is common, political scientists have begun only recently to study historical analogies in foreign policy decision-making settings. This neglect is partly because, in the quest for precise terms, most decision-making models are based on economic models, which usually preclude the influence of historical information. Most researchers also focus on the phase of decision making dealing with choosing among options and not on the phase where a problem is defined or framed, which can have a critical effect on policy choices and is when historical information and analogies often play a crucial role.[4]

Even though this area has been neglected, some excellent work has been conducted.[5] However, as is to be expected by pioneering research, much of this early work was anecdotal. It also focused on foreign policy failures and the misuse of history, neglecting the possible benefits of using historical information. Some of the research has also been tautological, in that a policy failure is traced back to a historical analogy, which is then labeled invalid, largely because the policy failed. Yuen Foong Khong's study of the U.S. decision to escalate involvement in the Vietnam conflict (*Analogies at War*) is the best recent work on historical analogies and foreign policy decision making. However, it focuses narrowly on decisions related to using different types of military force and not on the broader question of whether to use diplomacy, economic measures, covert operations, or military force. The present study analyzes this broader question.

Unlike political scientists, psychologists have studied analogical reasoning extensively. Although their research sheds light on the use of historical analogies by leaders, much of their work suffers from the drawbacks of the laboratory setting. It has focused on how people can use an analogy, which is provided, to solve an analogous, well-defined problem of the form A:B:: C:?. It has ignored the more complex, ill-defined, problem-solving tasks that are more common in foreign policy, where leaders often retrieve a historical analogy without the analogy being provided by someone else.

Most models of decisions to use military force in regional contingencies rely on some form of rational choice theory and, like political scientists, ignore the influence of historical analogies. There is a vast literature that analyzes the failings of the rational actor, *homo economicus*, who is generally seen as an ideal abstraction and is rarely used, except in game theory.[6] Therefore, the current study uses cognitive and bounded rationality models. The focus of the present study, historical information retrieved, primarily, by analogy, is a cognitive process and falls within a bounded rationality framework. The current study does not attempt to offer a comprehensive explanation of historical cases. The cases are used to analyze the role of historical information and analogies in foreign policy decisions.[7]

This book attempts to build on political science and psychological research by analyzing the influence of historical information, particularly historical analogies, on foreign policy decision making, particularly when leaders consider using military force in regional contingencies. The following research questions served to focus the study: Which situational and individual variables influence the use of historical information, particularly historical analogies, by leaders? What types of historical analogies are used in foreign policy decision making? What factors affect the retrieval of historical information via analogies? Why do leaders draw certain lessons from historical events, while ignoring other possible lessons? What is the process by which foreign policy decision makers use analogies to retrieve information from history? What is the process by which small groups debate and then accept or reject the validity of historical lessons? What are the common effects of historical analogies and under what conditions do historical lessons have their greatest, and least, impact on foreign policy? What is the influence of lessons from history on perceptions of an adversary's personality and rationality? What is the influence of such perceptions on decisions to use force? Under what conditions do historical analogies serve diagnostic, prescriptive, and legitimation functions? Under what conditions do historical analogies lead to valid, rational, effective, and specific lessons, which aid in making more effective foreign policy decisions? Succinctly, who uses historical analogies, when, how, and with what effects?

The following discussion focuses on the use of historical information by defining analogical reasoning, discussing types of historical analogies, the decision to reason using historical information, as well as the retrieval, functions, effects, and process of analogical reasoning, particularly in foreign policy decision making. The discussion of historical information and analogies is followed by a section that offers a definition of the use of military force and discusses psychological variables that influence the decision to use military force in regional contingencies.

WHAT IS A HISTORICAL ANALOGY?

Leaders use historical analogies to simplify novel and complex situations by transferring familiar categories and relationships from a familiar, past event to organize and explain an unfamiliar, but similar, current event. The analogy can be between two events or two people. Analogical reasoning suggests that if two things are known to be similar in certain respects, then they are also similar in other respects. For example, A and B share characteristic X; A also has characteristic Y, therefore it is inferred that B also has characteristic Y. Analogies explain through explicit, direct comparison and are used in abstract, deliberate phases of thought because they are too involved to be induced spontaneously. Although analogies are powerful rhetorical and diagnostic tools, analogies cannot prove something. Furthermore, they are offered as self-evident and the examination of differences only weakens or limits the analogy. The only way to support the validity of an analogy would be exhaustively to describe the two events. However, it is to avoid such an analysis that an analogy is offered.[8]

Historical analogies are not extrapolation, which is to infer that because something has occurred in the past, it will continue in the present. For example, the argument that Soviet attempts during the Cold War to extend their influence to the Indian Ocean were a continuation of Tsarist Russian attempts to achieve the same goal, were extrapolation, not analogical reasoning. Analogies rest on transfer from a historical event or person to a current event or person and assume some discontinuity between past and present, whereas extrapolation rests on the assumption of continuous trends.[9] Unlike extrapolation, a historical analogy is defined by separation in time. It is a comparison between a current event and an event that has been concluded before the current event began.

Analogical reasoning is a method policy makers use to attempt to learn from history. Learning is a general category. Learning by analogical reasoning from historical cases is a specific method or type of learning. Learning may be done on the basis of current information, practice, training, study, or instruction. Current information is from the here and now, not the past. Learning by analogical reasoning from history is based on comparing two events or people, one in the past and one current, to attempt to provide unknown information, policy prescriptions, or lessons for the current case. The crucial aspect is that the past is compared to the present.

TYPES OF HISTORICAL ANALOGIES

Historical analogies can be based on people[10] or events. A historical analogy based on a person compares a current person with a historical person, such as Iraqi President Saddam Hussein with German Chancellor Adolf Hitler. A historical analogy based on an event compares a current event with a historical event, such as Iraq's 1990 invasion of Kuwait with Nazi Germany's 1939 invasion of Poland. A series of events may form a script, such as the 1930s, which combines events and people.[11] Historical events and people are closely linked. For example, Hitler is linked to the 1939 German attack on Poland. However, when policy makers mention historical analogies, they focus on either an individual or an event. Whether a person or an event is mentioned is a measure of which a policy maker deems to be more important and leads to different frameworks, lessons and policy prescriptions. For example, in the Suez case, the British primarily compared people, Egyptian leader Nasser and Italian leader Benito Mussolini, and not events. Therefore, the British were more likely to personalize the crisis, to see Nasser as their adversary, and to seek his removal, than if they had focused on the event, the nationalization of the Suez Canal.

Historical analogies can be based on three types of history. Learned historical analogies are based on events or people that occurred or lived before the actor using the analogy became aware politically, usually in the late teens. Observed historical analogies are based on events or people that occurred or lived when the actor was politically aware, but was not personally involved in the events. Personally experienced historical analogies are historical analogies that are based on events or people that the actor was personally involved in, or with, as a member of a government.

Historical analogies can also be categorized by whether the lessons actors draw from them are micro and narrowly policy relevant (if U.S. forces approach the Chinese border during the Vietnam War, the Chinese will intervene militarily as they had in the Korean War), macro and support general principles (the United States should avoid a land war in Asia, based on the cost and restoration of the prewar status quo result of the Korean War), or are for creating myths, which create pride in a state (such as the battle for Vimy Ridge for Canada). Most historical analogies used in the decision-making process provide either micro- or macrolessons because myths are usually too broad to support specific policy options during a crisis.[12]

THE DECISION TO USE HISTORICAL ANALOGIES

Historical analogies can be used in a decision-making process either by an individual, a group, or by both.[13] Psychologists usually study the individual level, while political scientists focus on the group level. The current study integrates these two levels.

For analogical reasoning to occur, a policy maker must choose analogizing as the method to deal with all, or at least a part, of a problem. Analogical reasoning is often combined with other analytical and decision-making methods in a multiple-path decision-making process.[14] Policy makers usually think of an analogy by chance, but, on rare occasions, they may decide to reason by analogy after conducting a cost-benefit analysis to compare possible methods.[15] More commonly, individuals, especially when they are under intense time pressures, are overwhelmed by information and resort to shortcuts, such as historical analogies, to solve novel, complex, and dramatic problems, such as a foreign policy crisis. Leaders use historical analogies when a novel situation arises because it is easier to solve problems if an analogous problem has already been solved.[16] The analogous problem simplifies the current problem, as well as providing policy prescriptions. For actors to use historical analogies, the situation cannot be common enough to have led to the creation of standard operating procedures and thus have no need for analogical reasoning, nor can it be novel enough to have no perceived historical analogy. Analogies are also not used usually if the solution of the current problem can be reached easily through means-ends analysis,[17] although analogies can serve to confirm or justify a policy chosen by other means. However, almost all crises in international relations are novel, dramatic, complex, and have solutions that are not easily devised, which should lead to the use of historical analogies. For these reasons, historical analogies are often used in foreign policy crises, although individual variables, as well as a lack of time pressure in certain cases, may negate the inclination to use historical analogies, even for novel, dramatic, and complex crises. Unfortunately, there has been little, if any, research on the influence of situational compared to individual variables on the use of historical information and analogies in foreign policy decision-making situations. The present study addresses this issue by comparing the influence of situational and individual variables on the use of historical analogies.

Although culture and a state's history may influence whether policy makers use historical information and analogies,[18] there is a lack of rigorous, empirical research on this relationship. The current study will attempt to determine if there is a difference in the use of historical information between the leaders of Britain and the United States. Although whether states influence the use of historical information is still an open question, research has shown that administrations vary in their use of historical information and analogies. Individual differences in education, experience, training, and personality have a significant influence on the use of historical information, and prime ministers and presidents have a significant influence in setting the tone of an administration. For example, the approach of the administrations of U.S. Presidents Ronald Reagan and Jimmy Carter were ahistorical. They rarely used historical information, whereas Prime Minister Harold Macmillan often used historical information and analogies.[19]

Differences in the use of historical information by presidents, prime ministers, and their cabinets is shaped by individual variables. Legal and historical training may influence whether foreign policy makers use history. Although theories abound, rigorous empirical evidence is lacking about this issue. Leaders trained as historians or with a long experience in foreign policy may be more likely to use historical information than policy makers with legal training because historians and foreign policy experts have more potential historical analogies to draw from. However, they may also be less likely than lawyers to rely on history because they see more differences between historical analogies and the current case and are more aware of validity problems. Further complicating the issue is the argument that lawyers, whose training involves studying past decisions, may be more likely to use the same method in a foreign policy setting and analyze past, similar, cases. However, a lawyer who lacks any knowledge of history may not be able to recall any analogous events to compare to the current case.[20] There is also the further problem of spuriousness. An individual who studies history may be more interested in history to begin with and, therefore, more likely to use historical analogies than someone interested in law, regardless of what they study at school. Empirical analysis is the only means of sorting out the validity of these conflicting arguments, which is a goal of the present study.

Leaders who use historical information to frame international crises and to prescribe policy often use historical analogies because history is difficult to argue against. History seems credible, as if the interpretation of history is fact, not theory or opinion. History also seems certain and predictable, in that when people look at history they tend to believe that events had to turn out the way they did and that no other outcome was likely.[21] The decision to use historical analogies, whether conscious or not, brings an often powerful ally to a leader's arsenal to convince others of his chosen policy. But, how are historical analogies retrieved?

THE RETRIEVAL OF SPECIFIC HISTORICAL INFORMATION

Rigorous studies of the individual retrieval of lessons from history using analogical reasoning in a foreign policy environment are rare, in part because such research is intrinsically difficult. Minutes of meetings and memoranda provide little information beyond which analogy was retrieved. Even the lesson the leader drew from history is often only implied. Interviews can be unreliable sources of information on the influence of historical analogies because individuals often are unable to remember when they retrieved an analogy and, if they did, how they used it in their decision making.[22] However, psychological experiments and the limited amount of foreign policy research provides some information on the retrieval of historical analogies in foreign policy settings.

The intelligence and inclination of the individual to think of, and search for, possible analogies influences the size of the set of available historical analogies for retrieval. The range of historical analogies stored in a government's institutional memory also influences the size of the pool of possible historical analogies. Individuals tend to retrieve historical analogies from their own state's history, in part, because such analogies are in their government's institutional memory.[23] Individuals are more likely to retrieve a historical analogy that shares surface similarities, which are superficial and apparent at first glance, with the current case, rather than analogies that share structural, causal similarities, which are only noticed after prolonged analysis. How an event and an analogy are classified also affects retrieval. For example, if the 1938 Munich conference is categorized as appeasement, future acts labeled appeasement will remind the actor of Munich.[24] However, the more an individual analyzes and maps a historical analogy to a current case, the less the impact of surface similarities and the more actors focus on complex, causal similarities and differences that are not readily apparent from an initial comparison.[25] However, this in-depth analysis, common in laboratory experiments, rarely occurs in a foreign policy setting.

People retrieve certain types of analogies more than others, especially recent, vivid, salient, and emotional events experienced firsthand that had important consequences for decision makers and/or their state. Individuals tend to believe that an analogy that is easiest to recall is more representative and valid than other analogies. Such events are easier to remember and, therefore, easier to retrieve. Furthermore, such events are also more likely to be familiar both to the policy maker and to his or her colleagues. If an analogy is familiar, then the policy maker does not have to explain it. An obscure historical analogy leads to the very analysis to explain it that a historical analogy is used to avoid. For example, in the 1980s, when much was written about the relative decline of the United States, the most common analogies were to Britain and Rome. Comparisons to the decline of the Inca empire, Babylon, or ancient Egypt were rarely, if ever, mentioned because most readers would have gained little understanding from these unfamiliar analogies.

How rare an event is also influences the type of historical information retrieved. If an event is common, actors will probably be able to retrieve an analogy from their own recent experience, either on the basis of personal experience or observation. However, if an event is uncommon, they may have to delve deeper into learned history for an analogy. For example, the Bolshevik Revolution, a fundamental ideological change in a European great power, was something new and British leaders had to reach back into history to the French Revolution for an analogy.[26] Whereas in the 1980s, the civil war in Nicaragua appeared to be similar to a recent historical event that had been experienced personally and recently by many U.S. policy makers: the Vietnam War. There was no need to delve deeper into learned history to find a superficially similar analogy.

Leaders also retrieve foreign policy failures more often than successes. Failures tend to lead to examination and analysis far more than successes.[27] If a policy succeeds, there is little need for analysis. Events turned out as expected, or, at least, as hoped. However, policy failures are also failures of expectation. For example, the 1938 Munich conference is usually seen as a British foreign policy failure, as well as a failure of expectation. British policy failed to avoid a world war and, although many leaders at the time expected the policy to succeed, it failed. Analysis of failures leads to greater knowledge of failures than successes and, therefore, a greater likelihood that leaders will retrieve foreign policy failures than successes from history. Furthermore, the effects of a failure are usually more costly, clear, and memorable than those of a successful policy. Failures are usually clear-cut, while successes are often debated. For example, the American intervention in Vietnam led to a clearly negative result: American withdrawal and the fall of South Vietnam to the North Vietnamese. A successful policy, on the other hand, such as the American opening to China in the early 1970s, often avoids war and leads to outcomes that are more ambiguous. A success also tends to lead to the assumption that if a crisis was handled effectively in the past, there is nothing to learn, since the same policy can be applied to the next similar crisis to achieve the same success. Unfortunately, history does not repeat itself so precisely.

Age can also influence which historical information is retrieved. People may be more open to new ideas and concepts when they are young, because information acquired later in life must be assimilated into an existing mental framework. If the new information does not fit current beliefs, it may be ignored or given less weight than is warranted objectively. Therefore, events that a young policy maker is involved in are often used later in life as analogies for other crises. The variable of age is related to the generational effect model, which is based on the concept that attitudes and behavior are shaped by the common experiences of a cohort or generation when they are between the ages of 17 and 25. For there to be a generational effect, which has been found in elite groups,[28] an event's long-term impression must be common to a large group of people. According to this concept, great events will have an impact on policy about twenty years in the future, as those who were in their twenties during the event reach high office in their late forties. Thus, leaders may learn the lessons from an event decades before they apply those lessons to a crisis. However, a generational effect may be caused by a selection effect. A generation of leaders may hold a common set of views because they had to hold those views to reach high office.[29]

Although the underlying concept is valid, individual variation must be added to the generational hypotheses because the same aged leaders often use different analogies.[30] Furthermore, the generational model's emphasis on a specific age range is misplaced. The crucial factor is whether a dramatic, traumatic, life-changing event, such as World War II, Suez, or the Vietnam War, occurred during a policy maker's lifetime, regardless of his age, as long as he was old enough to be aware of world events. Such events are likely to become master analogies, which embody a broad, general lesson that is familiar to a large group of people.[31] For example, the Vietnam War provided the lesson that the United States should avoid military intervention in Third World civil wars. A master analogy can take hold of a generation or, more often, a series of generations, and is used as an analogy for many other crises, until a new generation, too young to remember the major event, and imbued with a different master analogy, rises to power. However, master analogies can linger for generations. For example, President George Bush and Prime Minister Margaret Thatcher, who both remembered World War II, used the 1930's analogy to frame Iraq's 1990 invasion of Kuwait, as did

President Bill Clinton and Prime Minister Tony Blair, who had no firsthand knowledge of the world war, during the Kosovo crisis in 1999. To test its validity, the generational model will be applied to the cases in this book.

To summarize, policy makers retrieve recent, vivid, salient, and emotional events, experienced firsthand that involved their own states, usually in a foreign policy failure, and that share surface similarities. Some historical analogies are so dramatic that they become master analogies for a generation of leaders, providing broad, general lessons that are applied to many crises.

FUNCTIONS OF HISTORICAL INFORMATION AND ANALOGICAL REASONING

Historical information retrieved by analogical reasoning serves three main functions: diagnosis, prescription, and justification. In diagnosing a crisis, historical analogies are used to frame a situation, evaluate causal relationships, choose between rival explanations of a current event, provide information on intentions based on past events where intentions are thought to be known, predict probable future events, and assess the stakes. Historical analogies also provide information on the roles, goals, core beliefs, and status of individuals and states. For example, British leaders in 1914 could draw the lesson from the 1800s that Britain's historical role was as balancer in the European balance of power. Historical analogies can prescribe policy and, even if policy options are derived by other means, not analogically, historical information affects the selection, attractiveness, and ranking of options by influencing how options are viewed in terms of the effectiveness of the past use of similar policies. Historical analogies can also justify policy either before, at the same time as, or after a policy option is selected. Historical information can be a source of normative legitimacy, which establishes the desirability of a policy as being consistent with personal, party, national or international values, and/or effective legitimacy, which supports the feasibility of a policy. Historical information can also delegitimize policy options by suggesting that past use of a similar policy failed.[32] For example, during the crisis over Iraq's invasion of Kuwait in 1990, the British and Americans wanted no hint of any appeasement of Iraq. In an August 8, 1990, speech, Bush said, "Appeasement does not work, as was the case in the 1930s."[33] Thatcher concluded, "Aggressors must never be appeased."[34] The 1930s delegitimized any form of appeasement of Iraq.

DIAGNOSIS AND PRESCRIPTION OR JUSTIFICATION?

Policy makers may, consciously or subconsciously, use historical analogies as justification to support whichever policies they have chosen by other means. Historical analogies may also serve diagnostic and prescriptive functions.[35] It is extremely difficult to determine which role of historical analogies is valid. Scholars have suggested ways to test whether historical analogies are used for diagnosis and prescription or solely for justification. For example, if historical information merely reinforced established beliefs, policy makers would not disproportionately use as analogies events they experienced firsthand.[36] However, recent events are easiest to retrieve from memory, so leaders are more likely to use historical analogies they experienced firsthand, whether for justification or diagnosis. Therefore, whether historical analogies are based on personal experience is not a valid indicator of whether an analogy is used for diagnosis and prescription or solely for justification.

More valid is the argument that if the interpretation of the past is clearly incorrect, present beliefs and preferences probably have influenced perceptions of the past. In such cases, historical information is only retrieved because it supports current beliefs and is used solely to justify policy chosen by other means. Unfortunately, it is difficult to determine which interpretations of the past are incorrect and to what degree. And, even if the interpretation is incorrect, historical analogies could still be used, albeit invalidly, for diagnosis and prescription. The individual may have based a policy on an invalid view of a historical event that was held before the policy was selected.

Other factors, especially underlying beliefs, and not the influence of history, usually explain instances in which people with different policy preferences and beliefs hold different interpretations of historical analogies. Conversely, a historical analogy probably had an effect on decision making if different people with different beliefs learned the same lessons from the same event or when an event changed a person's mind.[37] However, incidents of leaders changing their basic beliefs during a crisis, whether on the basis of a historical analogy or for some other reason, are extremely rare, if not nonexistent. In the present study, the beliefs of leaders will be analyzed across time to determine if beliefs changed in response to historical information, although it is far more likely that historical information influences perceptions of a crisis, as well as less deeply held beliefs, than basic, core beliefs.

Analysis of when historical information is mentioned during the decision-making process is dangerous to use as an indicator of whether a historical analogy was used to diagnose and prescribe or solely to justify policy. If a historical analogy is mentioned only after a policy has been chosen, the analogy was probably used to justify policy, although the analogy may have also influenced the choice of policy without actors mentioning the analogy. The analogy may have been on a policy maker's mind, yet he may not have mentioned the analogy. If a historical analogy is mentioned before a policy has been chosen, it may have influenced policy selection. However, a historical analogy may be used before a policy is selected, yet only serve a justification role within the debate as policy makers suggest different policy options and offer justification for their favored option. Therefore, timing is a weak indicator of whether a historical analogy was used for diagnosis and prescription or solely for justification.

If historical information is used only to justify policy, then the private use of analogies (when leaders choose policy) should differ from the public use of analogies (when leaders justify policy). For example, during the U.S. decision to escalate the intervention in Vietnam, the public use of historical analogies mirrored the private use and historical information was used to prescribe, as well as to justify, policy.[38] Furthermore, the public use of historical information to justify a policy strongly suggests that historical information was also used in private to diagnose a crisis and to prescribe policy.[39]

Laboratory studies in psychology have been unable to resolve this issue of diagnosis and prescription versus justification. In an analogical problem-solving experiment, it was unclear if subjects mentioned an analogy because they used the analogy for diagnosis and prescription or for justification.[40] In another laboratory study, subjects were unaware of the influence that historical analogies apparently had on their decisions,[41] making it questionable to rely on foreign policy decision makers to report whether historical analogies influenced their decisions.

This issue has not been resolved because in most cases diagnosis/prescription and justification are not mutually exclusive functions. Analogical reasoning serves both justification and diagnostic/prescriptive functions at different times, and both functions influence policy choices. Justification can influence the choice of policy. A government, except for covert operations, would not choose a policy that was effective, if the policy could not be justified publicly. The crucial question, which has largely been ignored, is the following: Under what conditions is historical information via analogical reasoning used, whether for diagnosis and prescription, or for justification?

MAPPING

Once a historical analogy is retrieved, whether for diagnosis and prescription or for justification, it is related to the current case by a process called mapping. Usually a conscious process, mapping involves finding a partial set of correspondences between the current case and the analogy and then extending the mapping by retrieving or creating additional information. Mapping has two parts: horizontal mapping between two aspects of two analogies (often causal factors in two events, such as the cause of two analogous events) and vertical mapping between two parts of the same analogy (the cause and the effect). Mapping includes attribute identification (labeling variables in the current event and in the historical analogy), attribute comparison (infer a rule to map the cause and effect relationship in a historical analogy, and then map the rule to the current event), and control (translate the rule into a chosen policy for the current event).[42]

In mapping, people seek coherence by matching elements one-to-one, such as objects (actors), predicates (actions), and propositions (causal links), between the historical analogy and the current case until the most similar match is made, although the degree of mapping can vary greatly. For example, comparing the Gulf War and the 1930s, President George Bush could be mapped to Prime Minister Winston Churchill, while the United States could be mapped to Britain. However, subjects may do one-to-many mapping, especially when there is strong support for many alternatives. For example, in the Gulf War/1930s comparison, actors may map Bush to Churchill, but could also map Bush to President Franklin D. Roosevelt, because all three leaders opposed, and fought wars against, aggressive dictators, among other similarities.

Although two analogies at the same level of abstraction are usually compared, mapping can be at multiple levels of abstraction. The degree of mapping required varies greatly depending on how much information is needed to solve the problem and which degree of mapping maximizes the correspondence between the historical analogy and the case. A detailed mapping will include aspects that do not appear to be analogous, while an abstract mapping may omit crucial information. The level of abstraction also affects recall: If it is too detailed, the analogy will not be retrieved because it will be seen as dissimilar; if it is too general, mapping may lead to overgeneralization that will be rejected by other policy makers. Individuals do not have to map every actor, action, and situational attribute in the analogy to the current case, although laboratory experiments show that subjects must map the causal elements between the analogy and the current case. Causal elements are the factors that make up the cause and effect relationship in the analogy and in the current case.[43] This argument is more valid in a laboratory than in a foreign policy environment. Foreign policy decision makers are willing to accept historical analogies even if the causal links are not explicitly mapped, given the difficulty of determining causal links in international relations, foreign policy, or in history, and the lack of precision in the real world compared to experiments in laboratory settings. However, as in laboratory experiments, in foreign policy, the greater the perceived similarities between the analogy and the event, the greater the perceived validity of the analogy, as well as the greater the resistance to disconfirming information.

From mapping, individuals conclude one of the following about the validity of the relationship between the historical analogy and the current case: identity—compared events resemble each other in almost every respect; similarity—main attributes are the same, while other attributes differ (the most common case); familiarity—broad, general similarities; contradiction—

the events are seen as mirror images that carry a lesson by counter-analogy; or irrelevance, the events are incomparable and therefore irrelevant. Irrelevance may help in seeing an event as unique and legitimize an innovative, new policy.[44]

Schema theory posits, on the basis of laboratory studies, that people accept all or none of an analogy as valid.[45] However, in a foreign policy setting an analogy can be accepted for diagnosis but rejected for prescription. For example, in the Suez case, Eisenhower agreed with Eden that Nasser was a negative influence and, possibly, similar to Mussolini. However, Eisenhower rejected the policy implications of the Mussolini analogy: to use force promptly. This difference between the laboratory and foreign policy emphasizes the gulf between the two environments.

Individuals vary in their beliefs about the validity of historical analogies in general, as well as their perceptions about specific analogies. If a leader views history as repeating or cyclical, then he will be more likely to accept historical analogies as valid than a leader who sees history as a series of unique events. There are three types of analogizers: perfectionists, who only will use a perfect analogy; satisficers, who accept the first historical analogy that is superficially similar to the current case (usually occurs if there is stress and time pressures); and pragmatists, who selectively adopt either a perfectionist or satisficing approach. It may be that the more demanding, committing, and risky the task, the higher the threshold for the level of validity demanded of an analogy, even for a satisficer.[46] However, cognitive dissonance theory suggests that the higher the risk, such as in a foreign policy crisis, the more desperately policy makers may want a historical analogy to fit the current case to ease the stress of decision making. Therefore, they may be less demanding than in less stressful cases. The current study will analyze the influence of time pressures, risk, and stakes, which influences how demanding a task is, on perceptions of the validity of historical analogies.

GROUP DISCUSSION

After a policy maker maps a historical analogy to a current case and judges that it is valid, he may mention it to the policy-making group. There is no rigorous research on the sequence of individual and group use of historical analogies in a foreign policy setting, and it is unclear how the two processes interact. Analysis of the group-level process itself has also been neglected even though the group level is crucial in foreign policy decision making as individual decision makers attempt to have the historical information they have retrieved via analogy adopted as the basis for diagnosis of a crisis, as well as to prescribe and justify a policy.

The common model is that a policy maker asserts the similarity of the analogy and the event, describes the relevant features of the analogy, and then describes the event using the same categories and relationships as were used to describe the analogy. A group may accept a historical analogy without debate or, like U.S. policy makers during discussions about escalating the war in Vietnam, may challenge the validity of the analogy. Whether historical analogies are questioned depends, in part, on the level of consensus about the interpretation of a historical analogy. If there is consensus, the interpretation of a historical analogy goes unquestioned and unanalyzed.[47] The historical knowledge, policy preferences, and governmental position of policy makers, as well as whether they have already decided on a policy, also influences whether a group debates the validity of a historical analogy. What people mean when they use an analogy can also influence whether others accept the validity of a historical analogy. If, for example, Hitler and Nasser are compared, does it mean that they have similar beliefs, behavior, and/or that their states have similar capabilities? Differences in intended meaning will lead to variations in perceived validity. There is also a difference between those who raise an analogy, only to abandon it quickly, and those who raise an analogy and defend its validity zealously. The latter phenomenon involves more mapping than the former and has a greater influence on policy making, especially if a president or prime minister, who usually has the greatest influence on foreign policy decisions, is the one zealously defending an analogy. However, there has been little, if any, empirical research on this issue. To remedy this lack of research, the present study will analyze the dynamics of group discussion of historical information retrieved by analogical reasoning in a foreign policy environment.

THE EFFECT OF HISTORY

In some foreign policy decisions historical information plays almost no part, such as Reagan administration decisions about policy toward the Soviet Union.[48] In other foreign policy decisions historical information is vitally important, such as the decision to escalate U.S. intervention in Vietnam,[49] and, in certain cases, history may be more influential than ideology and political beliefs.[50] By transferring categories and relationships from a historical case, analogical reasoning has a major influence on how a crisis is framed, which greatly affects the perceived stakes, as well as the attractiveness, morality, and possibility of success of, and dangers related to, various policy options. Historical information can also divert attention from relevant, current information, affect the judgment of other arguments based on other analytical tools, and block the generation of alternative solutions.[51]

Related to the question of whether historical analogies are used for diagnosis and prescription or solely for justification, is the question of whether historical analogies actually change behavior or are merely used post hoc to rationalize policy choices arrived at by other means. The answer is not mutually exclusive. Historical analogies, in some cases, change beliefs and alter policy, while, in others, merely rationalize policies selected by other means. However, even if historical analogies are merely rationalizations, then those who use them, at least, believe that mentioning a historical analogy may change the minds of other people and garner support for their policy. Although not the focus of this study, the use of historical analogies does help garner public support for policy. For example, Bush's use of the 1930's analogy helped win support for his Persian Gulf policy in 1990–91. Even so, historical analogies rarely, if ever, lead to a significant change in the basic beliefs of a policy maker. Such changes are rare, regardless of the cause. In most cases, historical analogies reflect and filter general, underlying beliefs. Historical analogies clarify and specify perceptions and beliefs about a current, specific case, especially perceptions of policy options, stakes, possible outcomes, adversaries, and the role of the state and other actors, as well as leading to the justification of certain policy options and the delegitimizing of other policy options. Overall, historical analogies simplify and clarify general beliefs policy makers already hold. However, absent the analogy, the general beliefs would have been applied to a specific case in a different way and form. Historical analogies filter basic, general beliefs so that they can be applied to a current, specific case and, in so doing, influence, often significantly, policy making.

The more historical information in the memory of a policy maker, the less the impact of any one piece of information on their decisions. Therefore, more knowledgeable statesman, because they know more history, should be less influenced by the last major event, such as a war or revolution.[52] Unfortunately, age is a weak indicator of how much history an individual knows. A knowledgeable young person may know far more history than an older, less knowledgeable person. Foreign policy experience and historical knowledge are more valid variables than age to predict the size of the pool of historical information in a leader's memory. Furthermore, this argument may be true during recall, but once information is retrieved, the affect of the analogy is the same regardless of the size of the pool of possible historical analogies from which it was drawn.[53]

Lessons from history based on events observed directly, early in adult life may be perceived as more valid than learned history. This is because events witnessed firsthand are easier to retrieve from memory, have helped form early perceptions, and seem more concrete and relevant.[54] However, although firsthand knowledge is easier to recall, that knowledge may seem analogous to fewer cases because it is context dependent and contains more information than knowledge learned secondhand. Therefore, leaders may see more dissimilar aspects than knowledge based on learned history that contains less information and is stored in a more context-free form.[55] Unfortunately, there has not been enough rigorous study of the use and effect of different kinds of historical analogies (personally experienced, observed, and learned) in a foreign policy setting to settle this argument. The present study analyses this issue.

HISTORY: THE UNCERTAIN GUIDE

"History abhors determinism but cannot tolerate chance."
—Bernard De Voto, *The Course of Empire* (1952)

Policy makers face a daunting task when they attempt to use history as a source of lessons for today. Although history is not random, it tends toward randomness and is far from simple or linear. Given the apparent ease with which subjects in psychological experiments in laboratories use analogies to solve problems compared to the ineffectual use of historical analogies by foreign policy decision makers, it is clear that the international environment is more difficult to learn in than a laboratory. In laboratories, subjects face far simpler problems than in a foreign policy environment. Laboratory experiments usually have clearly defined, unchanging problems and options, with clear and immediate feedback. International relations is extraordinarily complex, highly uncertain, and changeable, with infrequent, often delayed, and ambiguous feedback, as well as unclear chains of cause and effect.[56]

Analogical reasoning, because it is based on the assumption that if two events are similar in one respect they will be similar in other respects, is especially vulnerable to errors caused by the complexity of international relations. Even if two international crises appear the same, antecedent conditions never recur exactly, and slightly different antecedent conditions can lead to totally different outcomes.[57] Therefore, because foreign policy crises are often dissimilar, even when they appear similar, policy makers often attempt to reason analogically between two cases that are, in reality, fundamentally different. To make matters worse, cause and effect are often not proportional. In a nonlinear system a small cause can have a large effect. Even so, like most scientists, policy makers, when they reason analogically, focus on large causes to explain large effects, such as when policy makers argue that shifting balances of power, instead of small causes, such as the irrationality of a leader, cause war.[58] For these reasons, a policy maker can pursue the same policy in what appears to be two identical cases and experience vastly different outcomes because the cases are not identical and small differences in initial conditions can lead to significantly different outcomes.

Because of this complexity, research on attempts by foreign policy makers to draw lessons from history paints a bleak picture of a failure to learn and an inability to use historical information to improve decision making.[59] Even suggestions on how to improve the use of historical analogies by decision makers have failed to improve the effectiveness of policy.[60]

However, even in the face of such complexity, historical information retrieved by analogy is not irrational as a decision-making tool, especially when combined with other decision-making methods, such as cost-benefit analysis and means-ends comparisons, which can make up for weaknesses in analogical reasoning.[61] History is a source of information for policy makers and analogies are a valid method of retrieving historical information from memory. For example, it would be foolhardy for decision makers to ignore the history of a crisis or the past behavior of an opposing leader. It would also be foolhardy to ignore past, similar cases, even if they are not identical. The study of similar cases is the foundation of international relations, political science, and history, as well as law and medicine, even though cases do not repeat exactly in any of these fields. In one sense, much scientific thinking is based on analogical reasoning between past and current cases. To ignore the storehouse of the past is to doom policy makers to facing each new crisis as if it were unique with no possibility of learning. But, learning does occur because history does repeat to a certain extent, and there are some clear, albeit general, lessons from the past. For example, it is usually easier to intervene militarily than to withdraw from a civil war. Leaders can also learn on the basis of long-term, relatively linear, trends, such as economic growth, military production schedules, and population growth rates.[62] Historical analogies are a method of decision making and of learning, and they can sharpen, clarify, and add to analysis of a current crisis. Analogical reasoning itself fits various rational models, including limited rationality (historical analogies simplify reality), process rationality (analogies rank options and define preferences), and adaptive rationality (analogies guide choice).[63]

Given the prevalence of the use of historical analogies in foreign policy decision making, even with the drawbacks of historical analogies and attempts to learn from history, leaders will not stop using historical analogies to derive lessons from history. Therefore, the crucial area for research then becomes to try to understand how policy makers can improve their use of analogical reasoning to retrieve lessons from history. The foundation for such understanding is to analyze how, why, and what affects the use of historical information by various types of leaders. One of the most common areas in which policy makers use historical information and analogies, primarily because of the high level of drama, stakes, and time pressures, is during regional contingencies involving the potential use of force, which is the focus of the next section.

REGIONAL CONTINGENCIES AND THE USE OF FORCE

The use of force in regional contingencies is, like the use of historical analogies, common. There have been more than 600 military interventions by more than 100 states between 1945 and 1988.[64] The United States used military force in other states 163 times between 1776 and 1970,[65] and every president since 1945 has used force abroad. Military intervention also shows no sign of decreasing in frequency in the post–Cold War world. American and British forces have been active in recent regional contingencies. U.S. forces have intervened in Kosovo, Liberia, Somalia, and Bosnia, while British forces have seen action in the Gulf War, Bosnia, and Kosovo. The pace of interventions appears, if anything, to be increasing. During the Cold War the U.S. Navy and Marines responded by intervening militarily 190 times or about once every eleven weeks, while between 1990 and 1997 they intervened 80 times or about once every four weeks.[66]

The present study defines the use of military force as a decision by a government or governments to overtly use regular armed forces in another state's territory when decision makers perceive a possibility of opposition, combat, and casualties to the intervening force. It focuses on the intervening state and on cases where decision makers believe that the use of force will lead to a relatively brief, low-cost intervention in terms of casualties and money. Furthermore, leaders believe that the fighting will be on the target state's territory, not on their own. They also believe that while there may be uncertainty about the political outcome, the intervening force will not be defeated on the battlefield because the ratio of existing military power is greatly in their favor. Policy makers believe they will be able to rely on standing military forces and not have to initiate a draft or a war economy. In comparison, decision makers using force who believe their actions will lead to war usually believe that they will need to institute conscription and a war economy, may have to fight on their own territory, and will often believe that the battlefield outcome is uncertain.

The intervening state's goals can be limited, such as rescuing nationals, or unlimited, such as the unconditional surrender of another state's military forces coupled with fundamental changes to the target state's political structure and elite. However, the target of an intervention may be fighting a total, unlimited war, regardless of the goals of the intervening state.[67] The focus of this study, however, is the intervening state and its government's decision to use military force in another state with the expectation that the intervention will be brief and low cost, in terms of lives and treasure.

The present study analyzes four cases in the 1950s that involved the possible use of military force by Britain and/or the United States. Although the 1950s was a time of great change, from decolonization to the emerging Cold War, the variables that influence the use of historical information and analogies by policy makers, as well as how they arrive at decisions to use military force, remain similar, if not identical, today. The individual and situational variables that influence the use of historical information analyzed in this book are as applicable today as they were in the 1950s. The cases are not meant to provide comprehensive descriptions and explanations of the four crises. Undoubtedly, other variables had significant influences in all of the cases. The goal is to analyze the cases in terms of the use of historical compared to current information, the use of historical analogies, and the decision of whether to use military force in regional contingencies.

THE USE OF MILITARY FORCE IS NOT A LAST RESORT

Politicians often portray the use of force as a last resort. However, the concept of "a last resort" explains little. Does the term mean the least attractive option, the option tried last, or both? Furthermore, perceptions of when the "last resort" has been reached vary greatly. Policy makers decide early in a crisis, on the basis of the type and degree of threat, the stakes, and perceptions of an adversary's rationality and trustworthiness, all of which can be influenced by historical information, whether force is the preferred option. In some cases, force may be used promptly and not as a last resort in terms of attractiveness of options or time.

The type and degree of threat, as well as the stakes involved, effects the attractiveness of the use of force. Many military intervention studies group threats to a state's foreign interests under the all-encompassing category "instability" and do not analyze how the type of threat affects the form of the response. However, a sense of proportionality, in which morality plays a part, governs the use of force.[68] Means are proportional to the type, degree, and intensity of the threat, as well as to what is at stake.[69] Military threats are usually met with military means, such as Britain's military response to the Argentine seizure of the Falkland Islands, and economic threats with economic means, such as U.S. economic sanctions against Japan for not easing economic barriers to imports in the 1980s. The greater the threat and the stakes, the greater the response. For example, the perceived threat to Saudi Arabia after Iraq invaded Kuwait in 1990, and the stakes for the United States—oil—were much greater and led to a much larger response than the perceived threat and stakes when the 1996 civil war in Liberia threatened a small number of U.S. citizens. Only a small Marine force was sent to rescue the Americans in Liberia, while half a million troops were sent to Saudi Arabia in Operations Desert Shield and Desert Storm.

Furthermore, the less rational and trustworthy an opponent is perceived to be, the more likely leaders will decide early in a crisis that military force will have to be used and used promptly. Irrationality is defined by how other actors perceive the leader. Do policy makers state that the foreign leader is irrational, unreasonable, insane, megalomaniacal or use other terms implying an absence of rational calculation in the making of policy or that the adversary cannot be trusted to fulfill a negotiated agreement? Leaders who perceive an adversary as irrational are unlikely to think that the adversary is reasonable enough to negotiate and agree to, or fulfill the terms of, a negotiated compromise or to change policy in response to economic sanctions. The adversary will be seen as an untrustworthy madman motivated by nationalism, megalomania, or some other internal drive that will not allow for rational, cost-benefit analysis during a negotiation or in response to economic sanctions. Therefore, policy makers conclude that force will have to be used. However, the perception that an adversary is irrational increases the likelihood, but does not guarantee, that force will be used. Furthermore, leaders may decide to use military force even if they perceive an adversary to be rational.

Historical information can significantly influence decisions about whether to use force by influencing perceptions of the size and degree of threat, the stakes, and the rationality of an adversary. For example, Eden's comparison of Nasser to Mussolini led Eden to conclude that the threat and stakes during the Suez crisis involved the risk of another world war against powerful foes. Eden was not afraid of a war against Egypt alone, just as Britain probably could have fought Italy with minimal effort in the 1930s. The fear was that Egypt would be allied with the Soviet Union, just as Italy in the 1930s was allied with Germany and, later, Japan. The analogy also suggested that since negotiation had failed with the apparently unreasonable and irrational Mussolini, it would fail with, what the British believed, was a similarly irrational Nasser. The historical analogy greatly increased the probability that force would have to be used. Furthermore, Eden drew from the 1930s the lesson that force should be used promptly against aggressive dictators, which predisposed Eden to use force promptly against Nasser. This highlights the influence historical information can have on decisions about the attractiveness of force as an option and when it should be used.

To summarize, policy makers decide early in a crisis whether to use force on the basis of the type and degree of threat, as well as on the stakes and the perceived rationality and trustworthiness of an opponent, all of which may be influenced by historical information retrieved by analogical reasoning. On the basis of these factors, force is often not a last resort in terms of attractiveness of options or of time. The historical cases will test these propositions, as well as analyze the role of historical information and analogies in decision making during crises involving the possible use of force by the United States and Britain in regional contingencies.

A textual analysis of the documents relating to the cases will be conducted to determine which types of historical information and analogies were used by whom, when, for what functions, and, by tracing changes in beliefs and perceptions, their effects.[70] The documents will be analyzed using the congruence procedure: look for congruence between a policy maker's beliefs on the basis of a historical analogy and the policy they support.[71] Private and public utterances will also be compared. By comparing speeches to different audiences, changes can be found that reflect noncore beliefs, which are changed to fit an audience. In this way, the actual influence of historical information on beliefs, as well as on the diagnosis of a crisis, and the formulation and justification of policy, can be analyzed.

Each analogy will be counted once per document, even if it is mentioned more than once in the same document. A historical analogy involves the explicit comparison of a past event or person to the current crisis. However, axioms, lessons, or rules clearly drawn from a historical analogy are inferred to have been based on the historical analogy, even if the analogy is only mentioned later. Often a policy maker mentioned a historical analogy once, and it was never mentioned again during the crisis. Therefore, only historical analogies that have a significant impact on policy will be discussed extensively.

Individual and situational variables influence the use of historical information and analogies in foreign policy decision making. Part I analyzes individual variables. The leaders involved in the four case studies are analyzed, focusing on their use of historical information and beliefs about history in their careers before the crises analyzed in this study. Then, in Part II, the four case studies are analyzed, focusing on situational variables. A summary of the empirical evidence relating to the issues discussed in the introduction and a conclusion make up the remainder of the book.

NOTES

1. Kindleberger, *The World in Depression*; and Odell, *United States International Monetary Policy*.

2. Spellman and Holyoak, "If Saddam Is Hitler Then Who Is George Bush?," p. 913.

3. Ibid. Doyle, "Grenada," p. 139; Schoonmaker, *Military Crisis Management*, pp. 6, 35; May, *"Lessons" of the Past*, pp. ix-xiv; Fry, "Introduction," p. 16; and Khong, *Analogies at War*, pp. 3–6, 11.

4. Hybel, "Learning and Reasoning by Analogy," pp. 215–216, 233; Gilovich, "Seeing the Past in the Present," p. 797; Zashin and Chapman, "The Uses of Metaphor and Analogy," p. 292.

5. See Jervis, *Perception and Misperception*; Nuestadt and May, *Thinking in Time*; and Vertzberger, *The World in Their Minds*.

6. Karen S. Cook and Margaret Levi, eds., *The Limits of Rationality*; Green and Shapiro, *Pathologies of Rational Choice Theory*; and Hogarth and Reder, eds., *Rational Choice*. For rationality critiqued from a historical analogy model perspective, see Haslam, "The Boundaries of Rational Calculation," pp. 38–40; Hybel, "Learning and Reasoning by Analogy," p. 218; and Khong, *Analogies at War*, pp. 53–54. For violations of rationality in decisions to use force, see Jentleson, Levite, and Berman, "Foreign Military Intervention in Perspective," pp. 310–311.

7. Mercer, "Reputation and International Politics," pp. 59–61; and Snyder, *Myths of Empire*, pp. 133, 236, 279.

8. Khong, *Analogies at War*, pp. 6–7.

9. Vertzberger, *The World in Their Minds*, p. 309.

10. Also called stock characters or stereotypes. Vertzberger, *The World in Their Minds*, p. 310; and Fry, "Introduction," p. 11.

11. In comparison, Inoguichi analyzed historical scripts based on general princi-

ples and strategic concepts, not on specific historical events or people. Inoguichi, *Wars as International Learning*, pp. 12–16, 54, 474–475.

12. Cohen and Gooch, *Military Misfortunes*, p. 37. Macroanalogies are similar to master analogies.

13. History can also influence policy via society. For example, at the U.S. Civil War battle of Shiloh, a red sun rose and many Confederates called it, "The sun of Austerlitz," an analogy to Napoleon's great victory. Lewis, *Sherman*, p. 219. However, individual and group effects are more direct and significant for foreign policy decision making.

14. Stein and Tanter, *Rational Decision-Making*, pp. 63–87.

15. Vertzberger, *The World in Their Minds*, p. 311.

16. Hybel, "Learning and Reasoning by Analogy," pp. 219, 236; Mefford, "The Power of Historical Analogies," p. 185; Schank, *Dynamic Memory*, p. 110; Vertzberger, *The World in Their Minds*, pp. 322–323; Gick and Holyoak, "Analogical Problem Solving," p. 325; and Baron, *Thinking and Deciding*, p. 78.

17. Gick and Holyoak, "Schema Induction and Analogical Transfer," p. 4.

18. Vertzberger, *The World in Their Minds*, pp. 320–321; Jervis, *Perception and Misperception*, p. 270; and Henrikson, "Conclusion," pp. 239–241.

19. Dallin, "Learning in U.S. Policy Toward the Soviet Union," p. 418; and Neustadt and May, *Thinking in Time*, pp. xiv, 245. For Macmillan, see chapter 2 below.

20. Gilovich, "Seeing the Past in the Present," p. 802; Vertzberger, *The World in Their Minds*, pp. 296, 321, 330–338; and Neustadt and May, *Thinking in Time*, pp. xiv, 245.

21. Vertzberger, *The World in Their Minds*, pp. 320, 324–330; and Neustadt and May, *Thinking in Time*, p. 133.

22. Gick and Holyoak, "Analogical Problem Solving," p.327.

23. Etheredge, *Can Governments Learn?*, p. 108; and Heclo, *A Government of Strangers*.

24. Schank, *Dynamic Memory*, p. 65.

25. Schrodt, "Adaptive Precedent-Based Logic and Rational Choice," pp. 373–400; Vertzberger, *The World in Their Minds*, p. 313; Khong, *Analogies at War*, pp. 12, 35–36, 212–219; and Gilovich, "Seeing the Past in the Present," p. 798.

26. Fry, "Introduction," p. 16, n.2.

27. Levy, "Learning and Foreign Policy," pp. 304–305.

28. Schuman and Rieger, "Historical Analogies, Generational Effects, and Attitudes Toward War," p. 315.

29. Jervis, *Perception and Misperception*, pp. 239, 249–260; and Levy, "Learning and Foreign Policy," p. 304.

30. Khong, *Analogies at War*, pp. 33–34.

31. Fry, "Introduction," p. 11.

32. Vertzberger, *The World in Their Minds*, pp. 299–308; Khong, *Analogies at War*, pp. 20–22; Hybel, *How Leaders Reason*, p. 297; and Etheredge, *Can Governments Learn?*, p. 110. A fourth function of historical information, rare in foreign policy making, is to establish expertise. However, policy makers almost always use familiar analogies, which their colleagues already know, thus negating the ability to establish superior expertise through the retrieval of such information.

33. Kincade, "On the Brink," p. 295.

34. Thatcher, *Downing Street Years*, p. 817.

35. For justification, see Hybel, *How Leaders Reason*, pp. 217–218, 296–297; Tetlock, "Learning in U.S. and Soviet Foreign Policy," p.21; Henrikson, "Conclusion," p. 248; and Snyder, *Myths of Empire*, chapters 1, 6, 7. For diagnosis and proscription, see Khong, *Analogies at War*, pp. 7–8, 27; Jervis, *Perception and Misperception*, p. 217; and Mefford, "The Power of Historical Analogies," pp. 190–191.

36. Jervis, *Perception and Misperception*, p. 217.

37. Ibid., pp. 225–227, 248–249.

38. Khong, *Analogies at War*, pp. 10–11, 49, 59–61.

39. Neustadt and May, *Thinking in Time*, p. 32; Khong, *Analogies at War*, pp. 15–16; and Anderson, "Justifications and Precedents," pp. 738–761.

40. Gick and Holyoak, "Analogical Problem Solving," p. 327.

41. Gilovich, "Seeing the Past in the Present," pp. 805–806.

42. Spellman and Holyoak, "If Saddam Is Hitler Then Who Is George Bush?," pp. 915–916, 924–927; Gick and Holyoak, "Analogical Problem Solving," p.331; Gick and Holyoak, "Schema Induction and Analogical Transfer," pp. 2, 5; and Hybel, "Learning and Reasoning by Analogy," pp. 220–224.

43. Gick and Holyoak, "Schema Induction and Analogical Transfer," pp. 2, 5–9; Gick and Holyoak, "Analogical Problem Solving," pp. 314–315, 330, 349; Gilovich, "Seeing the Past in the Present," pp. 797–808; Vertzberger, *The World in Their Minds*, p. 313; and Jervis, *Perception and Misperception*, p. 220.

44. For a less comprehensive typology, see Gick and Holyoak, "Analogical Problem Solving," pp. 314–315; and Spellman and Holyoak, "If Saddam Is Hitler Then Who Is George Bush?," p. 914.

45. Spellman and Holyoak, "If Saddam Is Hitler Then Who Is George Bush?," p. 925.

46. Vertzberger, *The World in Their Minds*, pp. 311, 317–318.

47. Khong, *Analogies at War*, pp. 50–51, 219–220, 223, 262–263. If the validity of a historical analogy is not debated, it may be an indication of Janis's groupthink.

48. Dallin, "Learning in U.S. Policy Toward the Soviet Union," p. 404; and Larson, *The Origins of Containment*, pp. xi, 57, 350.

49. Khong, *Analogies at War*, pp. 148, 252.

50. Larson, *The Origins of Containment*, p. 354.

51. Khong, *Analogies at War*, pp. 10, 253; Simon, "Rationality in Psychology and Economics," p. 28; Einhorn and Hogarth, "Decision Making under Ambiguity," pp. 63–64; Vertzberger, *The World in Their Minds*, p. 339; Read and Cesa, "This Reminds Me of the Time When . . . ," pp. 4, 18; Jervis, *Perception and Misperception*, p. 226; and Gick and Holyoak, "Analogical Problem Solving," p. 323.

52. Jervis, *Perception and Misperception*, pp. 269–270.

53. Unless decision makers act like statisticians and consider the size of the set from which the information was drawn in determining the validity of the analogy. Tversky and Kahneman's work shows that such is not the case ("Rational Choice and the Framing of Decisions").

54. Fry, "Introduction," p. 16, n.2; and Jervis, *Perception and Misperception*, pp. 246–247.

55. Vertzberger, *The World in Their Minds*, p. 325. Differences between history

learned/observed and history personally experienced are based on two types of memory: episodic (based on personal experience) and semantic (based on the meanings of words and knowledge). Schuman and Rieger, "Historical Analogies, Generational Effects, and Attitudes Toward War," p. 325.

56. Breslauer and Tetlock, "Introduction," pp. 3–19; Larson, "Learning in U.S.-Soviet Relations," pp. 352, 389–390; Jervis, *Perception and Misperception*, p. 237; Tversky and Kahneman, "Rational Choice and the Framing of Decisions," p. 90; Vertzberger, *The World in Their Minds*, pp. 26–35; and Beyerchen, "Clausewitz, Nonlinearity, and the Unpredictability of War," p. 61.

57. Beyerchen, "Clausewitz, Nonlinearity, and the Unpredictability of War," pp. 64, 67–68. This is similar to a model of unanticipated consequences, although the present model also posits that it is difficult to predict even the probability of predicted consequences.

58. Prediction is also difficult, even for experts. Tetlock asked foreign policy experts, professors, journalists, scholars, graduate students, and government specialists to make specific one-, five- and ten-year predictions about foreign policy issues. Attesting to the difficulty of learning in international relations, the accuracy of experts did not appreciably diverge from chance, and they did no better than laymen. Tetlock, "Good Judgment in International Politics," pp. 518–519, 522–528, 532.

59. Khong, *Analogies at War*, pp. 12–14, 25, 30, 37–39, 45–46, 212, 220–221; Jervis, *Perception and Misperception*, pp. 220–221, 229–234; Kupchan, "Getting In," pp. 243–244, 252, 256; Etheredge, *Can Governments Learn?*, pp. 117, 142–143, 158–162; and Vertzberger, *The World in Their Minds*, pp. 329–339.

60. Khong, *Analogies at War*, pp. 12–14, 255–257.

61. For a multiple-path model of decision making see Stein and Tanter, *Rational Decision-Making*.

62. Foreign policy experts who base their predictions on long-term trends are more accurate than those who base their predictions on other variables. Tetlock, "Good Judgment in International Politics," pp. 518–519, 522–528, 532.

63. March, "Bounded Rationality, Ambiguity, and Engineering Choice," pp. 590–592.

64. Tillema, *International Armed Conflict Since 1945*, pp. vii, 6.

65. Foreign Affairs Division, *Background Information on the Use of United States Armed Forces*, pp. 50–57.

66. Truver, "The U.S. Navy in Review," *U.S. Naval Institute Proceedings*, p. 76.

67. Because the phenomenon must involve a vast difference in perceived military capabilities, the term "military intervention" is usually applied to the use of force by a First World state in the Third World. This is similar to the definition of low-intensity conflict, which usually occurs in the less developed parts of the world, rarely involves regular armed forces on both sides, and usually does not involve high technology weapons. Van Creveld, *The Transformation of War*, p. 20.

68. Proportionality is based on the moral principle of the punishment fitting the crime. Gaddis, *The Long Peace*, p. 146; Hart, *Strategy*, p. 343.

69. For a contrary argument, see Hybel, *How Leaders Reason*, p. 8. Also see Kaplan, *The Wizards of Armageddon*, p. 79; and Girling, *America and the Third World*, p. 144.

70. If analogies have their greatest impact during the framing of a problem, then analysis of early meetings before public statements about policy are made need to be analyzed for the purposes of this study. Khong, *Analogies at War*, pp. 10–11, 62–63.

71. Ibid., pp. 64–68.

PART I

INDIVIDUAL VARIABLES AND THE USE OF HISTORICAL INFORMATION

2

The Leaders

"The proper memory for a politician is one that knows what to remember and what to forget."

—John, Viscount Morley of Blackburn,
Bartlett, *Familiar Quotations*, p. 637

Individual variables have a significant influence on whether, how often, and with what effect, individual leaders use historical information and lessons from history to make foreign policy decisions. The next sections analyze the major decision makers in the four historical cases that follow. The purpose of these sections is not to provide a thorough description of the lives of the leaders, but to analyze the factors that influenced their use of historical information and analogies.

A range of variables influence the use of historical analogies and historical information by policy makers. A leader's date of birth and major experiences influences which historical events he observed or was personally involved in and, therefore, which events he is likely to retrieve as historical analogies for current crises. Training and education, especially subjects studied in university, can influence how leaders think and the likelihood they will use historical analogies, as well as their knowledge of history, which contributes to determining the size of the pool of historical analogies available to a decision maker in his memory. Foreign policy experience also influences the size of the pool of available historical information, as well as which historical analogies a policy maker is likely to retrieve, since personally experienced events tend to be drawn upon more than events learned secondhand. Leaders also vary in their use of rhetoric, their interest in writing, and their ability as orators. This cluster of interests and skills indicates a leader's interest in, and aptitude for, language. Since historical analogies are both a rhetorical and an analytical device, leaders who are interested in rhetoric and language are more likely to think of, and use, historical analogies than leaders who are not interested in rhetoric and language. However, historical analogies usually do not come to mind without some careful thought. Therefore, writers are more likely to think of an analogy than orators, especially orators who speak extemporaneously. Orators are, however, more likely to use historical analogies than individuals who have little, or no, interest in rhetoric and language. Leaders with a sense of drama, gravitas, and of their place in history are also more likely to use historical information because historical analogies are used in response to dramatic events. These variables are the most significant variables in explaining the variation between policy makers in their use of historical information and analogies.

Part I also discusses the use of historical information and analogies by policy makers in crises prior to those analyzed in this book, which indicates their individual propensity to use such information. This will allow an assessment of the relative influence of situational and individual variables in the use of historical information and analogies. For example, if an individual with a high propensity to use historical information does not use such information during a foreign policy crisis, then situational factors must have negated the individual variables that tended toward the use of historical information and analogies. Conversely, if a leader who rarely used historical analogies in his career uses historical information and analogies in a crisis, then situational factors must have exerted significant pressure to use historical analogies.

The following sections discuss the principal decision makers in the four cases analyzed in this study: for the British, Clement Attlee (Prime Minister [PM]—Korea and Iran), Ernest Bevin (Foreign Secretary—Korea, Iran), Winston Churchill (PM—Iran), Anthony Eden (Foreign Secretary—Iran, PM—Suez), Harold Macmillan (PM—Jordan), and Selwyn Lloyd (Foreign Secretary—Suez, Jordan); and for the United States, Harry S. Truman (President—Korea, Iran), Dean Acheson (Secretary of State—Korea, Iran), Dwight D. Eisenhower (President—Iran, Suez, Lebanon), and John F. Dulles (Secretary of State—Iran, Suez, Lebanon).

THE BRITISH

Clement Attlee

Attlee observed or personally experienced the major events of the end of the nineteenth century and early twentieth century, which he could have drawn upon later in life as analogies to current crises. Born in 1883, Attlee was old enough to remember the Boer War and the "Sun-never-sets" days of the British Empire. He volunteered for service in the First World War and served in France before beginning his political career as mayor of Stepney in 1919. Attlee became an alderman in 1920 and was elected to Parliament in 1922. As a member of Parliament (MP), he was an expert on local government and electricity. His experience as an MP would have limited his pool of potential foreign policy historical analogies to draw upon later in life. However, in 1927 Attlee moved into the realm of foreign policy as under-secretary in the War Office. He rose to become leader of the Labour Party in 1935 and, in the 1930s, was a leading critic of Prime Minister Neville Chamberlain's appeasement policy. Adding to his foreign policy experience, during World War II, Attlee served at the center of British foreign policy decision making in the War Cabinet. He was Lord Privy Seal (1940–42), dominions secretary (1942–43), and then deputy prime minister (1942–45), second only to Prime Minister Churchill. By the time he became prime minister in 1945, Attlee had a long experience of observed and personally experienced foreign policy events from which to draw on as historical analogies.

Even before he gained firsthand foreign policy experience as a politician, Attlee studied history at school. History was his favorite subject at prep school. At Oxford, he read history, specializing in the Italian Renaissance. He also developed a "keen knowledge" of British history.[1] However, even though Attlee loved history, he went into law. His legal background had a greater influence on his analytical style and use of historical information than his love of history. From his legal training, Attlee always reasoned "from what has been done to what may be done"[2] and he rarely used historical analogies to compare two cases widely separated in time.[3] Lawyers argue cases on the basis of what has been done before. They rarely set out to change established law. Attlee's reasoning followed a lawyer's incremental, extrapolative style. He used his knowledge of history to extrapolate recent trends, not to reason analogically by comparing events separated in time.

Attlee's decision-making style also decreased the need to use historical analogies to retrieve lessons from history. Attlee always wanted to avoid what he called "drift," or the error of not making a decision. To reach his goal of deciding on a policy swiftly, Attlee led by conciliation so that policies reflected the consensus of the cabinet and so that no time was wasted on policies that lacked broad cabinet support. This preference for consensus meant that Attlee usually did not need to use historical information retrieved by analogy to analyze an issue, because other cabinet members provided the framework in which Attlee fashioned a consensus policy. He did not need to use historical analogies as cognitive shortcuts, since he relied on others initially to analyze issues and to suggest possible policies. The consensual process also decreased the need to use historical analogies to justify his decisions, since the policy, reached by consensus, already had his cabinet's support by the time a decision was reached.[4]

Attlee also lacked an orator's skill in the use of rhetoric. He was not an inspiring speaker and liked to speak extemporaneously.[5] Therefore, he was less likely to use historical analogies, which are usually used in well thought out arguments or in writing. Analogies rarely spring to mind in whole form, such as when someone speaks extemporaneously, as Attlee liked to do. Furthermore, historical analogies are usually used for dramatic, exciting events and by individuals given to dramatics. Attlee was not dramatic. He was a "colourless [sic]," ordinary man,[6] further decreasing his inclination to use historical analogies.

Even though he had a wide range of personal experience in foreign policy, as well as a great knowledge of history, Attlee's legal training, consensus style of leadership, and lack of rhetorical and oratorical skills, as well as his colorless personality, led him to reason by extrapolating trends from the recent past. He rarely used historical information retrieved by analogical reasoning to analyze foreign policy crises.

Ernest Bevin

Before entering government, Ernest Bevin had no foreign policy experience from which to draw historical analogies. Born in 1881, Bevin, like Attlee, was old enough to observe the Boer War and the First World War, although he served in neither. A union organizer, Bevin rose to lead the largest union in Britain before he entered government during the Second World War. However, even in government, Bevin's focus was on domestic issues, not foreign policy. He served as minister of Labour and National Service in the Churchill government. This lack of experience in foreign policy meant that Bevin had a limited pool of personally experienced, foreign policy events from which to draw historical analogies.

Bevin also did not gain a knowledge of history, foreign policy, or international events from school or from books. He did not attend university, leaving school at age 11, and he did not read much.[7] Therefore, Bevin's reservoir of historical analogies for international events was smaller than other policy makers, such as Attlee, Churchill, or Eden, who had years of personal experience in foreign policy decision making from which to draw.

Bevin's analytical and decision-making styles also decreased the probability that he would use historical analogies. He had an imaginative, not a historical, mind. Bevin used intuition, based on his imagination, more than analysis, to make decisions. He also tended to draw on his personal experiences, not on information from books,[8] during arguments. His personal experiences were largely with trade unions, not foreign policy. Bevin's analysis of issues was also influenced by the complex and extremely detailed labor negotiations at which he excelled as a labor leader before becoming foreign secretary.[9] This attention to detail tended to make him critical of all but the most similar historical analogies. Bevin saw the small differences rather than the broad similarities between analogies. And, unlike Attlee, Bevin was not a consensus leader. He was a labor leader: tough, blunt, determined, and confident.[10] Therefore, he did not use historical analogies to persuade others or to justify his decisions. He relied on current information, details, and the force of his personality to win arguments.

Bevin was also more of a conversationalist and orator than a writer.[11] Historical analogies are used in writing more than speaking, since they do not come easily to mind during a conversation and require abstract thought, which is more common when someone is writing. Therefore, Bevin was less likely to use historical analogies than leaders like Macmillan and Churchill, for whom the written word was at least, if not more, important than the spoken word. Bevin was also not an intellectual and, therefore, not the type to spend time thinking of historical analogies. For these reasons, historical analogies were not in Bevin's rhetorical arsenal.

All of these factors, including Bevin's lack of foreign policy experience, low level of interest in history, his experience in detailed labor negotiations, his oratorical style, and style of arguing and decision making, meant that Bevin did not view the world historically and rarely used historical analogies.[12]

Winston Churchill

Unlike Bevin, Churchill perceived events in historical terms and often drew upon his long experience in foreign policy for historical analogies.[13] By the decade of the 1950s, which encompassed the cases analyzed in this book, Churchill had a vast reservoir of historical events to draw upon, both from long, personal experience in government in two world wars and from historical study.

Born in 1874, Churchill, after attending Aldershot and Sandhurst, became a cavalryman and fought in conflicts in the North-West Frontier Province in India. Unlike Attlee and Bevin, who only observed the Boer War from afar, Churchill served in the conflict. During World War I, as Attlee served in France, Churchill was First Lord of the Admiralty. After the war Churchill became secretary of state for War and Air. After serving in the opposition, Churchill rose to become prime minister during the Second World War and again between 1951 and 1955. Churchill is probably the only person who could have written an autobiography and entitled it, *The Second World War*.

Churchill was also a writer with a deep interest in literature and oration, which increased his tendency to use historical analogies. He was a war correspondent during the Boer War and wrote numerous books on a wide range of subjects, including history, and won the 1953 Nobel Prize in Literature. Churchill's stirring speeches and famous oratorical style helped buttress British resolve during the darkest days of the Second World War. One indication of his brilliant use of language is that Churchill has more than four pages of quotations in Bartlett's *Familiar Quotations*.[14] His writings and speeches are full of historical analogies and information. Churchill is the epitome of the educated, historically minded leader, with a sense of gravitas and of his place in history.[15]

Anthony Eden

Anthony Eden had a historical mind, a vast knowledge of history, and, by the time he became prime minister, significant foreign policy experience. Foreign affairs intruded on Eden's life at an early age. He was 17 when his brother was killed in World War I. Later in the war, Eden served in the trenches himself. Although World War I was traumatic for Eden, because of the death of his brother and other friends, the 1930s were a defining period for him: The period marked the high and low points of his political career. Opposing the Axis made Eden's reputation. Marking a high point in his career, after his 1923 election to Parliament, Eden rose to become foreign secretary, playing a major role in many of the 1930s crises. In February 1938, in one of the lowest points of his political career, he was ousted from the Chamberlain government for his opposition to the appeasement policy over Italy's invasion of Abyssinia. Eden's resignation was one of the most traumatic events in his life, and he did not speak in Parliament again for more than two months.[16] After Chamberlain's government fell in September 1939, Eden returned to the cabinet and became secretary of state for the Dominions, then secretary of state for War and, in December 1939, foreign secretary. The importance of the 1930s and of World War II to Eden were reinforced by his wife: Winston Churchill's niece, Clarissa Churchill. The legacy of the 1930s cast a shadow that would fall over the rest of Eden's life.

The impact of the 1930s on Eden's later decision making was reinforced by his historical mind and tendency to view current events in terms of the past. Eden liked history and read Oriental languages at Oxford, which included medieval history.[17] His interest in history and tendency to use historical analogies was reflected in his analytical style. When he wrote about issues he invariably began with a historical analysis of the problem. He believed the past provided lessons for the present and drew broad, general lessons from history, especially from the 1930s, to provide frameworks for current crises. For example, Eden perceived Suez in terms of the 1930s and appeasement, traced Soviet behavior in the 1950s back to the policies and goals of the Russian Empire, and argued that the history of the Cyprus question was the source of conflict in the 1950s. Eden made the theme of his memoirs that the lesson of the 1930s—to use force promptly against aggressive, expansionistic dictators—was applicable to many of the crises Britain was involved in during the 1950s.[18]

Although Eden perceived current affairs through the mirror of history, he rarely mentioned historical analogies.[19] This paradox is explained by Eden's tendency to focus on the lessons of a historical analogy, not the historical analogy itself. Once he had used an analogy initially to frame a crisis, the lessons of the analogy, usually from the 1930s, were so ingrained that he did not mention the analogy itself again. Indeed, he sometimes did not mention the analogy at all. For example, Eden applied the lessons of the 1930s to the U.S. response to the North Korean invasion of South Korea, but never mentioned the analogy itself.[20] Although he applied a lesson from an analogy to the 1930s (to use force promptly against aggressive dictators) to French involvement in Indochina in 1954, the Formosa Straits crisis of 1955, and other international crises in the 1950s, he did not explicitly mention this analogy. It is a subtle, but important, difference. Eden clearly and repeatedly mentioned lessons from the 1930s even though he did not explicitly mention the 1930s.

Eden had a historical mind and had a vast experience in foreign policy. However, his personal inclination to use historical information was skewed by the dominance of the 1930s in his life, the decade which he later often used as a historical analogy to current crises. The 1930s had such an impact because the period marked one of the lowest points in his political career, when he resigned from the government, as well as one of the highest points, when he served in the Churchill cabinet during World War II. The 1930s had such an influence on Eden that he framed almost every foreign policy crisis after 1945 using the 1930's analogy.

Harold Macmillan

Like Churchill and Eden, Macmillan viewed the world from a historical perspective. Of all the leaders in this study, Macmillan used historical analogies most often, and from a broader range of historical sources, than any other leader in his political career. His family's publishing business and his interest in rhetoric and writing strongly influenced Macmillan's inclination to retrieve historical analogies from his broad foreign policy experience to frame current crises.

Macmillan's major, early foreign policy experiences were the world wars. Macmillan was educated at Eton and at Oxford, although the First World War ended his university studies before he graduated. Like Attlee and Eden, Macmillan served in the First World War and lost many close friends in the conflict.[21] Elected to Parliament in 1923, he focused on economic issues. However, in the 1930s, Macmillan shifted his attention from economics to foreign policy. By the late 1930s he was a major critic of Chamberlain's policy toward Germany and Italy. Like Eden and Bevin, the Second World

War marked Macmillan's ascension to high office. During the war he served as parliamentary secretary for the minister of Supply, under-secretary at the Colonial Office, and then, in December 1942, he went to North Africa as minister of state. After the war Macmillan was in opposition during Attlee's Labour government before he served in Eden's cabinet and became prime minister after Eden's Suez disaster, in which he played a significant role.

The 1930s and World War II, which were dramatic, recent, and important events to both Macmillan and to Britain, had a significant influence on his later decision making. However, the influence of the 1930s was balanced by Macmillan's love of, and broad knowledge of, history, which was based on extensive reading.[22] This knowledge provided him with a vast pool of possible historical analogies from which to draw, ranging from antiquity to the recent past.[23] His historical knowledge also allowed Macmillan to speak in broad, historical contexts, which increased his inclination to use historical analogies.[24] Thatcher wrote, "Macmillan always prided himself on having a sense of history."[25] He used historical analogies to demonstrate his broad historical knowledge and foreign policy experience and, in so doing, dominated his cabinet through intellectual superiority.[26]

Macmillan was also fascinated by rhetoric and the tools of oration and writing, including historical analogies. He was heir to a publishing firm, and he worked at his family's Macmillan Publishing Company between 1919 and 1923. Rhetoric and the written word were important to him, and in 1938 he published a book on economics, *The Middle Way*. His interest in rhetoric also extended to a love of oratory and conversation. Macmillan was a gifted speaker[27] and had a personal view of diplomacy. He liked to meet other leaders personally, which put his speaking skills, including his historical knowledge, to best use.[28]

Macmillan's love and knowledge of history, rhetoric, writing, and oration, as well as his foreign policy experience, meant that he often used historical analogies in his papers, diary, speeches, and memoranda.[29] Biographies of Macmillan are full of examples of his use of historical information retrieved by analogical reasoning. For example, Macmillan compared Charles de Gaulle to Louis XIV and Napoleon. He said the British in the U.S. empire were like the Greeks in the Roman Empire. He compared an officer in World War II to Marlborough's Cadogan and Europe after World War II to Greece after the Second Pelaponnesian War.[30] During the 1938 Czech crisis, Macmillan said that Britain should make its intentions clear and not repeat the failure of Sir Edward Grey in 1914.[31] And on May 13, 1958, during the Lebanon crisis, Macmillan wrote, with great foresight, in his diary, if Lebanon falls, "after Austria—the Sudeten Germans. Poland (in this case Iraq) will be the next to go."[32] Unlike any of the other policy makers in this study, who restricted their historical analogies almost entirely to recent events and people, Macmillan's historical analogies ranged from ancient Rome and Greece to World War I and the 1930s, demonstrating his broad historical knowledge, especially given that most policy makers rely almost exclusively on personally experienced or observed events to retrieve as historical analogies. However, like Eden, although not to the same extent, Macmillan made his political career during the 1930s, and the 1930s exerted a significant influence on his beliefs. This influence was amplified because Macmillan was awestruck by Churchill. He even said he was Churchill's heir.[33] Macmillan often used historical analogies and of the analogies he used, lessons from the 1930s were the most common.

Selwyn Lloyd

Although interested in history, Selwyn Lloyd, because of his legal training and precise mind, rarely used historical analogies, although he had the knowledge to do so. Lloyd studied Classics at Cambridge, was in the History Tripos, and liked tracing his Welsh lineage. However, in large part, his lack of use of historical analogies can be traced to his legal background; he became a barrister in 1926. In cabinet discussions Lloyd usually provided a legal view. He was also precise by inclination, which made it more likely that he would see the small differences between historical analogies and deem them less valid than someone with a less precise mind, who would focus on the general similarities.[34]

On the rare occasions when Lloyd used historical analogies, he did not draw upon the 1930s, as Eden, his prime minister, usually did. Younger than Eden, Attlee, Bevin, Churchill, and Macmillan, Lloyd was in school in Edinburgh during World War I. Younger than the other prime ministers and foreign secretaries in this book, the hypothesis that leaders usually retrieve recent historical events as analogies would have predicted that Lloyd would have looked to more recent events than the other leaders for historical analogies. However, unlike Macmillan, who said he was heir to Churchill, and Eden, who looked to the 1930s for historical analogies, Lloyd's hero was from an earlier period: Lloyd George, who served as prime minister from 1916 to 1922. Also unlike Eden, Bevin, and Macmillan, who rose to political prominence during the 1930s and World War II, Lloyd came to political power after the Second World War.[35] His foreign policy experience was acquired in a brief period. In 1945, he was elected to Parliament, specializing in financial issues. He was minister of State (1951), minister of Supply (1954), minister of Defense (1955), and in 1956, the year of the Suez crisis, he was foreign secretary and then moved to the Treasury.

However, a prime minister or a president can overshadow his cabinet. Lloyd's individual traits were eclipsed by the prime minister he worked with, Eden, who dominated foreign policy decision making. Therefore, Eden's perspective and historical view, which focused on the 1930s, overrode Lloyd's decision-making style. Eden, in effect, acted as his own foreign secretary.

THE AMERICANS

Harry S. Truman

Harry S. Truman is an enigma. He had a historical mind. He loved to study history and "assumed patterns" in history. He believed these patterns repeated and were progressive.[36] Truman always wanted to know the history of a problem. He also had many years of experience in office before he was president, ten in the Senate and eight as vice president, on which to draw upon for personally experienced historical analogies. Truman thought about his place in history[37] and, in his memoirs, said he often used history.[38] His diary has many references to history, both ancient and modern. There are, however, surprisingly few historical analogies that compare a current event with a past event, in the diaries, speeches, minutes of meetings, or biographies of Truman.[39] Even so, many scholars argue, as did Cumings, that historical analogies were Truman's "stock and trade."[40] However, these scholars give few, if any, examples of Truman's use of historical analogies.[41]

This inconsistency between Truman's love of history and lack of use of historical analogies can be explained by Truman's legal work as a judge, which, like the lawyers Attlee and Lloyd, may have decreased his inclination to use historical analogies. However, a more valid explanation is that Truman, like Eden, did not mention historical analogies during the decision-making process because he relied on general, internalized lessons from history, not the analogies themselves, to frame crises quickly and prescribe policies. Lessons from history formed the basis for quick, or what Truman called "jump," decisions.[42] The lessons were cognitive shortcuts, just as historical analogies are cognitive shortcuts, that took the place of in-depth analysis of issues. "Jump" decisions, however, led to a need later to justify his decisions. Lacking in-depth analysis, Truman relied on history for justification.[43] It is noteworthy that Truman wrote that after he made a decision he would read history "to see if I could find some background of history which would affect what had to be done."[44] The key is that he read history after he made a decision. Truman made a decision, often on the basis of an internalized lesson from history, and then referred to history to justify the decision. Therefore, although Truman often relied on lessons from history to frame crises and prescribe policy, he usually mentioned historical analogies only after a policy decision had been reached in order to justify his chosen policy. Truman knew history and had internalized lessons from master historical analogies, especially from the 1930s. When a crisis arose, he framed it in terms of the analogy and applied the internalized lessons from the analogy. However, Truman did not mention the analogy when he applied the lessons. Instead, he only mentioned the historical analogy later to justify the chosen policy.

Dean Acheson

Acheson had an extensive knowledge of history. However, he only occasionally used historical analogies because his legal training was in conflict with his inclination to use historical information. In Acheson, British Ambassador Sir Oliver Franks perceptively observed that his broad, general view of history was at war with his narrowly focused, detail-oriented, legal training.[45]

Acheson served in World War I and, like Attlee and Lloyd, then became a lawyer. Acheson graduated from Harvard Law School in 1918. He clerked at the Supreme Court before joining a Washington law firm in 1921. Acheson's legal training, like that of Attlee and Lloyd, led to a way of thinking that decreased his reliance on historical information and analogies to analyze foreign policy crises. Acheson perceived the world from an economic viewpoint, reflecting his training and work as an international lawyer for some of the largest companies in America.[46] Historical analogies are usually used in national security issues. Therefore, Acheson's focus on economics decreased the probability that he would use historical analogies. Acheson's legal method, which he applied to foreign policy issues, was to think through the logic of a problem. He would then relate the problem to larger regional and global concerns, based on the interests of the United States and the global international political economy. His ultimate critique was, "It hadn't been thought through."[47] Acheson's logical mind only occasionally used historical analogies, which are cognitive shortcuts and the antithesis of a problem being "thought through." For example, in the chapter in his memoirs on the outbreak of the Korean War he does not mention any historical analogies,[48] even though the lessons of the 1930s were a powerful influence on the decision making of Attlee and Truman.

However, this legal and economic perspective was balanced by Acheson's interest in history. He had an excellent grasp of history, even giving a speech in 1966 to the Society of American Historians entitled, "History as Literature."[49] Acheson's memoirs begin with the 1815 Congress of Vienna[50] and in a collection of his letters he occasionally mentioned historical analogies.[51] Acheson also used historical analogies in his more literary books, such as *Morning and Noon*, although he used them more for imagery than to make an argument.

Acheson's legal training and precise mind, which noted the small differences rather than the general similarities between analogies, did not incline him to use analogies, even while his knowledge of, and liking for, history occasionally led him to use historical analogies. His method of thinking problems through logically also reduced the probability that he would resort to cognitive shortcuts, such as historical analogies.

Dwight D. Eisenhower

Although Eisenhower loved history and had an eye for his place in it, he rarely used historical analogies. Unlike Churchill, whose military training did not diminish his use of historical analogies, Eisenhower's professional training as a soldier, combined with his leadership style of using a staff to analyze issues, meant that he rarely used historical information or analogies to analyze a crisis or to prescribe or justify policy. The difference in the influence of military training on Churchill and Eisenhower was because Eisenhower remained a soldier for most of his adult life, retaining the style of leadership and decision making that he learned at West Point, while Churchill became a politician.

Eisenhower had the training and knowledge to use historical information and analogies. Ambrose wrote that Eisenhower was the best prepared president in foreign policy ever elected.[52] Eisenhower was educated at West Point and, later, at the Army Staff College. During World War I he trained troops in the United States. In the interwar period he served in Panama, the Philippines, and then, early in the Second World War, in Washington, planning the invasion of Europe. As commander of Operation Torch, the Anglo-American landing in North Africa, and Supreme Commander Allied Expeditionary Forces, Europe, Eisenhower was at the heart of Allied-American cooperation for the war in Europe. After the war he was commander of the North Atlantic Treaty Organization forces and then, in 1947, president of Columbia University, before he became president. Throughout his life, Eisenhower loved to read history. He also had an eye to history, which led to him writing notes to be used later by historians during major events in his life.[53]

Eisenhower was also a great communicator, which meant that he was interested in rhetoric and the use of historical analogies. He reviewed all of the major speeches by his secretary of state, John F. Dulles, and was intimately involved in writing and revising his own speeches.[54] Eisenhower had also been interested in psychological operations, including propaganda, during World War II and viewed rhetoric as a weapon in the Cold War to garner support for the West in Communist states.[55]

Eisenhower was also a rarity among the leaders studied in this book. He alone appeared to be able to control his use of historical information and analogies, as well as their influence upon him, to an extremely high degree. Although he rarely used historical analogies, Eisenhower used them for two specific purposes: to argue against an analogy when someone else had mentioned one and when he thought the person he was communicating with would be persuaded by a historical analogy. As an example of the former, in the late 1940s, Eisenhower often argued against those who posited a Pearl Harbor–type, surprise attack on the United States. He did not raise the analogy, although he did attempt to refute it. As an example of Eisenhower using an analogy for a specific audience, he said the best way to appeal to Churchill was through history. Eisenhower told Dulles to play on Churchill's "sense of history" to try to convince Churchill to stop promoting what Eisenhower called a "second Munich" by seeking a negotiated peace in Indochina. In an April 4, 1954, letter to Churchill, Eisenhower used a historical analogy to compare the West's failure to stand up to the Axis in the 1930s to Britain's reluctance to intervene with the United States in Indochina in 1954.[56]

Apart from using historical analogies for these two reasons, Eisenhower rarely used historical analogies. There are almost no historical analogies mentioned in his diaries, in biographies, or even in a volume on Eisenhower's use of rhetoric.[57] Eisenhower's military training decreased his inclination to use historical analogies to retrieve lessons from history. Reflecting his staff background, he wanted problems studied before making a decision. As president, the National Security Council (NSC) studied problems, gathered expert opinions and gave them to Eisenhower, who then made decisions.[58] This meant that Eisenhower did not need historical analogies as a cognitive shortcut to analyze most issues, since his staff studied and simplified the issues for him. Furthermore, his cabinet was composed almost entirely of lawyers and businessmen.[59] These men, as with the other lawyers in this study, Attlee, Acheson, and Lloyd, were less inclined to use historical analogies than if Eisenhower had included diplomats or academics in his cabinet.[60] The lack of interest of Eisenhower and Dulles in historical analogies was shown in a 1954 meeting with Eden, who called for a Southeast Asian version of the 1925 Locarno Treaty. Eisenhower and Dulles looked bored and Eden dropped the analogy. Neither American even mentioned that the Locarno Treaty failed to prevent war in Europe fourteen years later. Eisenhower was also detail oriented,[61] which meant that he tended to see the small differences between analogies, not the general similarities. Therefore, he did not see most historical analogies as valid and rarely used them, except in response to other people using them or when he thought a historical analogy would find receptive ears in a particular audience. Far more than other leaders, Eisenhower controlled his use of historical analogies and their influence upon himself because he discounted most analogies and because his decision-making style negated their usefulness as a cognitive shortcut.

John F. Dulles

Like Acheson, John F. Dulles's training as a lawyer and his love of history caused an inner conflict over the use of history and historical analogies. Dulles, like Acheson, Attlee, and Lloyd, was trained as a lawyer. He graduated from Georgetown Law School in two years, earning the highest grades in the law school's history.[62] Dulles was a Wall Street lawyer from 1911 to

1949, which led him, like Acheson, to have an international political economy view of world.[63] Given that historical analogies are usually used for security issues, this decreased the likelihood that he would use analogies to retrieve information from history. Dulles was also detail oriented,[64] further decreasing the likelihood that he would use historical analogies.

Balancing Dulles's legal training, detailed mind, and economic outlook, was his tendency to be dramatic and passionate. He was not "colourless [*sic*]" like Attlee. Historical analogies tend to be used for dramatic events, which inclined Dulles to use historical analogies. Dulles also had a wealth of personal foreign policy experience to draw upon for historical analogies. He worked for the Wilson administration (1917–19), and then at the Paris Peace Conference (1919), focusing on the reparations issue. Dulles also participated in foreign policy debates throughout the 1930s and 1940s. This sense of drama and long personal experience in foreign policy led him to sometimes use historical analogies.[65] For example, during the discussion about a peace treaty with Japan after World War II, Dulles stressed that the mistakes of the Versailles Peace Treaty after World War I must not be repeated.[66] However, Dulles, like Lloyd and Acheson, rarely used historical analogies. He instead generally used his legal training and detailed mind to analyze issues carefully from an economic standpoint.

CONCLUSION

The policy makers in this study were a diverse group of men who varied in their use of historical analogies throughout their careers. Macmillan used historical information and analogies the most often, followed by Churchill, Eden, and Truman, although Eden used analogies based mainly on one set of historical events: the 1930s. Eisenhower used historical analogies on rare occasions, usually for a specific audience or to refute an analogy raised by someone else, while Dulles and Acheson rarely used historical information and analogies. However, they used them more often than Attlee, Bevin, and Lloyd, who almost never mentioned historical analogies.

Certain variables influence the use of historical information and analogies by individuals. This limited sample of leaders suggests that legal training decreases the use of historical information and analogies. Military training, when the individual remains in the military as a career, like Eisenhower did, also decreases the use of historical analogies. Individuals who are interested in history, writing, rhetoric, or oratory are more likely to use historical analogies than those who are not so inclined. These factors can be broken down further. A leader must be interested in history to use historical analogies regularly during crises as a cognitive shortcut. Then, because historical analogies do not come easily to mind, policy makers who are interested in writing are more likely to retrieve historical analogies than those interested in oratory, especially those who speak extemporaneously. Leaders who draft speeches and, in a sense, write their own speeches are more likely to use historical analogies than orators who speak "off-the-cuff" or have others write their speeches.

Age, although in very broad bands, has a strong influence on which historical events are retrieved as analogies. Almost all of the leaders in this study, old enough to be aware of the 1930s and World War II, were influenced strongly by the traumatic, dramatic, and life-changing period and later drew upon lessons from that time to frame current crises. The 1930s and World War II became a master analogy. Even so, all of the leaders also observed or were involved in World War I. However, the First World War was not used often as an analogy to crises in the 1950s and did not become a master analogy. One reason is that the leaders in this study, while involved at low levels in World War I, rose to political prominence during the 1930s and World War II. The Second, not the First, World War marked high points in their lives, although Lloyd is an exception, in that he rose to power after 1945. Furthermore, as they faced crises as national leaders in the 1950s, their experiences in the 1930s and the Second World War, when they became leaders, appeared to be more analogous than their experiences in the Great War, when they were not involved in national decision making. And, the 1950s also appeared to be more similar to the 1930s and 1940s than to 1914–18. The First World War was a war of empires, kings, and trenches, while the Axis powers were non–status-quo powers who sought to overturn the entire system of international relations using air power, tanks, and submarines, just as the West believed the Soviets were attempting to do in the 1950s, with the added power of nuclear weapons.

The leaders in this study also varied greatly in the amount of foreign policy experience they had when they reached high office. Churchill had the most high-level, foreign policy experience, while Lloyd had the least. Experience in foreign policy correlates in a broad sense with use of historical analogies. Churchill, Macmillan, and Eden had far more foreign policy experience, and, therefore, used historical analogies more often, than Lloyd and Bevin. However, foreign policy experience alone does not automatically lead to the use of historical analogies. For example, the legal training of Dulles and Acheson overrode their foreign policy experience and knowledge of history, which meant that they did not use historical analogies nearly as often as Churchill, Macmillan, and Eden. Interest in history also influenced the use of historical information and analogies. Churchill, Macmillan, Truman, and Eden were interested in, and had greater knowledge of, history than the other leaders. They, therefore, used historical information and analogies more often than the other leaders when they faced foreign policy crises.

All of these leaders also were educated early in the twentieth century when history was taught as being progressive. Early in the century there was also a widely held belief that historical patterns repeated and that history could be looked to for answers to current problems. It was a belief contrary to the perception, held by many today, that rapid technological and social change have made history less relevant, or even, as Francis Fukiyama argued, that history has ended. This basic belief in the relevance of history made it more likely that the leaders analyzed in this book would use historical information and analogies than leaders educated later in this century.

There also is a relationship between dramatic leaders and the use of historical analogies, which tend to be used during dramatic, national security crises. Leaders with a sense of drama and gravitas, such as Churchill, Eden, Macmillan, and Dulles, use historical analogies more often than those who lack a sense of drama and flair, such as Bevin, Attlee, and Acheson. Eisenhower, who wrote notes for historians during crucial periods in his life, certainly had a sense of history and gravitas. However, his singular control of his use of historical analogies and their influence upon him, led him to use historical analogies as a tool of rhetoric, but only for certain audiences or in response to analogy-based criticisms.

However, given the small sample of leaders in this study, further research is needed to analyze the influence of individual factors on the use of historical information and analogies. Although individual traits influence the use of historical information and analogies, such influence must be balanced with specific situational variables, which are the subject of the following case studies.

Part II of the book deals with situational variables and their influence on the use of historical analogies and the decision to use military force. All four historical cases fall within the 1950s, a period when the Cold War heated up in Korea and the West responded to what it believed was a Soviet-sponsored probe by rearming and organizing alliances around the world to contain the Soviet Union. By 1949 both sides had nuclear weapons and the contest was set for the next forty years. However, even though the Cold War is over, the British and American decision making involved in the four cases relating to the decision of whether to use military force in regional contingencies and the influence of historical analogies on those decisions, is as relevant today as it was then. The threat of Soviet counterintervention is gone. However, the influence of situational variables on the use of historical analogies and, in turn, on the decision of whether to use military force, is the same today as it was in the 1950s. Historical analogies are still a cognitive shortcut used during certain types of situations to simplify chaotic events, as well as to prescribe and justify policies. The next four chapters focus on the types of situations that lead to the use of historical information and analogies, as well as on the types of situations that lead to the use of current information instead of the use of lessons from history.

NOTES

1. Brookshire, *Clement Attlee*, pp. 17, 147–148; and Burridge, *Clement Attlee*, pp. 12, 18.

2. Burridge, *Clement Attlee*, p. 143.

3. Almost no historical analogies are mentioned, for example, in Burridge, *Clement Attlee*, or Brookshire, *Clement Attlee*.

4. Burridge, *Clement Attlee*, pp. 1–2, 315–318; and Brookshire, *Clement Attlee*, pp. 3, 7, 13–14, 42, 186, 192.

5. Brookshire, *Clement Attlee*, pp. 8, 17.

6. Burridge, *Clement Attlee*, pp. 1–2, 315–318.

7. Bullock, *Ernest Bevin*, Vol. I, pp. 369–370.

8. Bullock, *Ernest Bevin*, Vol. II, pp. 101–103, 366.

9. Bullock, *Ernest Bevin*, Vol. I, pp. 369–370.

10. Bullock, *Ernest Bevin*, Vol. II, pp. 98–99.

11. Ibid., p. 103.

12. Biographies of Bevin contain few, if any, historical analogies. Bullock, *Ernest Bevin*, Vols. I, II, and III; and Weiler, *Ernest Bevin*.

13. Bullock, *Ernest Bevin*, Vol. II, pp. 102–103; and Gilbert, *Churchill*, p. 55.

14. Bartlett, *Familiar Quotations*, pp. 742–746.

15. Ashley, *Churchill as Historian*.

16. Aster, *Anthony Eden*, pp. 23, 50–54.

17. Ibid., pp. 4, 8; and Rothwell, *Anthony Eden*, p. 8.

18. Eden, *Full Circle*, pp. 3, 395.

19. For example, Aster mentions only one historical analogy apart from the Suez case. Aster, *Anthony Eden*, p. 127. Rothwell only mentions three historical analogies. Rothwell, *Anthony Eden*, pp. 32, 148, 183.

20. Aster, *Anthony Eden*, p. 141.

21. Horne, *Harold Macmillan*, Vol. I, pp. 33, 41.

22. Fisher, *Harold Macmillan*, p. 172.

23. Horne, *Harold Macmillan*, Vol. I, p. 116; Vol. II, p. 608; and Fisher, *Harold Macmillan*, pp. 103, 182, 366.

24. Fisher, *Harold Macmillan*, p. 182.

25. Thatcher, *Path to Power*, p.118.

26. Fisher, *Harold Macmillan*, p. 155.

27. James, "Harold Macmillan: An Introduction," p.2.

28. Aldous, " 'A Family Affair,' " pp. 9–35.

29. However, cabinet minutes are a questionable source for Macmillan's use of historical information. The minutes sometimes bore little relation to what had been said, sometimes appearing to have been prepared in advance. Fisher, *Harold Macmillan*, p. 185.

30. Ibid., pp. 95, 100, 106, 108, 134.

31. Horne, *Harold Macmillan*, Vol. I, p. 116.

32. Horne, *Harold Macmillan*, Vol. II, p. 92. For other examples, see Horne, *Harold Macmillan*, Vol. I, pp. 148, 160, 164–165, 201, 209, 247, 306, 307, 334, 364, 394, 397, 405.

33. Aldous, " 'A Family Affair,' ", p. 12.

34. Thorpe, *Selwyn Lloyd*, pp. 1, 2, 18, 22, 43, 146.

35. Ibid., pp. 19–20, 65.

36. Ferrell, *Harry S. Truman: A Life*, pp. 23–24; Hamby, *A Man of the People*, pp. 13–14.

37. Ferrell, *Harry S. Truman: A Life*, p. 183.

38. Truman, *Memoirs*, Vol. I, p. 121.

39. No official minutes were taken at his cabinet meetings, which may explain the lack of mention of historical analogies. However, this would not explain the lack of historical analogies in his memoirs, speeches or biographies. See *The Public Papers of the Presidents of the United States: Harry S. Truman* for 1950, 1951, 1952–3; Ferrell, *Harry S. Truman: A Life*; Ferrell, *Off the Record*; and Hamby, *A Man of the People*.

40. Cumings, *The Origins of the Korean War*, Vol. II, p. 630.

41. See chapter 3 of this book on Korea.

42. Ferrell, *Harry S. Truman: A Life*, p. xi.

43. Vertzberger, *The World in Their Minds*, pp. 321–323.

44. Ferrell, *Harry S. Truman: A Life*, p. 182.

45. Harper, *American Visions of Europe*, p. 251.

46. McGlothlen, *Controlling the Waves*, pp. 18, 29.

47. Cumings, *The Origins of the Korean War*, Vol. II, p. 630. Also see p. 411.

48. Acheson, *Present at the Creation*, chapter 44, pp. 402–420. Also see McGlothlen, *Controlling the Waves*, p. 90.

49. Acheson, *Fragments of My Fleece*, pp. 88–89.

50. Cumings, *The Origins of the Korean War*, Vol. II, p. 43.

51. McClellen and Acheson, *Among Friends*.

52. Ambrose, *Eisenhower: The President*, p. 18.

53. Ibid., p. 16; and Lyon, *Eisenhower*, p. 510.

54. Mark J. Schaefermeyer, "Dulles and Eisenhower on 'Massive Retaliation,' " p. 31.

55. Hogan, "Eisenhower and Open Skies: A Case in 'Psychological Warfare,' " p. 139; Griffin, "New Light on Eisenhower's Farewell Address," p. 281; and Medhurst, "Eisenhower's Rhetorical Leadership: An Interpretation," p. 289.

56. Ambrose, *Eisenhower: The President*, pp. 179, 205, 257, 430.

57. Ferrell, ed., *The Eisenhower Diaries*; *The Public Papers of the Presidents of the United States: Dwight D. Eisenhower, 1956*; *The Public Papers of the Presidents of the United States: Dwight E. Eisenhower, 1958*; and Medhurst, *Eisenhower's War of Words*.

58. Lyon, *Eisenhower*, pp. 531, 646–647.

59. Ambrose, *Eisenhower: The President*, p. 24.

60. Rothwell, *Anthony Eden*, p. 148.

61. Ambrose, *Eisenhower: The President*, p. 21.

62. Pruessen, *John Foster Dulles*, p. 12.

63. Ibid., pp. 73–74.

64. Ambrose, *Eisenhower: The President*, p. 21.

65. Pruessen, *John Foster Dulles*, pp. 164, 179, 213, 259, 272, 273, 286, 405, 445.

66. Miyasato, "John F. Dulles and the Peace Settlement with Japan," p. 194; and Pruessen, *John Foster Dulles*, p. 445.

PART II

SITUATIONAL VARIABLES AND THE USE OF HISTORICAL INFORMATION

3

The Toughest Decision: Korea

"This is the toughest decision I had to make as President."
—Truman about the Korean decision, Lowe,
The Origins of the Korean War, p. 169

When North Korea invaded South Korea on June 25, 1950,[1] the size and rapidity of the North Korean invasion convinced British and American policy makers that only one response had a chance of defending the Republic of Korea (ROK) successfully: the prompt use of military force. By the time diplomatic, economic, or military aid had an affect, North Korea would, they believed, have conquered South Korea. However, the United States also relied on lessons from the 1930s to frame the crisis, determine the stakes, the importance of time, the role of allies, and adversaries, to decide to use military force quickly and to justify the chosen policy. The British were more focused on current information, especially with maintaining the Anglo-American special relationship, than the Americans, although lessons from the 1930s and World War II about the prompt use of force against dictators, as well as the importance of the Anglo-American alliance, contributed to the British decision to respond quickly with naval forces. However, the British did not decide to commit ground forces until late July. For the Americans and, to a lesser extent, the British, military force was the preferred option, not a last resort, although they both also pursued diplomatic options and, after intervening militarily, imposed economic sanctions.

This chapter focuses on the influence of historical information on foreign

policy decision makers in London and Washington during the time period
when they decided to use force: June 25, the day of the invasion, until late
July, when the British cabinet decided to intervene with ground forces. The
first section outlines the major decisions relating to the North Korean invasion. It highlights the sequence of policy responses the British and Americans pursued: diplomacy and military force almost at the same time, and,
only later, economic sanctions. The use of historical information and historical analogies compared to current information on British and American
policies is then discussed. An analysis of why policy makers relied so heavily
on the 1930's analogy is followed by a discussion of the process by which
leaders used historical analogies. To highlight the influence of the 1930's
analogy, the remaining section discusses other possible historical analogies
that could have been applied to the North Korean invasion and would have
led to different policy prescriptions than the 1930's analogy.

THE AMERICAN AND BRITISH RESPONSES

American policy makers decided to respond to the North Korean invasion
with diplomatic measures and, at the same time, to intervene militarily. The
British also decided to intervene with naval forces at the same time as they
pursued diplomatic action against North Korea in the United Nations. It
was only long after pursuing diplomatic and military options that the British
and Americans resorted to economic sanctions against North Korea.

As soon as news of the North Korean invasion reached Washington, on
June 24, Secretary of State Acheson telephoned President Truman, who was
vacationing at his home in Independence, Missouri. Acheson's first recommendation was to take the issue to the United Nations.[2] Truman agreed
and asked if he should return to Washington. Acheson suggested that the
president stay in Independence until more information was available.

Following Acheson's recommendation, the United States presented the
case to the United Nations and on June 25, with British support, the U.N.
Security Council passed a 9–0 resolution, which stated that the invasion was
a breach of the peace and called for an immediate ceasefire.[3] A subsequent
U.S.–sponsored resolution recommended "that the members of the United
Nations furnish such assistance to the Republic of Korea as may be necessary
to repel the armed attack."[4] However, the United Nations was not crucial
to the American or British decisions to use military force. Both decided to
intervene militarily before the United Nations passed its resolutions, and
Truman and Attlee would have both intervened without U.N. support.[5]

Truman decided to use force soon after, if not at the same time as, he
decided to pursue the diplomatic option and long before implementing economic sanctions. Acheson and Truman decided to take the issue to the
United Nations and then, on the same day, Truman decided to use military
force, although this decision was not implemented until a few days later.
Only much later did the Americans decide to impose economic sanctions

on North Korea. After spending the day in Independence, Truman flew back to Washington. On the morning of June 25, the second day of the crisis, and in his first contact with his advisors other than the telephone conversation with Acheson, Truman showed he had already decided to use force if it was required. On June 25 Assistant Secretary of State James Webb rode with Truman, Acheson, and Defense Secretary Louis Johnson from the airport in Washington, where Truman had landed after his flight from Independence, to Blair House. Webb later said, "the President immediately stated that . . . this was a challenge that we must meet. . . . By God, I'm going to let them have it," which Webb believed meant that Truman was going to use military force. Webb told Truman that his advisors had three recommendations. However, Truman had made up his mind and said, "Well, O.K. of course, but you know how I feel." On June 25 Truman's daughter wrote in her diary: "Communist Korea is marching in on Southern Korea and we are going to fight." Other U.S. policy makers were also already considering introducing U.S. military forces to South Korea. Acheson and "a good many of the other officials felt [the commitment of U.S. forces] would have to come soon" within "another day or two."[6]

Truman had decided to use military force before imposing economic sanctions and well before diplomatic actions through the United Nations had any prospect of success. At his first meeting with his advisors, at Blair House on June 25 at 7:45 P.M., Truman decided that the United States had to do whatever was required to stop the attack. Joint Chiefs of Staff (JCS) Chair, General Omar Bradley, said, "we must draw the line somewhere," and Truman agreed. Truman and his advisors did not even debate whether to use force. Truman focused on what forces were available to defend South Korea. He asked where the 7th Fleet was, how many U.S. divisions and air units were in Japan, and how long it would take to move the Japan-based units to Korea. More concretely, Truman ordered the Commander in Chief Far East, General Douglas MacArthur, to use air and naval forces to protect the evacuation of U.S. dependents from South Korea,[7] "to send the suggested supplies [arms and ammunition] to the Koreans," and "to send a survey group to Korea" to determine what U.S. forces would be required to repel the invasion. Truman also ordered the JCS to draft orders for the "eventual" use of U.S. forces in Korea and to study U.S. capability to aid South Korea.[8]

Having decided on June 25, within twenty-hour hours of learning of the attack, to intervene with military force, Truman neither discussed with his advisors nor hesitated to approve escalating the size and scope of the military intervention as the crisis progressed. At first, Truman and his advisors thought air and naval forces would be enough to repel the invasion.[9] However, the North Korean advance quickly convinced them that ground forces would be needed. On June 26:

Mr. Acheson suggested that an all-out order be issued to the Navy and Air Force to waive all restrictions on their operations in Korea and offer the fullest possible support to the South Korean forces, attacking tanks, guns, columns, etc., of the North Korean forces in order to give a chance to the South Koreans to reform. The President said he approved this [escalation without discussion. Truman said] that no action should be taken north of the 38th parallel. He added "not yet."[10]

Truman preferred the military option over diplomatic and economic measures so much that he either ignored or accepted warnings from the military about expanding the intervention. When Secretary Johnson, Army Secretary Frank Pace, and Bradley warned against committing ground troops because of a fear of diverting forces to a remote area, which might leave Europe open to Soviet attack, Truman said nothing. And at a June 26 meeting, "General Bradley said that if we commit our ground forces in Korea we cannot at the same time carry out our other commitments without mobilization." Truman was not perturbed and said "he wished the Joint Chiefs to think about this and to let him know in a few days time" about mobilizing the National Guard to enable the United States to fulfill other commitments while fighting in Korea.[11] Truman had decided to intervene militarily with as much force as was required to repel the invasion and did not hesitate, or ask for advice, when he faced the decision to escalate the size and scope of the intervention a few days later. On June 30 MacArthur telegrammed, "the South Korea [sic] Army *was incapable of united action, and there was grave danger of a further breakthrough. He said further that the only assurance of holding the Han River line and to regain lost ground would be through the commitment of United States ground combat forces into the Korea battle area.*"[12] Truman did not hesitate, nor did he even consult his military or civilian advisors, to commit ground forces when the military commander in the area, MacArthur, requested them. On June 30, the day of MacArthur's telegram, Truman authorized the first U.S. ground forces, a regimental combat team, to engage in ground combat. Truman told his secretary, Miss Hachmeister, "Frank Pace called at 5 a.m., eastern daylight time [sic]. I was already up and shaved. Frank said MacArthur wanted two divisions of ground troops. I authorized a regiment . . . to be used at Mac's [sic] discretion."[13]

The focus on the military response meant that economic sanctions were even less of a priority for Truman and his advisors than a diplomatic response to the invasion. In early July, only after taking diplomatic action in the United Nations and intervening militarily, the United States finally implemented an embargo of strategic materials to North Korea and the People's Republic of China.[14]

Unlike Truman, Attlee's initial preference, supported by many officials in Whitehall, was not to intervene militarily, although he changed his mind quickly, primarily to maintain the close alliance with the United States, and decided to use military force. When Attlee first heard of the North Korean invasion he said, "It'll be alright so long as the bleachers [the Americans] don't join in."[15] However, as soon as the Americans intervened, Attlee's preferred response, like Truman's, was to intervene militarily, but, unlike Truman, with only naval forces.

The British committed naval forces before the U.N. request for aid to South Korea, although after the first U.N. resolution was passed condemning the invasion. This suggests that the British, like the Americans, would have intervened militarily even without U.N. support. When the full British cabinet finally met on June 27 to discuss Korea,[16] most of the members had already decided that force was the preferred option. After agreeing, with little discussion and with no dissent, to support the Americans, the cabinet decided on a two-pronged strategy of force and diplomacy. Diplomatically, the cabinet supported the second U.N. resolution calling for aid to South Korea. Militarily, British commitments elsewhere meant that the cabinet did not want to be drawn into another large military intervention in a distant land. Britain already had ground forces fighting in Malaya, units in Hong Kong facing a newly Communist China, and large ground formations in West Germany.[17] There was also concern about the costs of committing ground forces and what it would mean for the Labour government's ambitious domestic social programs.[18] However, the Foreign Office believed that a limited intervention would demonstrate Britain's capacity to act as a world power, as well as, most important, maintaining the crucial Anglo-American military, economic, and political relationship.[19] In keeping with these considerations of limited military resources and cost balanced against the relationship with the United States, the British Chiefs of Staff recommended committing only naval units already in Japanese waters to the Korean conflict.[20] Lagging Truman by three days, on June 28 Attlee agreed to commit the Far Eastern Fleet to service off Korea.[21] By early July the Royal Navy had a light fleet carrier, two cruisers, two destroyers, and three frigates operating in the Korean theater.[22]

In early July, after taking diplomatic action in the United Nations and intervening militarily, the British, under intense U.S. pressure, finally imposed economic sanctions. However, when the British Cabinet met on July 4 many members, including Foreign Secretary Ernest Bevin, feared that imposing economic sanctions against China would lead to retaliation in the form of an attack on Formosa or, worse for the British, Hong Kong. Bevin, who did not attend the meeting but responded to minutes from his hospital bed, concluded, "It is, however, certain that the psychological effect of our refusing to impose the controls proposed by the United States [will] create resentment out of all proportion to their practical effect, and would seem to have no advantage in the context of our policy towards China." Attlee agreed on the need to cooperate with the Americans, and Britain supported the embargo.[23] However, economic measures were only implemented after British naval forces had intervened. As with the Americans, for the British, force was not a last resort in terms of time or of options.

Although the British decided to intervene with naval forces in late June, they faced a second major decision in July as they came under increasing American pressure to commit ground forces. Through mid-July the Cabinet, Foreign Office, and the Chiefs of Staff continued to oppose such a widening of the intervention.[24] Attlee worried that the West was being tied down in Korea while the Soviets were free to intervene elsewhere. He wrote Truman on July 6, "the Russians have involved the Western Powers in a heavy commitment without themselves playing an overt part, and there are other areas in the Far East where the same tactics are open to them . . . Indo-China and Formosa . . . Malaya . . . Hong Kong."[25] On July 6 the Cabinet Defence Committee agreed not to intervene with air or ground forces.[26] On July 14 Air Chief Marshal Sir John Slessor argued against the commitment of British ground forces and worried about the prospect of an American Dunkirk and the subsequent need for a "minor Overlord" landing to retake South Korea:[27]

This will absorb enormous resources and take a long time. Meanwhile other danger spots in the Far East—such as Indo-China—to which those resources should be directed, will presumably have to go short. . . . Indeed, it is somewhat bizarre that, to liberate a country about which no-one cares very much (except on a point of principle) and restore a regime which was a pretty rotten one, the United Nations should have to undertake a major effort to weaken their ability to meet other "Koreas" elsewhere—to say nothing of a major Soviet attack.[28]

However, by mid-July the United States had three divisions in Korea and three more on the way. The North Koreans were not going to push the Americans and South Korean forces off the peninsula. The Americans pressed for British ground forces. Until late July the British believed that the fighting would be over before British troops could arrive. However, at Anglo-American talks in Washington on July 20 to 24, Acheson and Bradley convinced the British that the fighting would continue for months and that British troops were needed.[29] On July 23 British ambassador to the United States, Sir Oliver Franks, in an influential report from Washington, argued vigorously for British ground forces to be sent to Korea. "It was quite clear that the question of United Nations forces for Korea was foremost in the American mind." The British were sure they had been asked for forces by "the highest authority [Truman]."[30] Attlee chaired a July 24 meeting of the Cabinet Defence Committee where U.S. pressure finally succeeded.[31] Even the British military had come to agree that political considerations, primarily that of maintaining close relations with the United States, outweighed the potential military costs of weakening British forces elsewhere to intervene with ground forces in Korea. Sir William Slim, chief of the Imperial General Staff, said, "Although in their [General Staff] view it was still militarily unsound, they recognized the strong political arguments" and that "it would be wrong to send less than a Brigade Group. Nothing less would achieve the political objective." Although Slim attempted to rationalize the decision by discussing military advantages to the move, such as providing a "practical test for certain weapons, especially the Centurion tanks," it was clear the decision was made to appease the Americans and maintain the "special relationship."[32] On July 25 the cabinet agreed to send a brigade to Korea.[33] However, the British were still in no hurry to intervene with ground forces. Slim said, "The American Command . . . would probably not want reinforcements until the battle was stabilized."[34] By mid-August, however, the United States and ROK forces were still retreating and the Americans pressed for the immediate dispatch of British troops to Korea.[35] The first British ground forces, two battalions, arrived from Hong Kong in Pusan, Korea, on August 29, followed by a brigade on October 1. At their height, British forces in Korea grew to two infantry brigades and an armored regiment, as well as nineteen ships and air units.

In Korea, although Truman and Attlee both had some military training,[36] they acted as politicians and used limited and proportional, not overwhelming, force. Although the Americans and, to an even greater degree, the British were limited in their response to the Korean invasion by the size of their military forces in June 1950, Truman, Attlee and their advisors believed that the forces they employed were proportional to the stakes, as well as to the size and degree of threat, in Korea.

Truman and Attlee perceived that the stakes, at least specifically in relation to Korea, were not high. Therefore, they committed limited forces, proportional to their perception of the limited stakes in Korea itself. In a general, global sense, however, Truman and Attlee believed that the stakes were high in Korea, in that they believed that the North Korean invasion was a Soviet-backed attack to test the West's resolve. Even so, Truman and Attlee still believed that the European theater was the crucial area of the emerging Cold War. They did not see Korea as the primary theater in the Cold War. Both focused on Europe, although Britain, due to its proximity, was more concerned with Europe and even less with Korea than the United States. For this reason, the defense buildup by Britain and America after June 1950 focused on Europe, not Asia. Because of this perception of the stakes, low in Korea itself, high globally, in late June and early July, Truman and Attlee committed limited forces geared to avoiding defeat, not to achieving military victory or conquering North Korea. The Soviet-backed assault must be met and stopped. However, Korea was not where total victory over the Soviet Union and world communism would be won. Korea was not the center ring of the Cold War. Attlee, even more than Truman, severely limited Britain's use of force, at first using only naval forces. When British ground forces arrived they were also small, although British commitments elsewhere also severely constrained the size of the intervention. For Attlee, the primary goal was political, not military: to maintain U.S. support. The fewer forces Britain had to commit to far-off Korea, the better.[37]

The American and British responses in Korea were also proportional to the perceived degree of threat. They slowly escalated their interventions as their perceptions of the degree of threat increased. In late June Britain intervened with naval forces and it was only in late July, when North Korean forces threatened to push U.S./ROK forces off the Korean peninsula, that Britain enlarged the intervention and committed ground forces. The U.S. response also escalated from supplying ammunition and equipment to South Korean troops, to the commitment of air and naval forces. Finally, on the fifth day of fighting, after Seoul had fallen, Truman committed ground troops. Even then, U.S. troops were ordered only to defend Pusan and help resupply South Korean forces.[38] Only later were U.S. ground forces ordered into combat, which first occurred on July 5. At each point, U.S. policy makers were not thinking of overwhelming force, but of limited, proportional force and the minimum commitment necessary to halt the North Korean invasion. Dulles told Truman, "I am very glad that you have proposed measures that correspond to the magnitude of the danger."[39] Even later, Truman still followed the proportionality principle related to the perceived degree of threat. On August 22 Truman wrote that he believed there were enough U.S. and U.N. forces in Korea to stabilize the situation[40]—he focused on stabilization, not defeating North Korea. Truman and Attlee may have delayed sending ground forces in significant numbers to let South Korea attempt to repel the invasion and to reassure themselves that the Soviets were not massing elsewhere for an attack,[41] a belief in proportionality, however, meant that the scale of the U.S. and U.K. responses were limited, not overwhelming.

LESSONS FROM HISTORY

Truman and Attlee intervened with military forces in Korea even as their military advisors cautioned, and in some cases, opposed, the use of military force. A significant part of the reason why Truman and, to a lesser extent, Attlee promptly decided to use force was because of their reliance on the 1930's analogy to frame the invasion. From the moment they learned of the North Korean attack, Truman, Attlee, and their advisors relied on historical information to frame the crisis, as well as to prescribe and legitimate policy. Lessons drawn from history dominated American decision making and had a significant influence on British policy, although Attlee and his advisors balanced historical with current information, especially the need to maintain the Anglo-American special relationship.

Truman wrote in his memoirs that he relied on the 1930's analogy to determine his policy in response to the North Korean invasion. The 1930's analogy included a range of crises, events, and figures from the pre–World War II period, including, among others, the 1931–32 Japanese invasion of Manchuria, the 1935 Italian invasion of Abyssinia, the 1936 German re-militarization of the Rhineland, and the German invasion of Poland in 1939, as well as events that did not occur in the 1930s, such as the 1941 Japanese attack on Pearl Harbor. Truman, in describing his thoughts when he was on the airplane flying from Independence to Washington, wrote:

In my generation, this was not the first occasion when the strong had attacked the weak. I recalled some earlier instances: Manchuria, Ethiopia, Austria.[42] I remembered how each time the democracies failed to act it had encouraged the aggressors to keep going ahead. Communism was acting in Korea just as Hitler, Mussolini and the Japanese had acted ten, fifteen, and twenty years earlier. I felt certain that if South Korea was allowed to fall, Communist leaders would be emboldened to override nations closer to our own shores. . . . If this was allowed to go unchallenged, it would mean third world war, just as similar events had brought on the second world war.[43]

However, this evidence is based on Truman's memory of what he was thinking at the time. Unfortunately, there is little evidence in the relevant minutes of meetings, telephone conversations, and memoranda of the use of the 1930's analogy in the last week of June in U.S. policy-making meetings.[44] Truman's memoirs are supported by only four statements about the 1930s by three policy makers mentioned in documents in late June and early July 1950, as well as by one National Security Council (NSC) report. At a June 25 meeting with Truman, Air Force Secretary Thomas K. Finletter "stressed the analogy to the situation between the two world wars."[45] Also on June 25 John Foster Dulles, a consultant to the secretary of state, tele-grammed Acheson, "To sit by while Korea is overrun by unprovoked armed attack could start a disastrous chain of events leading most probably to a world war."[46] On June 29 Dulles wrote that the quick response by the United States in Korea had been the best opportunity to reduce the chance of a third world war.[47] Well after Truman's June 30 decision to commit ground forces, on July 10, Acheson wrote Bevin that North Korean aggression was like German aggression in the 1930s.[48] The NSC on July 6 reported, "The British refused to face up squarely to the menace of Nazism until the invasion of Poland. . . . The President carefully avoided that mistake."[49] The virtual lack of mention of historical analogies in the available documents apart from these exceptions might be due to a records problem, such as those taking the minutes of the meetings not deeming the mention of historical analogies worthy of note. However, such a problem did not occur during the Suez and Lebanon/Jordan crises, when there were more than a dozen historical analogies mentioned by more than ten policy makers on multiple occasions.

The British records also contain a similar lack of mention of the 1930's analogy. The official British history argued that Attlee and the British cabinet, like Truman and his advisors, were influenced strongly by the lessons of the 1930s during the Korean invasion crisis: "The memory of irresolution in stopping Hitler's aggression was fresh in their minds. The lesson there was to be firm at the outset."[50] However, like the Americans, no direct quotes are cited from policy meetings or memoranda in late June and early July 1950.

The public use of historical analogies reflects the private use of historical information and analogies. Furthermore, the use of historical analogies to justify a policy reflects the use of historical analogies to frame a crisis and to prescribe policy. Although policy makers rarely mentioned historical analogies in decision-making meetings, Attlee, Truman, and their colleagues repeatedly used the 1930's analogy both publicly and privately to justify their policies in Korea. The public was familiar with and, for the most part, accepted the lessons of the 1930s. On June 27, for example, Attlee said in the House of Commons, "The situation is of undoubted gravity, but I am certain that there will be no disagreement, after our bitter experiences in the past 35 years, that the salvation of all is dependent on prompt and effective measures to arrest aggression wherever it may occur."[51] On July 5, 1950, Attlee said in the House:

Surely, with the history of the last 20 years fresh in our minds, no one can doubt that it is vitally important that aggressors should be halted at the outset. . . . We all know the sequence of events—the Japanese aggression in Manchuria which was condoned and gave rise at once to aggression in other parts of the world such as the attack of Mussolini on Abyssinia, and to a general lack of faith in the preservation of peace by collective security under the League of Nations. From that start, that failure to check the first beginnings of aggression, there was a crescendo of violence, culminating in the Second World War, due to the fact that no one was willing to act when aggression first started.[52]

On July 23 Attlee said in a broadcast:

The attack by the armed forces of North Korea on South Korea has been denounced as an act of aggression by the United Nations. . . . If the aggressor gets away with it, aggressors all over the world will be encouraged. The same results which led to the second world war [sic] will follow; and another world war may result. That is why what is happening in Korea is of such importance to you. The fire that has been started in distant Korea may burn down your house.[53]

On June 27 Truman said, "If we let Korea down, the Soviets will keep right on going and swallow up one piece of Asia after another."[54] On July 17 Truman wrote the president of the Republic of Korea that the North Korean attack was "reminiscent of Poland and Pearl Harbor."[55] On July 19 Truman told Congress, "The fateful events of the 1930s, when aggression unopposed bred more aggression and eventually war, were fresh in our memory. But the free nations had learned the lesson of history."[56] On July 5 Acheson compared the 1930s to the Korean invasion,[57] and he wrote Bevin on July 10 that Korean aggression was like German aggression in the 1930s.[58] Truman told Attlee in December, "We were in complete agreement that there can be no thought of appeasement or of rewarding aggression, whether in the Far East or elsewhere."[59] Historical analogies formed the basis of the public justification for the British and American decisions to use military force in Korea, reflecting the importance of the lessons of the 1930s in framing the crisis, as well as in formulating American and British policies.

Although mentioned only a handful of times in British and American documents, the 1930's analogy had a greater impact on British and American decision making about Korea than if the analogy had been mentioned repeatedly. If a historical analogy is mentioned many times it usually means that a policy maker is trying to convince others of the validity of the analogy to the current case. If a historical analogy is mentioned only a few times, yet policy makers follow its lessons, then the policy makers have internalized the lessons of the analogy and accepted its application to the current crisis.

In the case of Korea, policy makers had internalized lessons from the 1930's analogy, and they did not have to mention the analogy in more than passing during meetings. When policy makers mentioned the lessons others already knew on which historical events they were based and accepted their validity: Korea appeared to be another case of 1930s-style aggression. These lessons strongly influenced decision making during the Korean invasion by framing the crisis in terms of the 1930s.

A distinction can be drawn between the use of the 1930's analogy and lessons based on the 1930s by policy makers. Lessons based on a historical analogy that are used without mentioning the analogy more than once, if at all, during policy making meetings, are internalized, more widely held, and accepted, and, therefore, are more resistant to change than lessons based on analogies that are repeatedly mentioned during a crisis. After a crisis, policy makers will mention the historical analogy that gave rise to the lesson that they relied upon during the crisis. Therefore, there are several mentions of the 1930s in relation to the Korean decision in memoirs and statements made after the Korean crisis by the top policy makers.[60] In Korea, Truman, Attlee, and their advisors used lessons from the 1930s without, in most cases, mentioning the analogy itself and rarely explained the lessons based on the 1930's analogy. The words themselves, such as the "1930s," "appeasement," "Abyssinia," and "Manchuria," had become code words for deeply—and widely—held beliefs about how to respond to aggression by nondemocratic states. Because of these shared beliefs and lessons, there was no debate in British or American policy-making meetings about how to interpret the 1930's analogy, its validity to the Korean invasion, nor even which historical analogy to retrieve to frame the Korean invasion.

Part of the reason the 1930's analogy enjoyed broad support was because it encompassed the following five themes: (1) to respond promptly to aggression against allies with force; (2) to support collective security against aggressors; (3) the belief that international communism, like Nazism, was ruthless and would use force to expand; (4) to use military force to prevent aggressive states from conquering small states in succession, like dominoes; and (5) the theme of alliance unity with like-minded states, with which Attlee and the British were deeply concerned. These related themes allowed different people to emphasize different aspects of the 1930's analogy, yet still support the validity and prescriptions of the 1930's analogy to the Korean case. The themes also reinforced each other, since they prescribed the same response to the invasion of a small ally by an undemocratic state: a prompt response with military force in alliance with other, like-minded states. The 1930's analogy provided a broadly accepted policy prescription, and there was little, if any, brainstorming in Washington or London to find either other possible policy options or possible historical analogies to frame the crisis.

This consensus was reinforced by other variables that influenced the British and American decisions to use force. For example, Truman feared that if he did not respond effectively to the North Korean invasion, he would be criticized domestically for having "lost" Korea, just as he had been criticized for "losing" China. Truman's fears were reinforced by Senator Joseph McCarthy's charges of Communist sympathizers or, worse, agents, in the State Department, which began in February 1950. For the British, the desire to maintain close relations with the Americans, especially the flow of financial aid, was of paramount concern. The British and the Americans also feared loss of credibility if they did not respond effectively to what was perceived to be a Soviet probe to test the West's resolve against unprovoked aggression. The Americans and British also wanted to support the fledgling United Nations, which they had helped create and which had been instrumental in the creation of the Republic of Korea.

Historical analogies do not change fundamental beliefs. However, they do affect perceptions of a current crisis and the way in which general beliefs are applied to a specific, current event. Historical analogies are the filter between general, broad beliefs and narrow, specific perceptions of a current crisis. British and American policy in Korea rested on a set of beliefs Attlee, Bevin, Truman, and Acheson held prior to the Korean invasion. Attlee's response to the Korean invasion mirrored his belief, held since 1946, that the West should respond promptly, with force if necessary, to what were seen as Soviet probes.[61] However, this belief rested on lessons Attlee learned in the 1930s and applied via analogical reasoning to the crises of the late

1940s and to Korea in 1950. The belief that a firm line should be taken toward the Soviet Union was not a separate analogy or extrapolation based on Soviet behavior, but a belief grounded on the 1930's analogy and applied to Soviet behavior since 1945. The comparison led to the term, "Red Fascism," which described the perceived similarity between Soviet behavior in the late 1940s and Axis behavior in the 1930s. The beliefs of Attlee and Bevin about collective security and the importance of the Anglo-American alliance during the Korean crisis can be traced even farther back. In the 1930s Attlee supported collective defense against Hitler, as well as league sanctions against Japan for the invasion of Manchuria and against Italy for the invasion of Abyssinia.[62] Bevin argued that Britain and the League of Nations should use economic sanctions backed by force, if necessary, against Italy for its invasion of Abyssinia.[63] Attlee also held strong beliefs throughout his political career about the importance of unity in the face of opposition and aggression. For example, during World War II, Attlee's major goal in the coalition government was to keep the coalition intact to win the war.[64]

Truman's beliefs, although filtered through the 1930's analogy, were also long held. In the 1930s Truman supported collective security,[65] which he again supported in 1950. By 1946 Truman had also adopted a harder line against the Soviet Union than he had supported previously and in 1947, on the basis of the Truman Doctrine, the United States had provided aid to the Greek government in its war against Communist rebels.[66] Truman would take another firm stand against what was seen as Soviet aggression in Korea. Acheson also acted on long-held beliefs when he favored supporting South Korea. From 1947 to 1950 Acheson, with the State Department, championed an active U.S. role in South Korea. The Pentagon and the Joint Chiefs opposed Acheson and favored a gradual withdrawal with, it was hoped, a minimal loss of U.S. prestige.[67] Supporting the argument that historical analogies rarely change basic beliefs, in the immediate aftermath of the North Korean invasion, both institutions supported the courses they had long championed. Acheson and the State Department favored military intervention, while the Joint Chiefs of Staff (JCS) and the Pentagon opposed intervention with ground forces and recommended, at the most, a strictly limited intervention. For example, at a June 25 meeting with the president, General Bradley "said that jets flying over her (Korea) would have a great morale effect on the South Koreans. . . . He said that naval action could help on the East Coast. . . . He questioned the advisability of putting in ground units particularly if large numbers were involved."[68] At a July 27 National Security Council (NSC) meeting Bradley reported, "the Joint Chiefs felt that we should not fight a major war in Korea."[69]

Although other variables and beliefs, such as the desire to maintain the Anglo-American alliance, concerns about Western credibility, fear of losing

Korea, and of damaging U.N. prestige, significantly influenced British and American policy, they were also themselves affected by historical information retrieved by analogical reasoning. The analogies not only reinforced general beliefs, but also helped shape the beliefs and significantly affected their application to the Korean case. The historical analogies filtered the general, basic beliefs. The existing beliefs were general, such as the need for a firmer line against the Soviets and the need to maintain close relations with the United States. These beliefs lacked specific policy recommendations, which the historical analogies provided. For example, the 1930's analogy reinforced Anglo-American support for the United Nations and emphasized the importance of the first test by an aggressor of a collective security organization, such as the League of Nations or the United Nations. On the basis of the 1930's analogy, Attlee and Truman wanted the first test of the United Nations to be a success to avoid repeating the failure of one of the first major tests of the League of Nations: No collective military action was taken against Italy after the 1935 Italian invasion of Abyssinia. Truman was especially concerned with persuading other states to contribute to the collective defense of South Korea under the U.N. flag. At a June 30 cabinet meeting, "He (Truman) wanted all of them to know that what we had done was being done under the auspices of the United Nations; and that offers of help which had come from countries like Canada, Australia, and New Zealand . . . were being made for the United Nations."[70]

The 1930s also filtered and clarified British beliefs. Attlee sought to maintain the Anglo-American relationship: a general goal. The 1930's analogy prescribed a specific policy: that the British would have to use military force to support the Americans in Korea, just as military relations and contributions had been at the foundation of the Grand Alliance of World War II. Lessons about the importance of the Anglo-American alliance during World War II, combined with an analysis of the current importance of the alliance, overcame the British reluctance to spread their overstretched military forces even further and to accede to U.S. demands to intervene, first, with naval units and then, later, with ground forces in Korea. Without the 1930's analogy and the lessons of maintaining the alliance from World War II, the British might have listened to the reservations of the military and stayed out of ground combat in Korea. The British believed that the Anglo-American alliance was crucial to their survival in 1950. However, this belief rested, in part, on the analogy to the Second World War. The British had needed American aid to defeat the Axis during World War II and believed they would require American aid to defeat the Soviet Union in the 1950s. The analogy ruled out other policies, especially a policy of appeasing the Soviets, since the 1930's analogy totally discredited any attempted appeasement policy.

The 1930's analogy also had effects independent of the beliefs already held by the principal decision makers. The Americans and British used the

1930s to frame the invasion, providing information that would not have been available if the invasion had been analyzed solely in terms of the pre-existing beliefs of the policy makers and of the current information. For example, by using the 1930s to frame the Korean crisis, Truman and Attlee viewed the North Koreans and the Soviets, who they believed were behind the invasion,[71] as similar to Hitler, Mussolini, and Japanese leader General Hideki Tojo. Diplomacy, such as the 1930's British appeasement policy, and economic measures, such as the 1941 American oil embargo of Japan, failed to prevent further aggression in the 1930s and helped contribute to the slide into world war. Therefore, Truman and Attlee believed, such measures would fail in 1950 against the North Koreans and their Soviet supporters. Force would have to be used, just as it had been in the late 1930s and 1940s, or Soviet-inspired attacks would occur elsewhere. Therefore, Truman and Attlee quickly decided on force as the preferred response, even though there was no evidence at the time to suggest that the North Korean invasion was anything more than a North Korean attempt to reunify Korea. Truman and Attlee, on the basis of the 1930s, went beyond the available information and perceived the North Korean invasion as part of a general, aggressive plan by Communist states to expand in a manner similar to the Axis expansion of the 1930s. This belief reinforced the increasing fear of an emerging Cold War and led to the massive buildup of the American and British militaries after 1950.

Reliance on analogies also shaped the belief held by Truman and Attlee that the North Koreans and the Soviets were irrational, ruthless, and untrustworthy, similar to the dictators of the 1930s. They were irrational in the sense that the Soviets would risk nuclear war, the British and Americans concluded, to expand communism. A State Department report said, "The events surrounding this crisis have served to emphasize the aims, purposes, and methods of international communism under Soviet guidance."[72] On June 27 Truman said, "The attack upon Korea makes it plain beyond all doubt that communism has passed beyond the use of subversion to conquer independent nations and will now use armed invasion and war."[73] Acheson agreed with Truman.[74] The North Koreans and their Soviet supporters could not be trusted to fulfill the terms of a diplomatic settlement, nor, given their apparent ruthless disregard for their own people, would they change policy under the pain of economic sanctions. The Soviets and their allies would only respond to force, just like the Axis of the 1930s.

Since the North Koreans were irrational, ruthless, and untrustworthy, the 1930's analogy also led Truman and Attlee to conclude that force was not a last resort in terms of attractiveness of options or of time. Waiting to use force in the 1930s had only encouraged further aggression, they believed, and had resulted in a world war. This historical lesson reinforced the argument, based on current information, that only the prompt use of military force could stem the rapid and large-scale North Korean invasion.[75] However, this preference for the use of force, in significant part on the basis of the 1930's analogy, led to a distorted view of the current situation in the early summer of 1950. Although there was a possibility of a negotiated settlement, the lessons of the 1930's analogy precluded any diplomatic solution. The aggressor must not be negotiated with, let alone appeased. On July 6 the Soviets approached the British about a negotiated settlement. This demonstrated that the Soviets, if not the North Koreans, contrary to the 1930's analogy, might have considered a diplomatic solution to the Korean conflict. It is debatable whether the Soviets would have adhered to the terms of any such diplomatic settlement, although the possibility did exist. However, the 1930's analogy scuttled the proposed negotiated settlement. When the Soviets suggested a trade of a seat for the People's Republic of China in the United Nations for a settlement in Korea, the Americans raised the specter of appeasement, Attlee balked, and any possibility of a settlement vanished.[76] Acheson later wrote, chiding the British for their attempted settlement, "The British Foreign Office had long believed, more than evidence seemed to warrant, that it understood the Russians and could negotiate with them compromise solutions of difficult situations."[77] In July India also unsuccessfully attempted to fashion a negotiated settlement, but again the lessons of the 1930s, that negotiations with dictators were futile and even dangerous, scuttled the plan.

Lessons from the 1941 Japanese attack on Pearl Harbor also influenced the U.S. response to the North Korean invasion, allowing the Americans to go beyond the information currently available. For example, Vice President Richard Nixon said, "Mind you, it wasn't just South Korea that was being attacked. It was our Army. It was small numerically, not well-equipped, and attacked by surprise, on a weekend, just like the Pearl Harbor attack."[78] The lesson of Pearl Harbor was that the United States had to respond promptly with military force and, although it would be a long, costly fight, victory was attainable. Pearl Harbor also taught the importance of readiness, which supported the huge American and British defense buildup after the Korean invasion, focused on Europe. Western Europe, the Americans and British feared, might be next to be attacked by a Communist state, just as Norway and Denmark had been attacked by Germany in 1940 after the 1939 attack on Poland. Reinforcing fears of a Soviet plan of global conquest, American and British policy makers framed the Korean crisis in terms of the 1930s and prepared for another world war. The response of the policy makers would have been fundamentally different if they had framed the invasion as part of a local, civil war. There certainly would not have been the massive military buildup by Britain and, even more notably, the U.S. focused on Europe after the North Korean attack.

Truman and Attlee also drew from the 1930's analogy the lesson that the stakes in the Korean crisis were extremely high, both personally and internationally, even though they did not believe Korea by itself was intrinsically important. Although the emerging Cold War made policy makers believe that Korea was crucial, the 1930s provided information that was not already in their belief systems and that allowed them to go beyond the information available in late June and early July 1950. An evaluation of the stakes on their own merits in 1950 would have relegated the Korean peninsula to a minor role in the emerging Cold War. Korea was weak industrially and American sea and air power could far more easily defend Japan, Formosa, and the Philippines than South Korea. This suggested the loss of South Korea might actually strengthen the West's position vis-à-vis the Soviet Union. However, the 1930's analogy provided the personal lesson that failure to deal effectively with an adversary's use of force could destroy a politician's career. Chamberlain failed to deter Hitler and fell from office even as Hitler invaded France. A similar fate could await Truman and Attlee if they did not respond effectively and forcefully to the North Korean invasion. The 1930s also provided an international lesson. The 1930's crises, many of which, like Korea in 1950, appeared peripheral to the United States and Britain, such as Abyssinia and Manchuria, were the prelude to World War II. Failure to respond promptly with force in Korea might lead to World War III. Even though no one knew what would happen if North Korea conquered South Korea, Truman and Attlee used the 1930's analogy to go beyond the available information and conclude that a failure to defend South Korea could lead to dire consequences, such as a Soviet invasion of Europe and, possibly, a world war.

The lessons of the 1930s led Truman and Attlee to conclude that they should intervene militarily to avoid a worse situation—world war—even though they recognized some of the serious risks and potential costs of intervention. Historical lessons overrode concerns based on an analysis of the current situation. Truman worried about becoming bogged down in Korea, fighting the Koreans and Chinese, while the Soviets stayed out of the fighting, free to intervene militarily elsewhere in the world unopposed by the United States. On June 29 Truman was afraid "the Russians are going to let the Chinese do the fighting for them."[79] Truman also believed, in part on the basis of the 1930s, that there was a risk of a world war with the Soviets. He discussed the possibility and accepted the risk because he believed the stakes globally in relation to Korea, also on the basis of the 1930's analogy, as well as the emerging Cold War, were high. On June 25 Truman ordered, "The Air Force should prepare plans to wipe out all Soviet air bases in the Far East. This was not an order for action but an order to make the plans . . . Careful calculation should be made of the next probable place in which Soviet action might take place. . . . The President again emphasized the importance of making the survey of possible next moves by the Soviet Union."[80] The orders sent to MacArthur on June 29 stated, "The decision to commit United States air and naval forces and limited army forces . . . does not constitute a decision to engage in war with the Soviet

Union if Soviet forces intervene in Korea. The decision regarding Korea, however, was taken in full realization of the risks involved."[81]

Like Truman, Attlee also accepted the 1930's framework and the belief that high risks must be run to respond promptly to the North Korean invasion with force to avoid further Soviet attacks elsewhere and a possible world war.[82] However, Attlee, like Truman, worried that if the United States and Britain became too involved in Korea, they would be unable to counter Soviet and Chinese threats elsewhere.[83] British forces were already stretched thin in Europe, Malaya, and Hong Kong. To Attlee and Bevin, the main threat was in Europe. Defense Minister Emmanuel Shinwell welcomed evidence that "the Korean affair was not distracting American attention from the vital European theatre."[84] Although current information warned against using force, historical information pushed Attlee to support the United States and to commit ground forces. Attlee feared the possibility of a world war, but drew the lesson from the 1930s that the British needed the United States in 1950, just as they had needed the Americans to prevail in World War II. The historical analogy reinforced the analysis of the current situation, which emphasized to the British the importance of the United States to Britain economically, politically, and militarily. The United States made it clear to the British ambassador in Washington, Franks, that the failure of Britain to provide troops to South Korea would strain Anglo-American relations and might decrease U.S. support of Britain's security in Europe, as well as her financial position.[85] Historical information and U.S. pressure overcame British fear based on current information of stretching limited military resources even farther and risking a costly war in a peripheral theater. Attlee concluded, "We'll have to support the Yanks."[86]

The Korean case illustrates the broad influence of historical information retrieved by analogy on foreign policy decision making. The use of lessons from history allowed Truman and Attlee to decide quickly on policy, without in-depth analysis. Truman and Attlee decided to intervene militarily within hours of learning of the invasion, with no time for rigorous analysis. Historical information also allowed them to go beyond the available information. They framed the North Korean invasion in terms of the 1930s and viewed the invasion as the opening gambit of a worldwide Communist plan to expand—not just as a Korean civil war. The 1930s prescribed one response: the prompt use of military force in coalition with other, like-minded states. The 1930s also suggested that the stakes were extremely high globally and that diplomacy and economic sanctions would fail. This belief precluded a negotiated settlement even though the Soviet Union and India had raised the possibility of acting as intermediaries in negotiations to end the war promptly. For the British, the lessons from the 1930s also prescribed the importance of the Anglo-American alliance for eventual victory, just as the alliance had been crucial to victory over the Axis. Combined with U.S. pressures and actual British dependence on the United States economically and militarily, the 1930's historical analogy contributed to the British decision to send ground forces to Korea. Although historical analogies did not change basic beliefs, the 1930's analogy significantly affected perceptions of the stakes, time, adversaries, the United Nations, allies, and of policy options.

THE USE OF HISTORICAL ANALOGIES

The personality of the decision makers, as well as the novelty, drama, and time pressures inherent in the Korean crisis, significantly influenced the use of historical information and historical analogies during late June and July 1950.

Personality strongly influences the use of historical analogies. Of the four primary decision makers, based on their use of historical analogies before Korea, Truman was the most predisposed to use analogies to retrieve historical information. Acheson sometimes used historical analogies, while Attlee and Bevin rarely, if ever, did. However, Korea showed that all four men understood, believed in, and used the lessons of the 1930's analogy to frame the crisis. This demonstrated the broad influence in both the United States and Britain of a master analogy: the 1930s. During the decisions to use force, none of the four policy makers mentioned the 1930s specifically, although all relied on lessons drawn from the 1930s to frame the crisis and to prescribe policy. After they decided to use force, Truman, who was most predisposed due to his decision-making style and interest in history to use historical analogies, mentioned the 1930s more often to justify his policies than Bevin, Attlee, or Acheson. However, Attlee and Bevin, who, in their earlier careers rarely used historical analogies, mentioned historical analogies as often to justify the intervention as Acheson, who used historical analogies more often than Bevin or Attlee. Therefore, situational variables increased the use of historical analogies by Attlee and Bevin, while the tendency of Truman and Acheson to use historical information remained high. In this case, situational variables increased the use of historical information and analogies by individuals, such as Attlee and Bevin, who rarely used such information. The situational variables in the Korean case that tended to cause policy makers to use historical analogies, overrode the influence of individual variables that decreased the use of historical analogies by Attlee and Bevin throughout their careers.

Situational variables in the Korean case had a significant influence on the use of historical analogies. Policy makers tend to use historical analogies when facing novel, complex problems. The Korean invasion was both novel and complex. Truman, who relied heavily on the 1930's analogy, later said the Korean decision was the most difficult decision of his presidency.[87] The British and American fear that the invasion was the first phase in a general war with the Soviet Union made the invasion novel, especially since it would be the first war with both sides armed with nuclear weapons. However, the Korean invasion was also seen as common. It was another case of one state attacking another. Therefore, given that the Korean invasion had common and uncommon aspects, it is difficult to determine if this variable had any influence on the use of historical analogies. The Korean case was also complex, involving more than just the two Koreas, Britain, and the United States. The U.S. response could have ramifications for the West's position in the Middle East, Asia, and Europe. However, complexity is a difficult variable to use to explain the use of historical analogies. Almost any foreign policy crisis is complex enough to lead to the use of historical analogies and, in some ways American and British policy makers did not perceive the Korean invasion as complex. Korea was seen as a simple case of one state invading another. Therefore, complexity is a poor variable on which to explain the use of historical information.

Time pressure can also lead to the use of historical analogies as a cognitive shortcut. Truman perceived intense time pressures as North Korean units raced south, so he relied on lessons based on the 1930s quickly to frame the crisis and to prescribe policy. Truman heard about the North Korean attack on June 24 and wanted to return to Washington from Missouri immediately. This showed that he believed that time was important and that he should be in Washington in order to act quickly with all of the resources of the government at his fingertips. Acheson told him that they did not have enough information to act so Truman, still concerned with speed, returned to Washington the following day instead of leaving immediately. Truman made a large military, economic, and political commitment within hours of hearing of the invasion. During the first phone call from Acheson, Truman authorized taking the case to the United Nations and within twenty-four hours Truman had decided to use whatever force was required to stem the invasion.

Attlee felt slightly less time pressure than Truman and, therefore, did not rely on lessons from historical analogies as a cognitive shortcut quite as much as the president. Attlee's first inclination was not to intervene. Then, when he learned that the Americans were using force, Attlee decided also to intervene militarily. This period when he changed his mind suggests that Attlee felt less time pressure than Truman, at least initially, when he believed that Britain would not intervene militarily. Even so, Attlee decided quickly and Britain intervened militarily with naval forces within forty-eight hours of the invasion. The decision to commit ground forces, made in late July, was made under far less time pressure. However, even though he faced less time pressure than Truman, Attlee still used historical analogies. Attlee used the 1930's analogy to emphasize the need to maintain a close alliance with the United States in the same way Britain had needed the Americans to win the Second World War. He also relied on the 1930's analogy to justify his decision to commit ground forces to Korea.

Policy makers are also likely to use historical analogies to analyze dramatic, important events. In addition to being novel and complex, the North Korean invasion was also dramatic and important. Both Truman and Attlee viewed the invasion as a Soviet-backed incursion into the Western sphere of influence, part of a global Soviet strategy to test the West.[88] International relations could not be more dramatic or important: The British and the Americans believed that the future of the world was at stake. Surprise increased the level of drama, as well as the perception of time pressures. The invasion caught Truman and Attlee by surprise, although it was not unexpected, in that before the invasion, the British and Americans believed the North Koreans might attack, but did not know when the attack would occur.[89]

Situational variables, including time pressures, surprise, and a high level of drama and importance, led Truman, Attlee, their cabinets, and their advisors to rely on lessons drawn from history to frame the Korean invasion as a cognitive shortcut to save time, as well as to prescribe and justify policy. These situational variables overrode the influence of individual variables. Attlee and Bevin, who, because of individual variables, rarely used historical analogies in foreign policy decision making, drew lessons from history during the Korean crisis because of the influence of situational variables.

RETRIEVAL AND TYPES OF HISTORICAL ANALOGIES

Attlee, Bevin, Truman, and Acheson retrieved the 1930's analogy and deemed it to be valid based on surface similarities. For example, the German invasion of Poland, the Italian invasion of Abyssinia, the Japanese invasion of Manchuria and attack on Pearl Harbor all shared surface similarities to the North Korean invasion of South Korea. All could be seen as one state attacking, unprovoked,[90] another state, and, except for Pearl Harbor, against a weaker foe. Most were also, to varying degrees, surprise attacks. North Korea, like the Axis powers, was viewed by American and British policy makers as a dictatorial state invading a Western ally. However, the deeper, causal similarities between the 1930s and Korea were less similar and less valid. Korea, unlike the 1930's cases, could be viewed as a civil war. The attack on Pearl Harbor, and the invasions of Abyssinia, Manchuria, and Poland were not civil wars. Furthermore, North Korea posed nowhere near the threat that industrialized Germany, Japan, and Italy presented during the 1930s. If North Korea was seen, however, to be a pawn of the Soviet Union, then it could be interpreted as being part of a larger threat. As with most cases involving analogical reasoning, however, general, surface similarities overrode deeper, specific, causal differences between Korea and the 1930s.

Leaders are more likely to retrieve recent, personally experienced events or people as analogies. If an event is uncommon, the odds are that a policy maker will not have experienced personally or observed a similar event during his life and will have to delve back into learned history for an analogy. Truman, Acheson, Attlee, and Bevin viewed Korea as novel and uncommon, in that a third world war appeared to be looming. However, they did not view Korea as unique, which would have led to the conclusion that there was no historical analogy for the singular invasion of South Korea. Dictatorial states had tested Western resolve in peripheral areas before and world war had resulted. Therefore, the British and Americans retrieved a recent, observed or personally experienced series of apparently similar events: the 1930s. They did not have to search through older, learned history to find an analogy. During the Korean crisis, British and American policy makers overwhelmingly retrieved historical analogies, particularly the 1930s, that they had personally experienced or observed within the past twenty years. They did not use historical analogies from learned history. In relation to the 1930s historical analogy, Truman was in Congress during the 1930s, although he was not involved in the neutrality debates of the period. Acheson was under-secretary of the Treasury briefly in 1933 before he returned to his international law firm. Attlee was elected leader of the opposition Labour Party in 1935 and, with Bevin, was a prominent critic of Chamberlain's appeasement policy. Furthermore, the 1930s marked a dramatic, vivid series of events that occurred during important periods in the lives of the decision makers, which increased the chance that they would retrieve the 1930s as a historical analogy. The 1930s marked the rise to prominence and power of Attlee and Bevin in Britain, and Truman and Acheson in Washington. For them, as well as for the American and British publics, the 1930s was a widely known and accepted master analogy, which meant that policy makers were more likely to retrieve it for later crises, than a less well-known analogy.

Leaders are also more likely to draw lessons from past foreign policy failures than from successes. The lesson from the foreign policy failure is based on avoiding what was done in the past, since that policy failed. In the Korean case, Truman and Attlee drew lessons from what they believed was the failed 1930's British appeasement policy, which was seen as having failed to avert World War II. In 1950 the analogy told Truman and Attlee who they should not be: Chamberlain. Chamberlain's policies must not be copied. The Americans and the British, in large part because of the 1930's analogy, rejected attempts by the Soviet Union and India to negotiate a peaceful settlement to the Korean conflict. Attlee and Truman must be Churchill: use force promptly and rearm. The British and Americans did exactly this when they used force promptly in Korea and began to rearm.

Policy makers also tend to use historical analogies that involve their own state. Within the 1930's cluster of analogies, Truman and his advisors mentioned Pearl Harbor,[91] which involved their own state, while the British did not. Instead, the British use of the 1930's analogy focused on the invasion of Poland, appeasement, and events in Europe,[92] which involved Britain.

Although historical events and people are closely linked, such as Hitler and the invasion of Poland, policy makers also tend to retrieve historical events to analyze a current event and historical people to analyze current political leaders. The invasion of Korea, an event, led to the retrieval of historical events, such as the Japanese attack on Pearl Harbor, and the German invasions of Poland and of Norway.[93] However, when current leaders were mentioned, they were compared to historical figures. For example, when Soviet leader Joseph Stalin was mentioned as the figure behind the North Korean invasion, he was compared to German Chancellor Adolf Hitler.[94]

The generational theory, that an actor will use events that occur when they were in their twenties as analogies later in life, would predict that Truman, Acheson, and Attlee would draw upon World War I, while Bevin would look to the Boer War, not the 1930s, as an analogy to Korea. Truman, Acheson, and Attlee were in their twenties during the First World War. Bevin turned 20 in 1901, as the Boer War raged in South Africa. However, references to World War I and the Boer War, which Truman, Attlee, Acheson, and Bevin, under the generational theory, should have retrieved as historical analogies, were almost totally absent in the case of World War I and were nonexistent in the case of the Boer War during the Korean invasion policy-making meetings.

Even more damaging to the generational theory, World War I was a major event in the lives of Truman, Acheson, and Attlee and, in some ways, more important and life-changing than the 1930s and World War II.[95] For Truman, volunteering for World War I was "the crucial event" in his life.[96] Soon after the war, through connections he made during the war, the Pendergast political machine launched him in politics.[97] Acheson also saw World War I as a major event in his life and of equal significance to the 1930s. He wrote that twice his world was "blown apart": August 1914 and September 1939.[98] Attlee's infantry service during World War I was a key formative experience and the most significant act of his political development.[99] This should have increased the likelihood that Truman, Acheson, and Attlee would retrieve World War I as a historical analogy to Korea. Under the generational theory, World War I should have had a significant impact on them, and they should have used often the First World War as an analogy later in their lives. However, none of them drew on World War I as an analogy for Korea.

Ironically, President Syngman Rhee of South Korea did draw on World War I as a source of analogies. He said he was trying "to avoid making Korea a second Sarajevo."[100] Korea could have been perceived easily as the spark that might ignite a world war. Truman, Attlee, and their advisors feared just such a possibility when they drew upon the 1930's analogy and as they wondered if the Soviets might attack elsewhere in the world. But, contrary to these similarities and to the predictions of the generational theory, British and American leaders in June 1950 did not retrieve analogies from World War I. Why? Level of involvement is a crucial factor. In the 1930s and during World War II, Truman, Attlee, Acheson, and Bevin were in the top ranks of their respective governments, in Congress, Parliament, or in the cabinet, while in World War I, none were directly involved in policy making. Therefore, their positions in the 1930s were more similar to their positions in the 1950s than during 1914–19. Furthermore, World War I did not appear to offer any specific, clear, broadly held lessons for policy about Korea in 1950. Top policy makers in London and Washington in 1950 did not widely hold any lessons from the First World War comparable to the lessons of the 1930s, which were widely known and agreed upon. It was far easier to gain support for a policy based on the 1930s than it would have been for a policy based on the lessons of 1914. The 1930s were also more recent than World War I and many of the top decision makers in government in 1950, especially the younger ones, were more knowledgeable, based on firsthand experience, about the lessons of the 1930s than about lessons from 1914. The monarchies of 1914–18 also appeared less similar to the world of 1950 than did the dictators and democracies of the 1930s. World War I just did not seem relevant. The world had changed too much.

Although neither Truman, Attlee, Bevin, or Acheson were in their twenties or early thirties during the 1930s, they mentioned the 1930s the most often to justify their Korean policy and used lessons from the 1930s to frame the Korean crisis, as well as to prescribe policy. The lack of use of World War I as an analogy and the use of the 1930s suggests that the generational theory must be expanded. Dramatic, large-scale events that occur during an individual's lifetime, such as a world war or revolution, are likely to be drawn upon later in life, regardless of the age of the individual when the event occurs. The individual must, of course, be old enough to be aware of world events. Acheson was born in 1893, Truman in 1884, Attlee in 1883, and Bevin in 1881. Therefore, Truman and Attlee were in their late forties and early fifties during the 1930s; Bevin was in his fifties; and Acheson was in his late thirties and early forties. A narrow generational theory would predict that these leaders should have drawn upon World War I as an analogy to the Korean invasion. However, a broader interpretation of the theory suggests that these men were also influenced significantly by the Second World War. This also suggests that if there are two such events, such as two world wars, then the more recent or the one in which the policy maker played a more important role, is more likely to be retrieved later as a historical analogy for a current crisis.

American and British policy makers retrieved the 1930s to frame the invasion of Korea because the 1930s was a recent, foreign policy failure involving their own states, which they had personally experienced, and which shared surface similarities with the North Korean invasion of South Korea.

The 1930s had also become a master analogy and seemed more similar to Korea than World War I, which the generational theory would predict should have been retrieved as a historical analogy. However, an expanded generational theory is valid.

THE PROCESS OF DRAWING LESSONS FROM HISTORY

Once Truman and Attlee decided, consciously or subconsciously, to use analogical reasoning to retrieve historical information, what was the process by which they used such information? The common model, of an actor asserting the similarity of a historical analogy and the current case, explaining the similarity, and then describing the current case in terms of the analogy, does not reflect what occurs in a foreign policy group. In the Korean case, an actor usually suggested, or implied, that the current case was similar to a historical analogy, often just mentioning an accepted lesson based on an analogy to apply to the current case. In the Korean case, the 1930's analogy, used by Truman and Attlee, was accepted from the beginning of the crisis as valid to frame the invasion, as well as to prescribe and justify policy. There was never any debate about the interpretation of the history of the 1930s in U.S. and U.K. policy-making meetings. Extended discussion of the similarities and differences between the current case and the analogy, or about the validity of the historical analogy also did not occur.

Another aspect of the process of analogical reasoning and drawing lessons from history is that once an analogy is retrieved, actors vary in their acceptance of it. In the Korean case, Truman and Attlee accepted the 1930's analogy as valid. Military force, in concert with other, like-minded nations, would have to be used promptly against North Korean aggression and to support the United Nations. North Korea and the Soviet Union were the new Axis, and the West must not repeat the errors of the 1930s that led to world war. There was no dissent about the validity of the analogy to the Korean invasion in late June and early July 1950 in British and American decision-making meetings. All agreed that the West must respond to the challenge, and all agreed that the response must be military, although the British favored naval forces only, while the Americans quickly escalated to a full-scale military intervention.

The process of analogical reasoning by the decision-making groups in London and Washington in June 1950 were remarkably similar. Truman and Attlee retrieved and then used the 1930's analogy to frame the North Korean invasion, as well as to prescribe and justify policy. The validity or applicability of the analogy was not debated, and its policy recommendations were followed almost without debate. The British debated what form the military response should take, but after a brief, initial period when Attlee wished to avoid intervention, the British, like the Americans, favored a prompt, united military response in concert with the United Nations, just as the 1930's analogy prescribed.

History is like a diamond: multifaceted. Therefore, historical events do not provide a single, specific, precise lesson, and there are numerous, credible lessons that can be drawn from the same historical analogy. To mention just one example, the 1930's/Korea comparison could have suggested that the United States and Britain should not fight in Korea but should build up their military forces, as Britain had done while Hitler remilitarized the Rhineland, integrated Austria and invaded Czechoslovakia, before declaring war when Germany attacked Poland. Even after declaring war, Britain still did little until the attack on France and the Low Countries. Attlee and Truman, even against domestic opposition, might have followed this course. They could have championed a military buildup, while arguing that the United States and Britain must defend Japan, Formosa, the Philippines, and Europe and not become bogged down in a war in strategically unimportant Korea. In fact, this policy was just what their military advisors had suggested before June 1950. The 1930's analogy could also have suggested the importance of investing in science and technology in response to the North Korean invasion, since World War II was ultimately concluded by the dropping of a new weapon: the atomic bomb. Improvements in weaponry since 1950 further highlight the importance of this lesson, as does the U.N. coalition's destruction of the Iraqi armed forces in the 1990–91 Gulf War.

Because it is possible to draw many valid lessons from the same historical analogy, it is extremely difficult to predict what lessons a leader will draw, and act on, from a historical analogy. However, there are some parameters about the types of lessons that will be drawn. The lesson should be simple and easy to explain publicly to justify the chosen policy. For example, the 1930's lesson about responding promptly to aggression with force was simple. In private and in public, Attlee and Truman could state clearly the lesson and its application in the Korean case. The lesson should also be well established and understood broadly, not one newly created. The audience for a historical analogy must be familiar with the analogy and its lessons to fulfill its simplifying function. If the audience is not familiar with the lesson then the communicator must explain the lesson, which negates the simplifying function of the analogy. For example, the lessons of the 1930s had been well enunciated and were known widely by 1950 when Truman and Attlee used them to frame the crisis, as well as to prescribe and justify policy in Korea. They did not suddenly use new lessons based on the 1930s. Historical analogies that provide macro-, rather than microlessons are also more likely to be used to frame a foreign policy crisis. Microlessons are narrow, specific, and are more likely to highlight small differences between the analogy and the current case, leading to their rejection. Macrolessons are broad, general, and are more likely to be perceived as valid for a current crisis. Macrolessons emphasize the broad similarities between the analogy and the current case. Furthermore, policy makers with a range of policy preferences can debate how to apply the macrolesson from an analogy, while a specific analogy excludes diverse views. For example, in the Korean case, the 1930's macrolesson—to use force in concert with allies promptly against aggressive dictators—allowed policy makers to accept the general principle, yet debate issues, such as when to use military force; whether to use only naval and air units, or to intervene with ground forces; and whether to recruit support from all friendly states or only from states that could supply militarily effective units.

It is difficult to determine if the use of the 1930's analogy led to a more effective policy in the Korean case than a policy based on other analogies or determined by some other method. The analogies that Truman and Attlee used to frame the crisis and to prescribe policy resulted in a policy that achieved the Anglo-American goal of repelling the North Korean invasion, restoring the territorial integrity of South Korea, and, for the British, maintaining the Anglo-American "special relationship." The use of the 1930's analogy to justify the policy also contributed to widespread support for American and British policy. However, without evidence on what would have happened if Britain and the United States had pursued different policies based on different analogies or other methods, it is nearly impossible to determine how valid and effective the 1930's analogy was compared to other possible, valid analogies or other decision-making methods. Neustadt and May offer an instructive example of the dangers of attempting to determine if a historical analogy offered valid and effective lessons. They argued that the 1930's analogy produced valid lessons for, and led to an effective policy during the initial U.S. decision to use force in Korea. However, they question the later decision to cross the 38th parallel. Their argument about how the 1930's analogy could have been used to warn Truman not to invade North Korea is logical. However, it is based on hindsight and the fact that the invasion of North Korea failed. If the invasion had succeeded, the 1930's analogy could just as logically have been used to support that policy. In 1945, the outcome of the Allied policy of using force against aggressors was the invasion and conquest of the Axis powers. Therefore, the 1930's analogy can provide the lesson that aggression must be rolled back until the source of the aggression is conquered and, therefore, that North Korea should have been invaded. Neustadt and May play an interesting mental game, but their argument borders on writing a fictional, alternative history because, especially after the fact, a range of lessons can be drawn from the 1930's analogy to fit either a successful or a failed policy.[101] The multiple facets of a historical analogy can often lead to lessons that support significantly different policies.

OTHER POSSIBLE HISTORICAL ANALOGIES

One measure of the influence of the 1930's analogy is that if the 1930's cluster of analogies had a significant impact on British and American policy in response to the North Korean invasion, then another historical analogy should have led to a different policy. One possible analogy that Truman and Attlee could have retrieved was the 1949 Communist Chinese victory over the Nationalists. The China case had attributes that made it a likely candidate for policy makers to use it as an analogy to the Korean invasion. The Communist victory was recent, had been personally experienced by Truman, Acheson, Attlee, and Bevin when they were in office, and was a foreign policy failure for the United States and, to a lesser extent, for Britain. Both China in 1949 and Korea in 1950 pitted Communist forces against a government allied with the West and supported by the United Nations. Both could also be seen as civil wars embedded in the Soviet-American Cold War. Both were also events involving national security, which were also dramatic and important to the United States and to Britain.

If the North Korean invasion had been framed using the Chinese civil war, it would have led to different policy prescriptions than the 1930s. The lesson of the Chinese civil war for Korea was that aid to South Korea would fail. Billions of dollars in U.S. military and economic aid failed to save the Chinese Nationalists. How could Western aid save South Korea when the North Koreans were already marching south at blitzkrieg speed? Criticism of Truman for "losing" China, often cited as a reason for why Truman intervened in Korea to avoid being charged with "losing" Korea, could have been used as a reason to avoid any further commitment to South Korea. Truman and Attlee could have argued, as the Pentagon had argued in the late 1940s, that the West had no national security interests in Korea. Truman and Attlee could have focused attention on strengthening Japan, Taiwan, the Philippines and other Western allies in Asia, as well as in Europe, instead of aiding Korea. The fall of Korea could have been a rallying cry for a defense buildup for the rest of Asia.

However, neither the British nor the Americans chose the Chinese civil war as a historical analogy for Korea. As often occurs, the master analogy, the 1930s, overrode the more recent analogy to China. The 1930s were more important and traumatic in the lives of the principal decision makers, as well as to the United States and to Britain, than the China case, which increased the probability that the decision makers would use lessons based on the 1930s instead of China to frame the North Korean invasion. In the 1930s, Attlee made his name as a critic of appeasement and rose to cabinet rank during World War II. Bevin also saw his star rise during the 1930s and the war years. Truman was in the Senate during the 1930s and became, first, vice president and, later, president during the war. It is no wonder that this period exerted such a strong influence on men whose careers were made during the 1930s and early 1940s. Furthermore, for the United States and Britain, the 1930s and World War II were a dramatic period when the future of the world hung in the balance, and they forged a Grand Alliance to defeat the Axis. The China case could not compete as a major event in the lives of the decision makers or in the history of the United States and Britain. Furthermore, domestic pressure, especially on Truman, and the perceived trend of increasing Soviet aggressiveness, also inclined policy makers toward a historical analogy that would lead to an active, strong policy, not a defensive one, such as the China analogy, that would abandon South Korea.

The Greek civil war of the late 1940s was another possible historical analogy for Korea. On June 26 Truman said Korea was the Greece of the Far East, in reference to the 1947 Truman Doctrine, which provided U.S. aid to the government of Greece in a civil war against Communist rebels.[102] Greece and Korea could both be seen as civil wars, and Truman was intimately involved in both crises. Both also involved Britain and the United States reacting to a threat from a Soviet-supported adversary in a peripheral region. Adoption of the Greece analogy would have prescribed furnishing financial aid and military equipment to South Korea, but not military forces. Greece may have been a valid analogy for Korea, but Truman and Attlee did not use Greece to frame Korea. Policy makers are more likely to draw upon foreign policy failures than successes as historical analogies, and Greece was viewed as a success for American and British foreign policy. This made it less likely to be retrieved as a historical analogy than a foreign policy failure, such as the 1930s. As with the China analogy, a master analogy, the 1930s, overrode the use of the more recent and, in some ways, more similar, analogy to Greece. In the Korean case, it was also quickly apparent, because of the rapid North Korean advance, that the provision of aid, without military intervention, would lead to South Korea's rapid defeat.

The Spanish civil war and the Vietnam War may be the most valid analogies to Korea, in that all were revolutionary civil wars.[103] Policy makers in 1950, of course, could not have drawn on Vietnam, since it had not yet occurred. However, the Spanish civil war (1936–37) offers a possible analogy Truman, Attlee, and their advisors could have used. Actually, the Spanish civil war could be seen as part of the 1930's analogy, with Spain as one of the events on the road to world war. However, policy makers during the Korean crisis did not use the Spanish analogy at first because it was not as much of a foreign policy failure for the United States and Britain as were the 1930s, nor were the United States and Britain as involved in Spain as in the other major crises of the 1930s. Furthermore, Attlee and Truman had less personal experience with, and probably knew less about, Spain than about the other major events in the 1930s, such as appeasement, Munich, and the Japanese attack on Pearl Harbor. Even so, in late July and August 1950, Truman and his advisors did discuss the Spanish civil war analogy in

relation to continued U.S. intervention in Korea. They drew the lesson that
the United States must not become bogged down in Korea in a bloody,
vicious civil war such as the Spanish civil war.[104] The analogy was clear: limit
involvement in a protracted civil war, which the British and Americans followed to a great degree. Most of the Anglo-American defense buildup after
June 1950 focused on Europe, not Korea. However, Truman and Attlee
did not retrieve Spain as a historical analogy during their initial decisions to
intervene in Korea.

A minor part of the reason why Greece, China, and the Spanish civil war
of the 1930s were not retrieved as analogies to Korea was that Greece,
China, and Spain were civil wars, albeit with foreign involvement. The
United Nations, with American and British support, had labored for years
to create a viable South Korean state and, if they compared the North Korean invasion to 1930's Spain, 1947 Greece, or 1949 China, then it would
destroy all that had been done to make South Korea an independent state.
However, this distinction, which colored American and British perceptions
to a limited degree, must be balanced against the fact that British and American policy makers viewed China, Greece, and Korea as all being parts of
the Cold War. They were thus seen as being similar in this major respect.

CONCLUSION

The American and British decisions to intervene in Korea were influenced
significantly by lessons from history, especially from the 1930s. Truman's
personality, as well as situational variables, including high drama, time pressure, surprise, and complexity, contributed to the use of historical analogies
in the Korean case. In fact, situational variables overrode individual variables.
Attlee, Bevin, and Acheson relied on the 1930s to frame the crisis, as well
as to prescribe and justify policy, even though Attlee and Bevin used historical analogies rarely and Acheson used them only occasionally. Surface
similarities, recency, and the influence of a master analogy, as well as the
perception that the 1930s was a foreign policy failure involving Britain and
the United States, led to the use of the 1930s to frame the Korean crisis,
as well as to prescribe and legitimize policy. The 1930s was also a crucial
period in the lives of the top policy makers who faced the North Korean
invasion. The 1930's analogy did not change basic beliefs. It did, however,
affect beliefs about the type and degree of the policy response (military force,
but limited), stakes (the world), risks (possible world war), and perceptions
of the adversary (irrational and untrustworthy), as well as predictions about
what would occur if the West did not intervene militarily in Korea (continued Soviet-supported attacks on the West leading to world war). On the
basis of the 1930's analogy, as well as increasing awareness of the threat
posed by the Soviet Union, Truman and, after a brief delay, Attlee, who
was also strongly influenced by the need to maintain the Anglo-American

alliance, favored the use of military force over other means. The decision to use force was made early in the Korean crisis, both in Washington and in London at almost, if not at, the same time as the decision to take the issue to the United Nations and well before economic sanctions were initiated. The North Korean invasion, especially when framed by the 1930s, called for a prompt military response as the preferred option before other options, such as diplomacy and economic sanctions, were tried or given a chance to succeed. Other factors, such as the size and rapidity of the North Korean invasion, domestic factors in America, the emerging Cold War, and British concern with continued American financial and military aid, also influenced British and American decision making significantly. However, historical information retrieved by analogical reasoning framed the crisis, reinforced and shaped perceptions and existing beliefs, allowed decision makers to go beyond the information currently available, and played a significant role in justifying the British and American military interventions.

NOTES

1. June 24 Washington time. Korean time is fourteen hours ahead of Washington time. For the rest of this chapter, all dates and times will be EDT.

2. Acheson, *Present at the Creation*, p. 405; and Cumings, *The Origins of the Korean War*, Vol. II, pp. 625–626, 631–632.

3. The Soviet Union was absent over the China-seat issue and, therefore, was unable to veto the resolution.

4. Farrar-Hockley, *The British Part in the Korean War*, pp. 31–32.

5. Cumings, *The Origins of the Korean War*, Vol. II, p. 634.

6. James E. Webb to John W. Snyder, April 25, 1975, Papers of James E. Webb, Box 456, Truman Library; and Truman, *Margaret Truman's Own Story*, p. 275.

7. Truman authorized what MacArthur was already doing. As soon as MacArthur received news of the invasion, in accordance with a prearranged plan, he began to evacuate U.S. personnel and moved naval and air units to protect the evacuees. Persons Present at the President's Meeting at 11:30 a.m., Tuesday, June 27, Papers of George M. Elsey, Truman Library.

8. Memorandum of Conversation, June 25, 1950, Subject: Korean Situation, Papers of Dean Acheson, Truman Library; Points Requiring Presidential Decision, Papers of George M. Elsey, Truman Library; and Truman, *Memoirs*, Vol. II, p. 335.

9. On June 26, the air force and the navy thought they alone could defend South Korea, although the army was doubtful. Acheson, *Present at the Creation*, p. 408.

10. Memo of Conversation, June 26, 1950, Subject: Korean Situation, Papers of Dean Acheson, Truman Library.

11. Ibid.; and Stueck, *The Korean War*, p. 44.

12. Papers of George M. Elsey, June 30, 1950, B File: Korea, Truman Library.

13. Miss Hachmeister's records, June 30, 1950, Subject: Call from Frank Pace, Papers of George M. Elsey, B File: Korea, Truman Library; Pelz, "U.S. Decisions on Korean Policy," pp. 128, 131.

14. There was already an embargo on strategic materials to the Soviet Union and its Eastern European allies.

15. Harris, *Attlee*, p. 454.

16. Cabinet Conclusions, 27 June 1950 (CAB 128/18); and Foreign and Commonwealth Office, *Documents on British Policy Overseas*, p. 3. At the start of the crisis Foreign Secretary Ernest Bevin was ill and Kenneth Younger, the minister of state at the Foreign Office, handled day-to-day affairs. However, Bevin read and commented on cabinet minutes and memoranda from early July onward. Lowe, *The Origins of the Korean War*, p. 162; and Lowe, "The Frustrations of Alliance," pp. 81–82.

17. Farrar-Hockley, *The British Part in the Korean War*, pp. 46–47; and Stueck, *The Korean War*, p. 72.

18. Farrar-Hockley, *The British Part in the Korean War*, chapter 5.

19. Cabinet Conclusions, 27 June 1950 (CAB 128/18).

20. Foreign and Commonwealth Office, *Documents on British Policy Overseas*, pp. 7–8.

21. Cabinet Conclusions, 28 June 1950 (CAB 131/9); Foreign and Commonwealth Office, *Documents on British Policy Overseas*, p. 10; and Farrar-Hockley, *The British Part in the Korean War*, p. 47.

22. Farrar-Hockley, *The British Part in the Korean War*, pp. 52–53.

23. Ibid., pp. 85–88.

24. Lowe, "Frustrations of Alliance," p. 82; and Farrar-Hockley, *The British Part in the Korean War*, p. 99.

25. Farrar-Hockley, *The British Part in the Korean War*, p. 98.

26. Boyle, "Oliver Franks and the Washington Embassy," p. 199.

27. Overlord was the code name for the Allied invasion of Normandy in June 1944.

28. Farrar-Hockley, *The British Part in the Korean War*, pp. 99–100. Also see Bullock, *Ernest Bevin*, Vol. III, p. 793.

29. Bullock, *Ernest Bevin*, Vol. III, p. 795. The U.S. State Department, which, for political reasons, favored asking every country that might be willing to commit troops, opposed the Defense Department, who favored asking only those states that could supply militarily effective units. Britain, however, fit the goals of both departments. Stueck, *The Korean War*, pp. 57–58.

30. Sir Oliver Franks (Washington) to Mr. Younger, 23 July 1950, pp. 76–78 in Foreign and Commonwealth Office, *Documents on British Policy Overseas*; Farrar-Hockley, *The British Part in the Korean War*, pp. 102–103; and Boyle, "Oliver Franks and the Washington Embassy," p. 200.

31. Morgan, *Labour in Power*, p. 423.

32. Although there was still opposition within the military to the decision. Farrar-Hockley, *The British Part in the Korean War*, pp. 103–104, 121.

33. Foreign and Commonwealth Office, *Documents on British Policy Overseas*, pp. 81–82; MacDonald, *Britain and the Korean War*, p. 21; Lowe, "The Frustrations of Alliance," p. 81; and Farrar-Hockley, *The British Part in the Korean War*, p. 104.

34. Farrar-Hockley, *The British Part in the Korean War*, p. 104.

35. Cumings, *The Origins of the Korean War*, Vol. II, p. 655; and Stueck, *The Korean War*, p. 72.

36. Truman joined the Missouri National Guard in 1905 and was an artillery officer in World War I. Attlee joined the cadet corps at prep school, was active in a

regiment at Oxford, and served as an officer in World War I. Brookshire, *Clement Attlee*, p. 148; and Hamby, *Man of the People*, chapter 4.

37. Farrar-Hockley, *The British Part in the Korean War*, pp. 103–104.

38. Kaufman, *The Korean War Challenge*, pp. 37–38.

39. J. F. Dulles to Truman, July 20, 1950, Miscellaneous (1948)-471B: Korean Emergency, June-July 1950, PSF, Box 1305, Truman Library.

40. Truman to Mrs. Roosevelt, August 22, 1950, Miscellaneous (1948)-471B: Korean Emergency, June-July 1950, PSF, Box 1305, Truman Library.

41. Pelz, "U.S. Decisions on Korean Policy," p. 127.

42. Austria was not attacked militarily by a stronger neighbor. A plebiscite was held, albeit under severe German pressure, and the Austrians voted to join Germany.

43. Truman, *Memoirs*, Vol. II, pp. 332–333. Also see Ferrell, *Off the Record*.

44. The Korea volume of the *Foreign Relations of the United States* series, in the period from June 25 through early July 1950, provides no mention of the 1930s and only a few allusions to the lessons of the 1930s about responding to aggression promptly with force to avoid a world war. Others also mention the influence of historical analogies on Truman and rely on his memoirs as evidence with little, if any, other supporting evidence. See Paige, *The Korean Decision*, p. 171; Neustadt and May, *Thinking in Time*, p. 89; Jervis, *Perception and Misperception*, pp. 218–220; Khong, *Analogies at War*, p. 22; Cochran, *Harry Truman and the Crisis Presidency*, p. 313; Hamby, *Man of the People*, pp. 536–537; and Lowe, *The Origins of the Korean War*, p. 169.

45. Memorandum of Conversation, June 25, 1950, Papers of Dean Acheson, Truman Library. Also see Paige, *The Korean Decision*, p. 137.

46. J. F. Dulles and John Allison to Acheson and Rusk, June 25, 1950, Subject File: Korea, 25 June 1950, Truman Library.

47. *Foreign Relations of the United States, 1950, Korea*, Vol. III, p. 238.

48. Lowe, *The Origins of the Korean War*, p. 167.

49. Memo for the NSC, Subject: Suggested Action by the NSC for Consideration of the President in Light of the Korean Situation, July 6, 1950, PSF, Truman Library.

50. Farrar-Hockley, *The British Part in the Korean War*, p. 32. Others make the same argument. See Sanders, *Losing an Empire*, p. 69; Ovendale, "Britain and the Cold War in Asia," p. 131; Pelling, *The Labour Governments*, p. 243; Morgan, *Labour in Power*, p. 425; and Macmillan, *Tides of Fortune*, p. 326.

51. *Parliamentary Debates*, Commons, 5th Series, vol. 476 (June 27, 1950), col. 2160.

52. *Parliamentary Debates*, Commons, 5th Series, vol. 477 (July 5, 1950), col. 493.

53. Farrar-Hockley, *The British Part in the Korean War*, p. 113.

54. Persons Present at the President's Meeting at 11:30 A.M., June 27, 1950, Papers of George M. Elsey, B File: Korean War, Response to North Korea's Invasion, Box 1 of 2, Truman Library.

55. Truman to President of Korea, July 17, 1950, PSF: Korean War File, Truman Library.

56. Special Message to the Congress Reporting on the Situation in Korea, July 19, 1950, *The Public Papers of the Presidents of the United States: Harry S. Truman, 1950*, p. 529. In radio and television addresses on July 19 and Sept. 1 Truman

compared the 1930s and Korea. "Radio and Television Address to the American People on the Situation in Korea," July 19, 1950, *The Public Papers of the Presidents of the United States: Harry S. Truman, 1950*, p. 538 and "Radio and Television Report to the American People on the Situation in Korea," Sept. 1, 1950, *The Public Papers of the Presidents of the United States: Harry S. Truman, 1950*, pp. 609–614.

57. Acheson, "Charging South Korea as Aggressor Reminiscent of Nazi Tactics" (released July 5), *Department of State Bulletin*, vol. 23, no. 576, July 17, 1950, p. 87.

58. Lowe, *The Origins of the Korean War*, p. 167. Also see Acheson to Clarence E. Moullette, stamped Feb. 23, 1951, Moullette Papers, Box 1, correspondence file, Truman Library.

59. NSC Report, Results of Conversations between the President and the British Prime Minister, Dec. 12, 1950, PSF NSC Files, Meetings 71 to 79, Box 210, Truman Library.

60. Another example is the Vietnam analogy. In many arguments about military intervention in the 1980s and 1990s, the lessons of Vietnam were discussed, although the analogy often was not mentioned.

61. Burridge, *Clement Attlee*, pp. 227–233.

62. Ibid., pp. 96–115; and Brookshire, *Clement Attlee*, p. 159.

63. Bullock, *Ernest Bevin*, Vol. I, pp. 526, 562–563.

64. Brookshire, *Clement Attlee*, p. 172; and Burridge, *Clement Attlee*, p. 149.

65. Hamby, *Man of the People*, p. 266.

66. Ibid., p. 345.

67. Cumings, *The Origins of the Korean War*, Vol. II, pp. 45, 58–61; Stueck, *The Korean War*, pp. 24–25; and McGlothlen, *Controlling the Waves*, pp. 51–78.

68. Papers of Dean Acheson, Memorandum of Conversation, June 25, 1950, Subject: Korean Situation, B File: Korea, Truman Library.

69. Memorandum for the President, July 27, 1950, IPSF, NSC Meetings, Box 220, File: Memos for the President's Meeting Discussions, Truman Library.

70. Papers of George M. Elsey, Cabinet Meeting, June 30, 1950, B File: Korea, Truman Library.

71. Truman, *Memoirs*, Vol. II, p. 340; MacDonald, *Korea: The War Before Vietnam*, pp. 30–32; Kaufman, *The Korean War*, pp. 33–35; Pelz, "U.S. Decisions on Korean Policy," pp. 119–127; Foot, *The Wrong War*, pp. 42, 58–62; Williams, *Twilight of Empire*, pp. 230–232; Lowe, *The Origins of the Korean War*, p. 165; and MacDonald, *Britain and the Korean War*, pp. 1, 5.

72. Dept. of State, "The Conflict in Korea," October 1951, Published Background Material, Harry S. Truman Papers, Box 1, Selected Records Relating to the Korean War, Truman Library.

73. Statement by President on Situation in Korea, June 27, 1950, *The Public Papers of the Presidents of the United States: Harry S. Truman, 1950*, p. 492.

74. Jervis, *Perception and Misperception*, p. 34.

75. Truman, *Memoirs*, Vol. II, pp. 334–335; President's News Conference, June 29, 1950, *The Public Papers of the Presidents of the United States: Harry S. Truman, 1950*, p. 503; Paige, *The Korean Decision*, p. 143; Cabinet Conclusions, 27 June 1950 (CAB 128/18); and Foreign and Commonwealth Office, *Documents on British Policy Overseas*, p. 3.

76. Bullock, *Ernest Bevin*, Vol. III, pp. 793–795; Stueck, *The Korean War*, pp.

50–51; Farrar-Hockley, *The British Part in the Korean War*, pp. 88–96; and Acheson, *Present at the Creation*, pp. 416–420.

77. Farrar-Hockley, *The British Part in the Korean War*, p. 89.

78. Richard G. Nixon, Oral History, No. 265, Security Copies, Volumes I-III, Box 44, Nov. 4, 1970, p. 729, Truman Library.

79. President's Meeting, June 29, 1950, Papers of George M. Elsey, Box 71, Korea File Folder, Truman Library. Also see Pelz, "U.S. Decisions on Korean Policy," p. 132.

80. Memorandum of Conversation, Korean Situation, June 25, 1950, Papers of Dean Acheson, B File, Truman Library; Blair House Meeting (also labeled JCS Instructions to MacArthur), June 25, 1950, Papers of George M. Elsey, Subject File: Korea, Truman Library; Oral History, John J. Muccio, Dec. 27, 1973, p. 21, Truman Library; Oral History, Frank Pace, Jr., February 17, 1972, p. 77, Truman Library; and Oral History, Robert L. Dennison, Nov. 2, 1971, p. 115, Truman Library.

81. Outgoing Classified Message, JCS to CINCFE (Command), June 29, 1950, Papers of George M. Elsey, B File: Korea, Truman Library.

82. *Parliamentary Debates*, Commons, 5th Series, vol. 477, cols. 493–494 (Attlee). Also see Farrar-Hockley, *The British Part in the Koren War*, p. 44; MacDonald, *Korea*, pp. 4, 16–17, 30–32; Lowe, *The Origins of the Korean War*, p. 165; and Pearce, *Attlee's Labour Governments*, pp. 64–66.

83. Williams, *Twilight of Empire*, p. 230; and Lowe, *The Origins of the Korean War*, p. 177.

84. Lowe, *The Origins of the Korean War*, p. 202.

85. Ibid., p. 177.

86. Harris, *Attlee*, p. 454 quoted in MacDonald, *Britain and the Korean War*, p. 4.

87. Lowe, *The Origins of the Korean War*, p. 169.

88. Truman, *Memoirs*, Vol. II, p. 340; MacDonald, *Korea*, pp. 30–32; Kaufman, *The Korean War*, pp. 33–35; Pelz, "U.S. Decisions on Korean Policy," pp. 119–127; Foot, *The Wrong War*, pp. 42, 58–62; Williams, *Twilight of Empire*, pp. 230–232; Lowe, *The Origins of the Korean War*, p. 165; MacDonald, *Britain and the Korean War*, pp. 1, 5; and Lowe, "The Frustrations of Alliance," p. 80.

89. Lowe, "The Frustrations of Alliance," p. 80; Farrar-Hockley, *The British Part in the Korean War*, p. 37; and McGibbon, *New Zealand and the Korean War*, Vol. I, p. 65.

90. Attlee and Truman did not mention South Korean raids into the North or South Korean propaganda against the North, which may have provoked the invasion.

91. Truman to the President of South Korea, July 17, 1950, PSF: Korean War File, Truman Library; and Richard G. Nixon, Oral History, No. 265, Security Copies, Volumes I-III, Box 44, Nov. 4, 1970, p. 729, Truman Library.

92. *Parliamentary Debates*, Commons, 5th Series, vol. 477. MPs mentioned Manchuria (col. 563), 1939 (col. 504), 1914 (col. 505), Hitler and the 1930s (cols. 564–565) all July 5, 1950. Also see July 5, 1950: col. 493 (Attlee); cols. 584–585 (Eden); and cols. 588–589 and 594–595 (Herbert Morrison, Lord President of the Council).

93. Memo for the NSC, Suggested Action by the NSC for Consideration of the President in Light of the Korean Situation, July 6, 1950, PSF, Truman Library; Truman to the President of South Korea, July 17, 1950, PSF: Korean War File,

Truman Library; and Richard G. Nixon, Oral History, No. 265, Security Copies, Volumes I-III, Box 44, Nov. 4, 1970, p. 729, Truman Library.

94. J. F. Dulles, "U.S. Military Actions in Korea," *Department of State Bulletin*, vol. 23, no. 576, July 17, 1950, p. 88.

95. World War I was not a major event in Bevin's life. The major point in his life was in 1910 when he organized a union. He did not serve in World War I. Bullock, *Ernest Bevin*, Vol. I, p. 44, Vol. II, pp. 11, 36, and Vol. III, p. 848.

96. Ferrell, *Harry S. Truman: A Life*, pp. 56, 70; and Hamby, *Man of the People*, chapter 4.

97. Ferrell, *Harry S. Truman: A Life*, pp. 116–160.

98. Acheson, *Morning and Noon*, p. 215.

99. Brookshire, *Clement Attlee*, p. 147; and Burridge, *Clement Attlee*, pp. 41–42.

100. He was referring to the city where Archduke Franz Ferdinand was assassinated in 1914, which ignited the First World War. *Foreign Relations of the United States, 1950, Korea*, p. 131.

101. Neustadt and May, *Thinking in Time*, pp. 35–48.

102. Cumings, *The Origins of the Korean War*, Vol. II, p. 629.

103. Ibid., pp. 412, 770.

104. See *Foreign Relations of the United States, 1950, Korea*, late July, August, and September items.

4

A Twisted Tail: The Iranian Oil Nationalization Crisis

Current information dominated British and American decision making at the expense of historical information during the Iranian oil nationalization crisis. Almost no historical analogies were mentioned in memoirs or in available government records and neither British nor American leaders used historical analogies to frame the crisis or to prescribe or legitimize policy. Eisenhower was an exception when he mentioned the "loss" of China as an analogy, although it had little influence on policy. Unfortunately, the finding that historical information and analogies were not used to influence policy significantly in the Iran case is weakened, although only minimally, by the numerous deleted portions of key documents, as well as missing documents related to the crisis in the U.S. and U.K. archives. However, given the lack of mention of historical analogies by British or American policy makers in the public record[1] and the proposition, supported by three other cases in this study (Korea, Suez, and Lebanon/Jordan), that the public use of historical analogies mirrors the private use of analogies, it is logical and valid to argue that policy makers did not use historical analogies or information much, if at all, in the Iran case.

For historical analogies, Iran is a case of the hound that did not bark. All too often such cases are ignored, yet the lack of use of historical information and analogies is as important to study as cases when historical information is used. Both types of cases shed light on the central issues of this study: who uses historical information and analogies, when, why and with what effects? Therefore, the major issues relating to historical information in the Iran case are to explain the reliance on current information and lack of use of historical analogies, as well as the effects of not relying on lessons of the past to make policy. Situational variables, including the lack of time pressures and surprise and a low level of drama, as well as individual variables, led to the predominance of current over historical information.

Given the lack of use of historical analogies in this case, historical information does not provide an explanation for the British and American policy choices. However, the lack of use of historical analogies contributes to an explanation of the general trend of British and American policies. Historical analogies are a cognitive shortcut and usually provide policy makers with a specific policy to pursue from diplomatic, economic, and military options. For example, in the Korea and Suez cases, the 1930's analogy proscribed the prompt use of force. During the Iran crisis, the lack of use of historical analogies as a cognitive shortcut to simplify the crisis and prescribe a specific policy left policy makers without a single, broadly supported, policy response. Therefore, the British and Americans pursued a range of policies in succession. As each policy failed, the British and Americans escalated their responses. Within the broad model—that lack of reliance on a historical analogy leads to a succession of policies until the crisis is resolved—a bounded rational actor model, combined with alliance politics, fear of Soviet counterintervention, and personal beliefs about the use of force, provides a valid explanation of the escalation of successive American and British policies toward Iran during the crisis. When Iran nationalized its oil industry, the British and Americans faced a range of policy options, embracing, broadly: diplomacy; economic and financial measures; covert action; and military force, either threatened (compellence) or used (military intervention). On the basis of alliance politics, especially U.S. opposition, and political beliefs, Attlee ruled out the use of force. He then pursued a compellence strategy combined with negotiation and, when those strategies failed, he escalated the crisis by imposing economic and financial sanctions and initiating covert action in an attempt to overthrow Iranian prime minister Mohammed Mossadegh.[2] Truman also supported negotiation and, when talks failed, escalated U.S. actions by supporting a British-led oil embargo. When Eisenhower came to power, the Americans further escalated the crisis by initiating covert operations against Mossadegh, although Truman also tried to topple Mossadegh by asking the shah to remove his prime minister. Gradual British and American escalation of diplomatic, economic, and then covert means was the result, to a significant degree, of the lack of a historical analogy to provide a single, clear policy prescription.

Just as studies of historical analogies exclusively focus on cases where policy makers relied on historical information, the 1951 Iranian oil nationalization is a rare case in studies of the use of military force in regional contingencies, because such studies predominantly analyze cases where states decided to use force. In the 1951–53 Iran case, the United States did not consider using force, while Britain debated intervention, but decided not to use force. The British decided not to use military force because of U.S. opposition, Attlee's personal beliefs, and the type and degree of threat. Although British pressure on Iran escalated in degree and form during the crisis, the original decision not to use force never changed. Even after diplomacy and economic sanctions failed to solve the crisis and, even after a new, Conservative government took office, the British did not decide to use military force because the underlying causes for the decision did not change, except that Attlee's personal beliefs were removed from the equation when he left office.

American and British perceptions of Mossadegh's rationality significantly influenced their views on the use of force, as well as on the effectiveness of covert operations, negotiations, and economic sanctions. Policy makers who view an adversary as irrational, whether based on a historical analogy or not, are more likely to use force or covert operations than those who view their adversary as rational. If policy makers view an adversary as rational, then they are more likely to support negotiations or economic sanctions instead of the use of force.

This chapter begins by outlining the major events in the long and complex Iran crisis, as well as British and American goals. The British decision not to use military force is then analyzed, followed by a discussion of British alternatives to the use of force. A section on U.S. decision making is followed by an analysis of the relationship between the perceptions of British and American policy makers of Mossadegh's rationality and their views on the use of force. The chapter then analyzes the reasons why current information dominated decision making and why historical information and analogies were not used, with one exception: Eisenhower's use of the China analogy. A conclusion summarizes the major findings of the chapter.

THE CRISIS AND WESTERN GOALS

On March 15, 1951, the Iranian Majlis (parliament) passed a bill nationalizing the Iranian oil industry.[3] The British cabinet met repeatedly between March and October 1951 to decide whether to use military force against Iran to achieve its goals. The British goal was, at first, to secure the return of the Anglo-Iranian Oil Company's (AIOC) concession. Although Prime Minister Attlee accepted the principle of nationalization, he did not accept Iran's right unilaterally to repudiate a contract without compensation. Because of this the British goal was later modified to seeking compensation for the nationalization of AIOC property and operations in Iran, as well as for future lost earnings as a result of the loss of the concession.[4] In May 1951 the Foreign Office instructed the British ambassador to Iran "to suggest to Mossadeq [sic] that the British are willing to cooperate in Iran's national aspirations in regard to their oil . . . but that UK cannot accept Persia's right to repudiate contracts . . . it is prepared to negotiate a settlement which . . . involved some form of nationalization."[5] Attlee wrote Truman on June 5, 1951, "Furthermore, a breach of contract of this nature might well jeopardize other overseas contracts, not merely those held by British and United States companies for the development of Middle East oil resources, but contracts for other products elsewhere."[6] While Attlee would have accepted a negotiated settlement that fell short of the restoration of the concession, Prime Minister Churchill and Foreign Secretary Eden, who both took power in October 1951, wanted to regain the concession and, almost to a greater extent, punish Mossadegh. However, by the time Churchill became prime minister, the use of military force was not a justifiable option, either domestically or internationally, since the provocation, the nationalization, was so long in the past.

Throughout the crisis, the principle American goal was to prevent Iran from slipping into anarchy, which might have led to increased Soviet influence in Iran or, worse, a Communist government in Iran, which Eisenhower especially feared. A greater U.S. role in Iran would not be unwelcome, but the Americans did not, in 1951, want to decrease British influence just to increase their own. The Americans were at war in Korea and were struggling to build a military capable of defending Western Europe against possible Soviet invasion. If the British could keep the Middle East out of the Soviet orbit, the Americans saw no need to interfere. Therefore, the United States sought a negotiated settlement that appeased their British allies, but did not turn Iran against the West. However, the Americans did not want to reward the Iranians for unilateral nationalization by giving them a better deal than those received by other states with other foreign oil companies, such as Saudi Arabia had with the Arab American Oil Company. At an October 10, 1951, meeting Acheson told Eisenhower, "The Iranians should not result in doing better than Saudi Arabia has in its deal. Probably about a 50% split in profits is a reasonable result. . . . The President agreed to this."[7] The Americans believed that these goals could best be achieved without the use of military force by the British or by the United States.

A DIVIDED CABINET: THE BRITISH DECISION NOT TO USE MILITARY FORCE

The British decided not to use military force, although it remained an option of last resort throughout the crisis, especially if Iran threatened British nationals. The British considered using force from March 1951, during the initial nationalization, to October 1951, when Iran ordered British nationals out of the country and seized the AIOC oil refinery at Abadan. Talk of military intervention was not just saber rattling. The British developed multiple military plans to intervene, code named Jagged, Midget, Companion, and Plan Y, among others.[8] The most well-developed plan, Buccaneer, was drafted and changed repeatedly between April and September 23, 1951, when the operation was finally cancelled.[9] The British were not merely planning. At one point British forces were put on three hours' warning to be ready to intervene[10] and in April 1951 the British sent the cruisers *Gambia* and *Mauritius* to Abadan, Iran. By May 1951 two frigates joined the cruisers and the 16th Paratroop Brigade Group was ordered to Cyprus to relieve any troops that might be used to intervene in Iran.[11] On August 8, 1951, the cruiser *Mauritius* and four British destroyers conducted firing practice off Abadan, while British troops in the Middle East were put on alert.[12] British military deployments were not a military intervention as defined by this study because British policy makers did not view them as a military intervention. Royal Navy ships were routinely off Abadan, and there was no expectation of casualties nor was there any Iranian defense. The Iranians also did not perceive the British warships off their shores as a military intervention, although they did see them as a threat. Therefore, because of the views of both parties, the British warships in Iranian waters were not a military intervention.

Throughout the crisis, when the British considered using force, the same factors influenced the decision. Therefore, the decisions can, to a great extent, be analyzed together.[13] There was, however, a change in the dynamics of the crisis, which influenced the decision to use force. Early in the crisis, Herbert Morrison, who supported intervention, played a more prominent role in the crisis because Ernest Bevin, the foreign secretary, was in the hospital. By July, however, Attlee, supported by the now healthy Bevin against Morrison, asserted his role as prime minister and his opposition to intervention slowly took precedence.[14] Although it took months for Attlee to impose his decision on his cabinet, he decided early that the crisis did not warrant the use of military force. Only after Attlee decided not to use force did the British pursue diplomatic and economic measures against Iran.

Throughout the crisis in 1951 the British cabinet was divided over the use of military force. Morrison and Defense Minister Emanuel Shinwell were the leading supporters of the use of force, while Attlee, the Chancellor of the Exchequer Hugh Gaitskell, and the military chiefs opposed intervention.[15] In Parliament, Morrison said the government "reserve[s] the right to act as we see fit to protect British lives and property."[16] He later said, "My own view was that there was much to be said in favor of sharp and forceful action."[17] Shinwell said, with great foresight, "If Persia was allowed to get away with it, Egypt and other Middle Eastern countries would be encouraged to think they could try things too. The next thing might be an attempt to nationalize the Suez Canal,"[18] which happened five years later. On April 1, 1951, Shinwell warned that "the sport of twisting the British lion's tail might produce undesirable reactions."[19] And during the crisis over the threatened eviction of British personnel from Abadan, the British ambassador to Washington, Sir Oliver Franks, said Britain "would in no circumstances abandon Abadan."[20] For Morrison, Shinwell, and the hawks in the cabinet, military force was the preferred response to the Iranian nation-alization from the beginning of the crisis.

However, Attlee overruled the promilitary intervention cabinet members. Attlee, Bevin, and Gaitskell believed that military intervention was obsolete in what they believed was the more enlightened world of 1951, with the United Nations fighting aggression in Korea and the decline of colonial empires. Gaitskell also argued that a military attack would be costly and would inflame the Arab powers against the West.[21] Attlee agreed and later said:

I think if we had used force we would have raised the whole of Asia against us and a great deal of public opinion in the rest of the world too. And it would have been quite wrong morally and politically. It was impossible for us as a Labour Government to say that you couldn't nationalize the oil industry. . . . At this time of day it was quite out of the question to think you could revert to old form and act as a big nation throwing in its forces to defend its commercial interests. Quite wrong, and certainly quite impossible for us, of all people.[22]

Attlee had nationalized the British iron and steel industries and could hardly criticize the Iranians for doing what he had done domestically. Bevin agreed and said, "What argument can I advance against anyone claiming the right to nationalize the resources of their country? We are doing the same thing here."[23] Therefore, Attlee told the Foreign Office to accept the principle of nationalization. However, Attlee and Bevin opposed the manner in which the Iranians implemented their nationalization. They wanted the Iranians to compensate the AIOC.[24]

Attlee's opposition to the use of military force also reflected his broader beliefs about the Middle East. Oil was crucial to Britain, but Attlee, as early as 1946, believed the British could not maintain control of the oil by force. Therefore, he reasoned, the British must keep the area politically stable through other means. The principle other means, Attlee believed, had to be the United States. In 1947 the Americans assumed the British role in Greece, and Attlee hoped the Americans would take over from the British in the Middle East.[25] Attlee's belief about the ineffectiveness of using British military force to maintain control of Middle Eastern oil contributed to his opposition to the use of force against Iran in 1951.

The opposition of President Truman and Secretary of State Acheson to the use of military force also significantly influenced Attlee's decision not to use force. Their opposition was probably sufficient to scuttle any British plans to use military force. On January 20, 1953, Truman and Acheson were succeeded, respectively, by Dwight D. Eisenhower and John F. Dulles, al-though they too opposed the British use of military force.

The British also decided not to intervene because of the unsettled situa-tion in newly independent India, conflict over Kashmir, and the ongoing crisis in Egypt that put British interests at risk and threatened to stretch British military resources to the breaking point. With these other commitments, Attlee did not believe that Britain had the resources to conduct a quick and decisive military intervention.[26] Fear of Soviet counterintervention also influenced British decision making. The Russo-Persian Treaty of 1921 gave Russia and, the British feared, the Soviet Union as the successor to Russia, the right to move troops into Iran under certain circumstances.[27]

The personal beliefs of Attlee and Bevin in support of the principle of nationalization and against the use of military force, combined with fear of Soviet counterintervention, limited British military resources, and, most significantly, U.S. opposition to the military option, led to the British decision not to use military force when Iran nationalized its oil industry.

BRITISH ALTERNATIVES TO MILITARY FORCE

Even though the Attlee cabinet decided not to use military force, it was under intense domestic pressure to do something. The U.S. embassy in London emphasized "the extensive frustration and anger which have grown up in England as a result of the growing Near East practice of 'twisting the lion's tail.' "[28] In August 1951 the U.S. State Department reported, "Prime Minister [Attlee] and others were concerned that inaction by the British for protracted period is embarrassing politically in UK and indicates signs of weakness abroad. They are acutely aware of possible approaching elections."[29] With no historical analogy to prescribe a single, specific policy, such as the prescription of the 1930s analogy to use military force promptly, Attlee pursued a succession of policies in an attempt to resolve the crisis. Attlee first pursued negotiation by various means and in different forms. In April 1951 the Foreign Office was exerting "greater pressure than ever before" on the AIOC to offer Iran a generous deal,[30] and Morrison said that he "was anxious that every avenue for peaceful negotiations should be explored."[31] On May 26, 1951, Britain took the case to the International Court of Justice. Mossadegh rejected the initial British proposal in June 1951, and in August 1951 Sir Richard Stokes, the Lord Privy Seal, went to Tehran for further negotiations, which also failed. In September the British again tried the negotiation route and took the case to the United Nations. However, that avenue also failed to produce a settlement. By October 1951 Attlee and Morrison had abandoned negotiation. Morrison said the British "did not wish to be made fools of once more,"[32] with another failed negotiation attempt.

The failure of negotiation led to Attlee's escalation of the crisis to economic and financial sanctions. Even before negotiation failed, in July 1951, the AIOC and six other major oil companies took legal action against anyone buying Iranian oil, viewing it as "stolen oil."[33] After talks failed, in September-October 1951, the British government, in a major step, escalated the crisis by organizing an international boycott of Iranian oil. Even if the Iranians managed to operate their oil industry, they would be unable to sell any oil. The British also banned the sale of iron, steel, sugar, and oil-processing equipment to Iran. After the failure of the Stokes mission in September 1951 the British also cancelled Iran's Sterling conversion privileges.[34]

Economic sanctions, however, also failed to elicit any major change in the Iranian position. Although Mossadegh believed the world needed Iran's oil and, therefore, the United States would pressure Britain to reach a negotiated settlement, he was wrong. The world oil market was glutted, and neither the British nor the Americans needed Iran's oil. As the British escalated their policies, Mossadegh matched their moves. For example, the failure of the initial Anglo-Iranian negotiations in June-August 1951 led to his demand, in September 1951, for the eviction of British technicians from Abadan.

Having decided not to use military force, with negotiations failing and economic sanctions apparently unable to change Iran's course, Attlee adopted the next best option to appease the public and the hawks in his cabinet: covert action aimed at overthrowing Mossadegh combined with a compellence strategy. As early as June 15, 1951, after the failure of the first round of negotiations, but before Britain imposed severe economic sanctions in the form of the oil boycott, Morrison sent Christopher Woodhouse, chief MI6 officer in Iran, and Robin Zaehner, an academic expert on Iran, to Iran to engineer Mossadegh's political demise.[35] However, the British were unable to find an alternative to Mossadegh. Iranian politicians Qavam es-Sultanah and Fazlollah Zahedi, both supported by the British, failed to oust Mossadegh. Even after their diplomats had been evicted in October 1951 British agents remained active in Iran cultivating Iranian politicians to overthrow Mossadegh.[36] On September 28, 1951, as Mossadegh, who was also escalating his policies, threatened to evict British technicians from Iran, Attlee tried his hand at toppling Mossadegh. Attlee sent a message to the shah through the British ambassador:

The message stated that, although Attlee could understand the hesitation of the Shah heretofore to intervene, Attlee thought the Shah must now appreciate that a political situation has arisen which he alone can redress. . . . Attlee trusts that the Shah will take immediate action to ensure that expulsion measures against the British technicians are not carried out. Shephard [British ambassador] explained to Ala [minister of Court], upon the latter's direct query, that by "immediate action" Attlee had in mind the removal of Mosadeq [*sic*]. [However, the Monarch declined because] Mosadeq [*sic*] might, by open denunciation of the Shah, and by appeals to religious and national fanaticism, create such an atmosphere that the Majlis would be completely cowed and the Shah's position irretrievably ruined.[37]

The British request failed, and in October 1952 Mossadegh expelled British nationals from Iran.

The British compellence strategy made military forces available near Iran if Britain decided to intervene on a limited scale to protect British lives or, if the cabinet changed its mind, to intervene on a larger scale to protect British and/or AIOC property. Throughout the crisis Attlee and the cabinet favored the use of military force on a small scale if British nationals were threatened. For example, in June 1951 Morrison said, the British will not "stand by idle if the lives of British nationals are in jeopardy."[38] Preparing for a possible rescue mission of British nationals dove-tailed nicely with a compellence strategy: "the British intend to send troops into Iran only if necessary to protect British lives, [sic] they admit that the present troop movements are being made with an eye on the salutary effect it will have on Iran."[39] However, the troop movements, planning, and threats did not compel Iran to rescind the nationalization or even to discuss compensating the AIOC. Even so, Attlee did not reverse his initial decision not to use military force.

Churchill and Eden succeeded Attlee and Bevin in October 1951. Churchill, without drawing specific lessons from history to guide him, continued the policies Attlee had initiated as the British tried different means to resolve the crisis. In a way, Attlee had already framed the crisis for the public and for many top policy makers. Churchill would have faced an extremely difficult chore to change basic perceptions of the crisis, as one that did not justify the use of military force. The task was probably impossible unless the Iranians committed a provocative act that Churchill could then react to by using military force. Even though Churchill won the 1951 elections, in part, by charging the Attlee government with "scuttle" over Iran, he told Acheson, "the British had been kicked out of Abadan in a most humiliating way. If he [Churchill] had been in office, it would not have occurred. There might have been a splutter of musketry, but they would not have been kicked out of Iran." There was no attempt to revive the military intervention option under Churchill.[40] There was actually no drastic change in policy between the Labour and Conservative governments. Churchill continued to keep warships off Abadan as part of a compellence strategy, even though it had obviously failed, maintained Attlee's financial sanctions, and intensified covert action against Mossadegh by enlisting American participation in the operation, which later led to Mossadegh's fall.

U.S. DECISION MAKING

Truman, like Attlee, without relying on lessons from history to simplify the crisis nor to narrow down his policy options, also tried a range of policy options in succession as each policy failed to resolve the crisis. The Americans did not even consider military intervention. In 1951 the United States had little direct investment or national interest in Iran, which was viewed as being in the British sphere of interest. Oil was important, but the United States was far more involved in Saudi Arabia and, in fact, there was a glut on the world oil market at the time. Therefore, Iran's nationalization could not justify U.S. military intervention.[41] Furthermore, Truman, and later Eisenhower, accepted the Iranian's right to nationalize, although they opposed the manner in which it was done and wanted Iran to compensate the AIOC. Truman did not believe that nationalization, even uncompensated nationalization, justified the British use of military force and favored negotiation backed with economic aid to Iran to ensure that Iran did not collapse into turmoil and fall to the Soviets. However, as the crisis progressed and attempts at negotiation failed, Truman changed his mind about Mossadegh's rationality and the possibility of a negotiated settlement. Truman then turned to economic sanctions and covert operations to settle the issue. In October 1951 in a major change from economic aid to economic sanctions against Iran, Truman supported the British oil embargo and, in February 1952, agreed with the British to cut off all military, and almost all economic, aid to Iran. Truman also initiated covert action to weaken and, possibly, overthrow Mossadegh.[42]

Truman and Acheson opposed British military intervention[43] because they feared a Soviet counterintervention and believed that the British use of force might turn Iran against the West. The Americans tried to prevent British military intervention. In April and May 1951 the British began to plan operation Buccaneer, which envisioned a large-scale intervention in Iran. Truman and Acheson "expressed [to the British] our serious concern over any use of British forces which might lead to Soviet intervention."[44] And on May 17, 1951, Acheson told U.K. Ambassador Franks that the United States opposed the use of force unless there was a Communist coup or a Soviet military intervention.[45] On May 30, 1951, Acheson urged Truman to cable Attlee to emphasize "the importance of taking no action in this critical situation which might imperil world peace."[46] The warnings succeeded and Attlee, acting on his own beliefs against the use of military force, as well as fears of Soviet counterintervention, decided not to use military force.

During the September-October Abadan crisis, as Iran threatened to evict British technicians from the AIOC oil facility, Truman and Acheson again exerted pressure on the British not to use military force. During Anglo-American talks in August 1951 the Americans "emphasized [the] danger of disastrous consequences of military action beyond that absolutely necessary in landing forces solely to evacuate British personnel."[47] The British again received the message and Morrison publicly said he was well aware that the United States was "absolutely clear in opposition to the use of force."[48] Churchill later said that "The reason for the weakness of the Labour Government [and its decision not to use force], he was informed by that Government, had come from the refusal of the American Government to support strong measures."[49] In September Attlee said there would be no military intervention without U.S. support. With the use of force ruled out, in significant part by U.S. opposition, Britain withdrew from Abadan and pursued a diplomatic solution through the United Nations.[50]

MOSSADEGH'S RATIONALITY AND THE USE OF FORCE

Perceptions of Mossadegh's rationality played a significant role in British and American beliefs about the use of military force. Leaders who believe that an adversary is irrational are more likely to use military force than leaders who believe their adversary is rational. Early in the crisis, Truman and Acheson believed that Mossadegh was rational and this belief significantly influenced their early opposition to the British use of armed force and their support for negotiation. Truman wanted to act as an "honest broker"[51] and even applied diplomatic pressure on the British to make concessions to aid negotiations. For example, on May 31 Truman wrote Attlee:

Recent information which has reached me has led me to believe that the Iranian government is willing and even anxious to work out an arrangement with His Majesty's government which would safeguard basic British interests. . . . The United States government has expressed to His Majesty's government in recent days its firm conviction that an opportunity is now presented by the Iranian government for negotiations which should be entered into at once. . . . I am confident that a solution acceptable both to Britain and Iran can be found.[52]

Truman recognized, however, that Mossadegh was under intense nationalist pressure, which might sway the Iranian leader's rational judgment during a negotiation. Truman said, "with the passage of time and with wisdom on our part we believe it possible that the present extreme nationalist pressures may moderate and a more realistic attitude may be assumed by the Iranian government."[53] Averell Harriman, who Truman sent to Iran on July 15, 1951, to negotiate a settlement, supported Truman's beliefs and on July 19, 1951, reported, "There is a chance . . . that his [Mossadegh's] emotions can to a degree be tempered with realism." Harriman believed that conditions existed for Britain to make a satisfactory agreement.[54]

However, by the fall of 1951 the Americans began to change their view of Mossadegh's rationality as their hopes for a negotiated settlement diminished. They began to think that Mossadegh might not be rational enough to reach, nor fulfill, a reasonable negotiated settlement. For example, on September 14, 1951, a discouraged Harriman concluded that the "only hope for settlement of [the] Iran oil question is a change in government of

Iran. Present government is impossible to deal with."[55] By December 1951 Assistant Secretary of State George McGhee concluded that Mossadegh was "warped by his extreme suspicion of everything British."[56] As Truman changed his view of Mossadegh's rationality and concluded that a deal could not be negotiated, he concluded that Mossadegh would have to be removed by means other than diplomacy and economic sanctions. The United States lacked a pretext or justification to use military force, so covert operations, clandestine force, would have to be used. A coup would not be crippled by Mossadegh's perceived irrationality, which had appeared to doom negotiations and economic measures. The British and Americans concluded that Mossadegh was too irrational even to negotiate a settlement to avoid the crippling economic sanctions that had been inflicted on his country. In September 1951 even as Attlee pressed the shah to oust Mossadegh, Truman asked the U.S. ambassador in Iran "to urge the Shah to replace Mosadeq [*sic*] if he feels he is in a position to do so. He will assure the Shah that the US [*sic*] will assist Iran in obtaining an agreement which would eliminate any interference in internal Iranian affairs on the part of the oil company and which would provide to Iran a net profit as high as that received by any other country under comparable circumstances."[57] Unfortunately for Truman, the shah was as hesitant to act in response to American urging as he had been under British pressure. Mossadegh was too popular domestically and the shah too timid.

Unlike the Americans in the early days of the crisis, Attlee and most of his advisors believed that Mossadegh was irrational, unreliable, and, possibly, insane from the beginning of the crisis. An influential group in the Foreign Office, led by Morrison and Eric Berthoud, assistant-under-secretary, believed it was useless to negotiate with Mossadegh because he was irrational and would not agree to, nor meet the obligations of, a negotiated settlement.[58] Some in the British government went so far as to consider all Iranians "lunatics."[59] For example, Sir Francis Shepherd, British ambassador to Iran from March 1950 through October 1951, repeatedly said Mossadegh was a "lunatic" or, at best, "a buffoon."[60] The British believed that Mossadegh was not even rational enough to realize that the British oil embargo and economic sanctions were devastating the Iranian economy and people. Morrison said, "It seems that the present Persian Government is blind to the needs of their own country."[61] The British believed that the embargo should have led Mossadegh to agree to their offers of a negotiated, albeit a pro-British, settlement.

Attlee and his advisors viewed Mossadegh as irrational and, according to the propositions outlined in this book's introduction, should have favored the use of military force. Although some in the cabinet, most prominently Morrison and Shinwell, believed Mossadegh was irrational and favored the use of military force, Attlee's personal beliefs against the use of military force, combined with American opposition, limited U.K. military resources, and the possibility of Soviet counterintervention, overrode the preference of using military force. Similarly to Truman, Attlee, because of his personal, as well as U.S., opposition to the use of military force, at first hoped a negotiated settlement could be reached, even though Attlee questioned Mossadegh's rationality. However, after the rejection of the first British negotiating proposal in June 1951, Attlee's belief that Mossadegh was irrational came to the fore and led him to conclude that a negotiated settlement was impossible. Attlee still did not want to use military force but was willing to try clandestine force if diplomacy and negotiation failed. In a covert operation against Mossadegh, the Iranian's perceived lack of rationality would not influence the outcome, as it had appeared to doom negotiations and cripple the influence of economic sanctions. Attlee ordered Morrison to intensify covert action against Mossadegh.[62] At this time, Attlee, like Truman, also vainly urged the Shah to replace Mossadegh.

Churchill, Eden, and their government, like Attlee and Bevin, believed that Mossadegh was irrational. Eden wrote: "Dr. Mosadeq [*sic*] was a dubious character on whom too much reliance could not be placed."[63] Eden later wrote that "Musaddiq's [*sic*] megalomania was described as verging on mental instability. He had never been very amenable to reason, and lately it had been necessary to humor him as with a fractious child."[64] Eden also believed that Mossadegh would not accept a reasonable negotiated agreement because the Iranian was fervently anti-British. George Middleton, charge d'affaires to Iran from January 1952 until relations were severed in October 1952, said, "He [Mossadegh] is surrounded by a gang as little amenable to reason as himself. . . . Musaddiq [*sic*] appears to be beyond reasonable thought and to be swayed entirely by emotion."[65] The actions of Churchill and Eden support the argument that those who view an adversary as irrational are more likely to use military force. Churchill later said that he would have used military force if he had been in office at the time of the nationalization. However, by the time he took office, too much time had passed since the act of nationalization, which would have been the pretext for intervening, and compellence had already failed, so he turned to covert action, or clandestine force.

Like the British and Truman late in his term, Eisenhower, his cabinet, and his advisors viewed Mossadegh as irrational. Eisenhower, therefore, supported the use of clandestine force against Mossadegh. For example, at the June 25, 1953, meeting that approved the "Ajax" plan to overthrow Mossadegh, Dulles said, "So this is how we get rid of that madman Mossadegh!"[66] Loy Henderson, Eisenhower's ambassador to Iran, said, "We are confronted by a desperate, a dangerous situation and a madman who would ally himself with the Russians."[67] Henderson said Mossadegh sounded "not quite sane and that he should therefore be humored rather than reasoned with."[68] Because they viewed Mossadegh as irrational, Eisenhower and his advisors did not believe diplomacy and negotiation would succeed, especially given the domestic political forces in Iran. At a February 18, 1953, National Security Council (NSC) meeting, "Dulles stated his opinion that Prime Minister Mossadegh could not afford to reach *any* agreement with the British lest it cost him his political life."[69] With negotiations apparently doomed to failure and insufficient justification to intervene militarily, Eisenhower choose to conduct a covert operation to remove Mossadegh. Eisenhower had also been impressed by the Office of Strategic Services, the forerunner of the Central Intelligence Agency, and its covert operations during World War II.[70] Even though Eisenhower believed the chance for a negotiated settlement was negligible and the Dulles brothers were already planning with the British to overthrow Mossadegh, Eisenhower sent Ambassador Henderson to Tehran in December 1952 in a final attempt to negotiate with Mossadegh. Henderson's failure cemented Eisenhower's belief that Mossadegh was irrational and that further negotiations would fail. Mossadegh would have to be overthrown.[71]

Operation Ajax was the CIA name for the covert action to overthrow Mossadegh, which the British called Operation Boot. Anglo-American discussions of a plan to overthrow Mossadegh began even before Eisenhower took office. Eisenhower's early decision to try to overthrow Mossadegh shows that because Eisenhower believed that Mossadegh was irrational, he believed that negotiation and economic sanctions would not be effective in reaching a compromise settlement. Instead, Mossadegh would have to be removed by clandestine force: a coup. After initial meetings with the British in the final months of 1952 and in February 1953, on June 25, 1953, Dulles approved Ajax. On July 22, 1953, Eisenhower gave final approval for Ajax,[72] although the operation was already well underway. Churchill gave final British authorization for Operation Boot. "Churchill enjoyed dramatic operations and had no high regard for timid diplomatists."[73] A coup toppled Mossadegh between August 13 and 20, 1953.[74] Finally, clandestine force succeeded and Mossadegh, who Attlee, Truman, Churchill, and Eisenhower had concluded was irrational and could not be reasoned with, was removed. An oil deal between Iran and an international consortium of oil companies was reached in August 1954.[75] The crisis was over.

HISTORICAL INFORMATION

Although American and British decision makers mentioned a few historical analogies during the Iran crisis, the analogies had little, if any influence on policy. For example, Truman compared Iran's financial troubles to U.S. economic problems in the depression year of 1933.[76] In Parliament, in July 1951 a Labour member of Parliament (MP), arguing against intervention, compared the difficulty of holding the Suez Canal and Palestine against a hostile population to attempting to hold Abadan if Britain intervened.[77] Labour MPs also compared the use of force in Korea to possible intervention in Iran, with Iran seen as a more dangerous and risky situation. The fear was that the Soviets might counterintervene in Iran.[78]

However, the only historical analogy that influenced British or American policy decisions during the Iran crisis, although only to a limited degree, was Eisenhower's use of the analogy of the "loss" of China in 1949.[79] Eisenhower retrieved the China analogy because it was a recent, U.S. foreign policy failure that involved Eisenhower's own state and was similar superficially to the Iran case. China and Iran were both Third World states threatened, Eisenhower believed, by communism. Both were also seen as important, as well as friendly at some level, to the United States: China for its long missionary, trade, and economic relations with the United States; Iran for its oil and strategic location. However, the causes of the conflict in China were different fundamentally from those in Iran. The Chinese case was a civil war between Nationalists and Communists, while in Iran, Mossadegh, a nationalist, struggled against the shah and his court, as well as against British influence and economic power. The Iran crisis was ignited by the nationalization of the oil industry, which led to the subsequent international dispute between Britain and Iran, and was not, as in China, a civil war.

However, the most important factor that led Eisenhower to raise the China analogy was that he had to respond to other politicians who mentioned the same historical analogy. Throughout his career, Eisenhower rarely used historical analogies. However, he did use them when he believed a particular audience was conducive to arguments based on history or to argue against historical analogies that were used, or he feared might be used, by his domestic political opponents. In the Iran case, Eisenhower used the China analogy because he feared others might use the analogy against him. Eisenhower feared he would be criticized by domestic opponents for "losing" Iran, just as Truman had been criticized for "losing" China. Eisenhower did not say that he would apply the China analogy to Iran, nor did he say that the analogy was valid. However, he feared that others would use the China analogy against him.

Even so, the China analogy influenced Eisenhower's view of the Iran crisis, although only to a limited degree. The China analogy highlighted the importance of Iran to the West and to Eisenhower. The loss of China had, many in the West believed, strengthened the Communist bloc significantly. It had also helped lead to Truman's defeat at the ballot box. The lesson for Eisenhower was clear: The loss of Iran might lead to a more powerful Communist bloc and result in Eisenhower losing the next election. In early 1953 Mossadegh reinforced the China analogy and U.S. fears when he warned that if Washington did not provide aid to Iran, he would instead turn to the Soviets for support.[80] Eisenhower believed that the Communists might take control of Iran through Mossadegh. For example, Eisenhower said on August 4, 1953:

Iran . . . is in a weakened condition. I believe I read in the paper this morning that Mossadegh's move toward getting rid of his parliament has been supported and of course he was in that move supported by the Tudeh, which is the Communist Party of Iran. All of that weakening position around there is very ominous for the United States, because finally if we lost all that, how would the free world hold the rich empire of Indonesia? So you see, somewhere along the line, this must be blocked. It must be blocked now.[81]

The China analogy also provided the lesson that U.S. economic and military aid to Iran would not remedy the situation. The United States provided substantial aid to the Nationalist Chinese, yet the Communists defeated them anyway. American economic and/or military aid to Iranian moderates or nationalists other than Mossadegh would, the China analogy predicted, also fail. This lesson had already been supported by Truman's failure to entice Mossadegh into a more moderate bargaining position by providing aid to Iran. Eisenhower's use of the China analogy also framed the crisis in terms of the Cold War. It blinded him to the strong nationalist feelings in Iran which, although dampened by the overthrow of Mossadegh in August 1953 and the strengthening of the shah's position, would burst forth anew in the 1979 Iranian revolution.

THE PRESENT AND THE PAST

The fundamental questions concerning the Iran case are to explain why British and American leaders relied almost exclusively on current information and did not use historical information to frame the crisis or to prescribe policy, as well as the consequences of the lack of use of historical analogies. The reliance on current information meant that factors such as Attlee's beliefs about nationalization and the use of force, U.S. opposition to the use of military force, fear of Soviet counterintervention, and limited British military resources, had a greater impact on British policy than would have occurred if the crisis had been framed using a historical analogy. Current information was not balanced by historical information and, therefore, had greater influence.

There were other valid historical analogies to Iran, such as Mexico's 1938 nationalization of its oil industry. Mexico was, in fact, mentioned during the Iran crisis. At an April 27, 1951, meeting Acheson "went on to draw the analogy between the experiences of our oil companies in Mexico and the actions of the AIOC in Persia."[82] However, the analogy gained no support and was not mentioned again. The Mexico analogy would have prescribed a moderate and peaceful response. In 1938 the United States did not use either military force or covert action against Mexico. The Mexico analogy would also have lowered the perceived stakes of the Iran case, since the nationalization of the Mexican oil industry did not cripple the U.S.

economy, as some in Britain feared that their own economy would be severely harmed by Iran's nationalization. The Mexico analogy did not, however, significantly influence policy making during the Iran crisis, if it had any effect at all. Why? Policy makers tend to use historical analogies based on foreign policy failures, and Mexico was not a British, or indeed much of an American, foreign policy failure. Policy makers also tend to retrieve historical events with which they are familiar as analogies. American and, even more so, British, policy makers in 1951–54 were not familiar with the Mexican nationalization. Furthermore, actors overwhelmingly retrieve historical events that their own state was involved in and, for the British, the Mexico analogy did not fulfill this requirement. Policy makers also tend to retrieve dramatic, high-stakes events and the Mexico case, viewed from 1951, appeared to lack both these variables. The Mexico crisis was also not a national security issue. Iran, by contrast, was considered to be so by the British, who planned to intervene militarily. For all of these reasons, Mexico was not used as a historical analogy to Iran.

A second possible analogy was the 1930's master analogy, particularly the remilitarization of the Rhineland. Truman, Acheson, Attlee, Morrison, Churchill, Eden, Eisenhower, and Dulles all were aware certainly of the 1930's master analogy, having lived through the decade. Many of them also experienced personally the major events of the 1930s as adults. Mossadegh's nationalization of the Iranian oil industry could have been perceived as superficially similar to Hitler's 1936 remilitarization of the Rhineland. Both cases involved states taking control of something within their borders: In Hitler's Germany it was territory, and in Iran it was the oil industry. Both violated legal documents: an international treaty (the Versailles Treaty) and a commercial contract (Iran's concession to the AIOC). Both Mossadegh and Hitler, especially in 1936, could be seen as nationalists. Both leaders also posed a threat to Britain: Germany's threatening posture toward Britain's ally, France, by remilitarizing the Rhineland; and control of Iran's valuable oil. If the Rhineland analogy had been applied to Iran, the prescription would have been, on the basis of the widely held lessons of the 1930s, to use military force promptly to avert further aggression and possible war. In fact, five years later Eden applied the 1930s to another nationalization in the Middle East: that of the Suez Canal, and the analogy led to Eden's decision to use military force. The 1930s prescribed a very different policy than the British or the Americans, relying on current information, pursued during the Iran crisis.

Individual variables, time pressures, and the level of drama and surprise must be analyzed to explain why, except for the China analogy, policy makers did not use historical analogies, such as the 1930s or the Mexican oil nationalization, to frame the Iran crisis or to prescribe or justify policy. Individual variables contribute to explaining why policy makers did not use historical analogies in the Iran case. Eisenhower, Attlee, Dulles, and Acheson rarely, if ever, used historical analogies in their careers. However, personality factors do not explain why Churchill, who often used historical analogies, as well as Eden and Truman, who used historical analogies occasionally during their careers, did not apply this type of reasoning in the Iran case. Situational factors overrode the individual factors that often led Churchill, Eden, and Truman to use historical analogies to draw lessons from history. Therefore, situational variables must be examined to explain their lack of use of historical analogies.

Policy makers tend to use historical analogies when faced with complex, novel situations. The Iran case, like almost all foreign policy crises, was complex enough to warrant the use of historical analogies. It involved multiple actors, including the Iranian, British, and American governments, strong nationalist forces in Britain and Iran, as well as the AIOC. The negotiations became extremely complex over various compensation packages, production, and distribution plans, and the role of technicians from different countries. Domestic Iranian politics were complex and confusing as factions supporting the Shah, Mossadegh, the Tudeh, and religious parties maneuvered for power. In many ways, the Iranian oil nationalization was more complex than the North Korean invasion of South Korea, which, although simpler in many ways, led to the use of historical information by Truman, Acheson, Attlee, and Bevin. Yet Iran did not lead to the widespread use of historical analogies.

The Iran case had both novel and common aspects. Novelty often leads to the use of historical analogies, while familiar events rarely lead to such reasoning. Therefore, this combination of novel and common aspects did not point strongly to the use or nonuse of historical analogies. The case highlights the difficulty of using novelty as a causal variable to explain the use, or lack of use, of historical analogies. Nationalization was not novel. Attlee's government had nationalized industries and companies in Britain after the Second World War. However, international nationalization was a comparatively new situation. Iran was only the second Third World state to nationalize its oil industry. The first had been Mexico in 1938, although Iran's was novel to the extent that Iran's oil reserves were far vaster and were considered to be crucial to Britain in general and the Royal Navy in particular. The Royal Navy purchased Iranian oil from the AIOC at bargain prices. The British had also dealt with nationalists, like Mossadegh, before, including Mahatma Gandhi in India and Michael Collins in Ireland. The United States had also dealt with nationalists in the Philippines and Central America. The Soviet threat lingering in the background of the Iran crisis was also not uncommon during crises in the 1950s. From all of these mixed and varying factors it is difficult to determine if the Iran crisis was novel or common to the British and American decision makers of 1951–53.

Time pressures often lead policy makers to use historical analogies as cognitive shortcuts to diagnose crises and to prescribe policies. However, the thirty-month Iran crisis allowed ample time to analyze the crisis, as well as to pursue different policy options, and Truman, Attlee, Eisenhower, and Churchill felt little time pressure. At the start of the crisis, the Attlee government felt a need to respond in some fashion, yet, unlike the Suez crisis, where Eden felt intense time pressures, Attlee did not perceive the same sense of time working against Britain. In part, this was because Mossadegh waited weeks to implement the nationalization bill and nationalization had already been a major issue in Iran for months. The British knew what was coming. Furthermore, trends in the Middle East had been toward renegotiated deals between Middle Eastern states and Western oil companies, such as the Aramco 50/50 profit sharing deal with Saudi Arabia and a recent British-Iraqi deal.[83] Attlee also did not frame the Iran crisis in terms of the 1930s, as Eden framed Suez, which, for Eden, reinforced the belief that time would weaken the British position in relation to the Arab world in general and Iran and Egypt, with its crucial canal, in particular. In the 1930s the Axis had grown increasingly stronger with time, and Eden feared that delay would provide Nasser time to increase his power. Attlee did not want the Iran crisis to drift indefinitely, but there was no talk of needing to act right away as in the Korea (for Truman and Attlee), Suez (for Eden), or in the Lebanon/Jordan (for Eisenhower and Macmillan) cases.

The Abadan crisis, in the fall of 1951, also did not put intense time pressure on the British. The Iranians threatened to expel the British from Abadan weeks before they did so, giving the British time to develop their response. A few weeks may not seem like a long period, but it was longer than the time period British and American leaders had during the Korea or the Lebanon and Jordan cases, where Truman, Attlee, Eisenhower, and Macmillan, respectively, decided to intervene within twenty-four to forty-eight hours after the crisis erupted and caught the Americans and British by surprise. In the Iran case, a few weeks was enough time to negate any feelings of urgency felt by the British policy makers, which would have contributed to the use of historical analogies as a cognitive shortcut. The Americans, with much less at stake in Iran than the British, felt even less time pressure than the British. For most of the crisis the Americans believed that Iran was a British responsibility and Truman and Eisenhower consequently felt little, if any, time pressure. Although he wanted the issue settled, Eisenhower had years to analyze the issue from the time the crisis erupted in 1951 until he attained the White House in 1953. Therefore, there was no pressure to use historical analogies as a cognitive shortcut to find a solution rapidly.

Related to the lack of time pressure, the low level of drama and lack of surprise in the Iran case also helps to explain why historical analogies were not used. Policy makers used historical analogies in response to the full-scale North Korean invasion of South Korea, the bloody Iraqi coup that triggered the U.S. intervention in Lebanon, and the British intervention in Jordan, and Egypt's surprise nationalization of the Suez Canal. However, the Iran case lacked the drama and surprise of the Korean invasion, the Iraqi coup, or the Suez nationalization, which were all surprises. Furthermore, the other three cases were more dramatic and had higher stakes than the Iran case. The Americans and British thought the North Korean invasion might be the opening salvo of a third world war. The coup in Iraq appeared to herald the spread of Nasserism across the Middle East, and Egypt's nationalization of the Suez Canal seemed, to the British, to mark the demise of British power and influence in the Middle East. However, the level of drama and degree of surprise was lower in the Iran case, which helps explain why historical analogies were not used to formulate policy. No world war threatened, and the threat to British commercial interests in Iran was nonviolent. The Iran case also lacked surprise since the nationalization bill and the plan to evict British personnel from Abadan were discussed publicly long before they were passed or implemented.

In the Korean, Suez, and Lebanon/Jordan cases, the invasion, the nationalization of the canal company, and the Iraqi coup, respectively, were dramatic events that triggered the use of historical analogies. Once policy makers used analogies to frame the crises that prescribed the prompt use of military force, the level of drama increased because force was involved, which, in turn, reinforced the use of historical analogies. Historical analogies tend to be used for national security issues. In the Iran case, however, the lack of use of historical analogies and low level of drama was reinforced by the decision not to use military force unless British nationals were threatened. With force ruled out as an option early in the crisis, the already relatively low level of drama in the case declined even further. Any chance that historical analogies would be used later in the crisis, for example, during the crisis over the British eviction from Abadan, decreased to near zero.

The British should have been more likely to use historical analogies than the Americans in the Iran case, because the British perceived the stakes to be greater than did the Americans. The stakes were, for the British, high, including: British reputation and position in the Middle East, such as in Iraq, Jordan, Kuwait, and Aden; the effect of nationalization of a British company on other U.K. companies around the world; as well as the loss of revenue from the AIOC and the special, low rates the Royal Navy paid for Iranian oil. Attlee wrote Truman on June 5, 1951, "a breach of contract of this nature might well jeopardize other overseas contracts, not merely those held by British and United States companies for the development of Middle East oil resources, but contracts for other products elsewhere."[84] If Britain was not firm toward Iran, it would, the British feared, also undermine confidence in the British economy and the pound. The Americans said "that the British really believe that to yield in Iran is to write a vitally important chapter in the decline of the U.K. [*sic*]"[85] Even though the British perceived the stakes to be high, they did not use historical analogies. The lack of drama, surprise, and time pressure in the crisis overrode the tendency of policy makers to use historical analogies when the stakes are high.

In Iran, the stakes for the United States were lower than for the British. Truman was aware that there was a great deal at stake in Iran, including access to oil and Iran's geostrategic position neighboring the Soviet Union and on the Persian Gulf. He was also concerned, although not as much as Eisenhower was, about the apparent increasingly powerful position of the Tudeh Party. In May 1951 Truman said he had "serious concern" about the situation in Iran and said it was of "great importance" for the British to settle it. "I am acutely aware that it is essential to maintain the independence of Iran and the flow of Iranian oil into the economy of the free world."[86] However, the Iran case involved the nationalization of a British, not a U.S., company. Therefore, the stakes for the United States in the Iran crisis were not on par with the stakes in Korea, in which Truman used historical analogies. Korea involved potential world war and the invasion of a state that the United States had, to a significant degree, helped create: South Korea. The chance of a world war over Iran was negligible, especially once the British decided not to intervene and the chance of a Soviet counterintervention was eliminated. The low stakes for the United States meant that, with the limited exception of Eisenhower, U.S. policy makers did not rely on historical analogies to frame the crisis or to prescribe or legitimize policy.

In summary, situational factors, including the lack of drama, surprise, and time pressures, overrode the influence of individual personality, training, and experience, as well as the influence of the high stakes for the British, in determining whether policy makers would use historical analogies. No policy makers, except for Eisenhower, used historical analogies significantly to frame and diagnose the crisis or to prescribe policy. Reliance on current information predominated. There was also no use of historical analogies to justify the policies chosen by the British and the Americans after Operation Ajax/Boot succeeded. However, there was no need for either the United States or Britain to justify a coup in which they denied any role.

CONCLUSION

In analyzing the balance between the influence of situational and individual variables on the use of historical analogies in the Iran case, situational variables, including the influence of the lack of time pressure, drama, and surprise, outweighed individual inclinations to use historical analogies. Truman, Eden, and Churchill often used historical analogies in their careers. In the Iran case, however, because of the lack of time pressures and surprise, as well as the low level of drama, they did not do so. The complexity and debatable novelty of the Iran case did not counterbalance the influence of the absence of time pressure, surprise, and drama. Even so, Eisenhower used the China analogy. However, he used the analogy because of the fear that others would use the analogy against him. This fit the pattern of Eisenhower's past use of historical analogies and his uncommon ability to consciously choose to use or not to use historical analogies, as well as to control their influence upon him. Eisenhower, unlike Truman and Attlee during Korea, Eden during Suez, or Macmillan during Lebanon/Jordan, never appeared to be under the sway of a historical analogy.

The lack of use of historical analogies led to a prolonged search for a policy option that would resolve the crisis. Policy makers did not retrieve a historical analogy that prescribed a single policy response in the Iran crisis, as occurred with the 1930's analogy during the Korea and Suez crises. Policy makers relied on current information to shape policy. Without a clear lesson from the past, Attlee and Truman tried a range of policies in succession in an attempt to resolve the crisis. Their search for an effective policy is best explained by a bounded rationality model. Attlee believed that the use of military force was outdated and, combined with U.S. opposition to military intervention, limited British military resources, and the threat of Soviet counterintervention ruled out the British use of military force. With military force ruled out, Attlee attempted to negotiate a solution and, when negotiations led nowhere, domestic pressure for action combined with pro-military intervention cabinet members led him to impose economic sanctions and to pursue a compellence strategy combined with covert operations to attempt to remove Mossadegh by using clandestine force. Truman also changed his policy over the course of the crisis. He attempted to act as an honest broker and, while supplying economic aid to Iran, to negotiate an Anglo-Iranian settlement. When talks failed, Truman supported economic sanctions against Iran and then, finally, covert operations to overthrow Mossadegh. Eisenhower and Churchill continued the policies of Truman and Attlee, culminating in the coup.

The Iran case also shows that decisions not to use military force, like decisions to use military force, are made early in foreign policy crises at the same time as, if not before, the decision to use diplomacy and/or economic sanctions. Furthermore, the Iran case highlights the relationship between the views leaders hold of an adversary's rationality and the policy preferences of the leaders. Attlee, Churchill, and Eisenhower viewed Mossadegh as irrational and, therefore, believed he was not amenable to negotiation or to the influence of economic sanctions. Churchill favored the use of military force, while Attlee came to support what might be called the clandestine use of force: covert action. Eisenhower supported the use of clandestine force even before he took the oath of office. Truman, who viewed Mossadegh as rational, favored negotiation, at least until his views of Mossadegh's rationality began to change, when he too attempted to use a form of covert force against Mossadegh by asking the shah to remove his prime minister. Asking was not enough and Operation Ajax/Boot was required to overthrow Mossadegh, a leader whom the British and Americans believed was irrational, through the clandestine use of force.

NOTES

1. For example, see *The Public Papers of the Presidents of the United States: Harry S. Truman, 1951; The Public Papers of the Presidents of the United States: Harry S. Truman, 1952–3; The Public Papers of the Presidents of the United States: Dwight D. Eisenhower, 1953*; and *Parliamentary Debates*, Commons, 5th Series, vol. 486, 489, 491, 494 (March 1951 to August 1953).

2. There are eight different ways to spell Mossadegh, however, this is the way he spelled it. Diba, *Mohammad Mossadegh*, p. 1.

3. The Senate passed the bill on March 20.

4. Katouzian, *Musaddiq and the Struggle for Power in Iran*, p. 144.

5. Summary of Telegrams, May 17, 1951, Naval Aide Files, State Dept. Briefs, State Dept. Summary Telegrams, Truman Library.

6. Attlee to Truman, June 5, 1951, Folder, Iran, PSF, Subject File, Foreign Affairs File, Iran, Truman Library.

7. Memo of Conversation, Subject: Iranian Oil Problem, Oct. 10, 1951, Papers of Dean Acheson, Memos of Conversations, Aug.–Dec. 1951, Box 69, Truman Library; and Bill, *The Eagle and the Lion*, p. 78.

8. Cable, *Intervention at Abadan*, p. 45.

9. Morgan, *Labour in Power*, p. 471.

10. Cable, *Intervention in Abadan*, p. ix.

11. Ibid., pp. 45–52.

12. Memo for the President, Subject: Luncheon Meeting with Prime Minister Mossadeq, Oct. 22, 1951, Papers of Harry S. Truman, PSF, Truman Library.

13. For the tortuous evolution of British policy about the use of force, see Cable, *Intervention at Abadan*.

14. Cable, *Intervention in Abadan*, p. 38; and Morgan, *Labour in Power*, pp. 482–483.

15. Brookshire, *Clement Attlee*, p. 226; and Goode, *The United States and Iran*, p. 93.

16. *Parliamentary Debates*, Commons, 5th Series, vol. 486 April 13, 1951, cols. 1333–34.

17. Northedge, "Britain and the Middle East," p. 174.

18. Louis, "Musaddiq and the Dilemmas of British Imperialism," p. 228.

19. Goode, *The United States and Iran*, p. 93.

20. Memo of Conversation, Aug. 2, 1951, Subject Iran, Papers of Dean Acheson, Memos of Conversations, Aug.–Dec. 1951, Box 69, Truman Library.

21. Pearce, *Attlee's Labour Governments*, p. 72; and Morgan, *The People's Peace*, p. 90.

22. Williams, *Twilight of Empire*, p. 255.

23. Bill and Louis, "Introduction," pp. 5–6.

24. Burridge, *Clement Attlee*, p. 65; and Brookshire, *Clement Attlee*, pp. 53–54, 57–59, 226.

25. Burridge, *Clement Attlee*, p. 259; Bullock, *Ernest Bevin*, Vol. III, p. 839; and Brookshire, *Clement Attlee*, pp. 201–203.

26. Bill, *The Eagle and the Lion*, p. 75; and Williams, *Twilight of Empire*, p. 254.

27. Bill, *The Eagle and the Lion*, p. 75. The Americans shared the same fear: see Probable Soviet Courses of Action in the Middle East, 1952, National Intelligence Estimate (NIE) 25, August 2, 1951, PSF, Intelligence File, Box 253, Truman Library; and CIA, Current Developments in Iran, May 22, 1951, Special Estimate-6, PSF, Intelligence File, Box 258, File Special Estimate 1, Reports, Truman Library.

28. Summary of Telegrams, May 10, 1951, Naval Aide Files, State Dept. Briefs, State Dept. Summary of Telegrams, Truman Library. Also see *Parliamentary Debates*, Commons, 5th Series, vol. 494 (November 19, 1951), cols. 145–146.

29. Incoming Telegram, Dept. of State, from Tehran (Grady) to Sec. of State, August 28, 1951, PSF, Subject File, Box 180, Truman Library.

30. Summary of Telegrams, April 2, 1951, Naval Aide Files, State Dept. Briefs, State Dept. Summary of Telegrams, Truman Library.

31. Summary of Telegrams, June (no date), 1951, Naval Aide Files, State Dept. Briefs, State Dept. Summary of Telegrams, Truman Library.

32. Summary of Telegrams, Oct. 8, 1951, Naval Aide Files, State Dept. Briefs, State Dept. Summary of Telegrams, Truman Library.

33. Summary of Telegrams, June 14, 1951, Naval Aide Files, State Dept. Briefs, State Dept. Summary of Telegrams, Truman Library. A small Italian company bought Iranian oil, was sued, and their ships held in Aden and Naples. Mosley, *Power Play: Oil in the Middle East*, p. 210.

34. Painter, *The United States, Great Britain, and Mossadegh*, Part A, p. 4.

35. Woodhouse, *Something Ventured*; Katouzian, *Musaddiq and the Struggle for Power in Iran*, p. 177; and Painter, *The United States, Great Britain, and Mossadegh*, Part A, p. 4.

36. Gasiorowski, *U.S. Foreign Policy and the Shah*, pp. 66–67, 73; and Louis, "Musaddiq and the Dilemmas of British Imperialism," pp. 233–235.

37. Summary of Telegrams, September 28, 1951, Naval Aide Files, State Dept. Briefs, State Dept. Summary of Telegrams, Truman Library. Also see Summary of Telegrams, Nov. 29 and Dec. 28, 1951, Naval Aide Files, State Dept. Briefs, State Dept. Summary of Telegrams, Truman Library.

38. *Parliamentary Debates*, Commons, 5th Series, vol. 489 (June 19, 1951), col. 522.

39. Summary of Telegrams, May 25, 1951, Naval Aide Files, State Dept. Briefs, State Dept. Summary of Telegrams, Truman Library.

40. Memo of Conversation, Jan. 7, 1952, Papers of Dean Acheson, Memo of Conversations, Truman Library. Also see Morgan, *The People's Peace*, p. 129.

41. Although the Department of Defense studied the possibility of using force in 1952, the department concluded that military actions would be "extremely difficult to implement" and neither Truman nor Eisenhower ever seriously considered the use of force against Iran, unless the Soviets intervened. Secretary of Defense Foster, Memo for the Pres., Nov. 19, 1952, President's Secretary's File (PSF), NSC Files, Meetings, Box 220, Truman Library; and NSC, Report to NSC by Executive Secretary on United States Policy Regarding the Present Situation in Iran, Nov. 20, 1952, White House Office, Office of the Special Assistant for National Security Affairs

(OSANSA), NSC Series, Policy Papers, Box 3, Dwight D. Eisenhower (DDE) Library.

42. Gasiorowski, *U.S. Foreign Policy and the Shah*, p. 69.

43. Unfortunately, the initial U.S. decision in early 1951 to oppose the use of force and to try to convince the British not to use military force is blacked out in the documents or missing from the archives at the Truman Library.

44. Summary of Telegrams, April 13, 1951, Naval Aide Files, State Dept. Briefs, State Dept. Summary of Telegrams, Truman Library.

45. Bill, *The Eagle and the Lion*, p. 75; Roosevelt, *Countercoup*, p. 88; and Lytle, *The Origins of the Iranian-American Alliance*, p. 201.

46. Memo for the President, May 30, 1951, Subject: Iranian Situation, Box 180, PSF Subject File, Foreign Affairs File, Iran, Truman Library. Also see Draft Personal Message from President Truman to Winston Churchill, July 31, 1951, File: State Dept. Correspondence, 1951–52, Papers of Harry S. Truman, WHCF: Confidential File, Box 42, Truman Library; and Summary of Telegrams, May 16, 1951, Naval Aide Files, State Dept. Briefs, State Dept. Summary of Telegrams, Truman Library.

47. Incoming Telegram, Dept. of State, from Tehran (Grady) to Sec. of State, Aug. 28, 1951, PSF, Subject File, Box 180. Truman Library.

48. *Parliamentary Debates*, Commons, 5th Series, vol. 494 (Nov. 19, 1951), col. 65.

49. Memo of Conversation, Jan. 7, 1952, Papers of Dean Acheson, Memo of Conversations, Truman Library.

50. Roosevelt, *Countercoup*, pp. 88, 101; Painter, *The United States, Great Britain, and Mossadegh*, Part A, p. 5; and Mosley, *Power Play*, pp. 204–205. Roosevelt criticizes Mosley's book as inaccurate.

51. Memo of Meeting with Oil Company Representatives, Dec. 30, 1952, Papers of Dean Acheson, Memo of Conference, Box 72, Truman Library.

52. Signal from USS *Williamsburg* to Signal Center, White House, 31 May 1951, Iran File, PSF, Subject File, Foreign Affairs File, Iran, Box 180, Truman Library. Also see "The President's News Conference of May 24, 1951," *The Public Papers of the Presidents of the United States: Harry S. Truman, 1951*, item 113, pp. 296–320.

53. Draft Reply by President to Attlee, Aug. 1951, File: State Dept. Correspondence, 1951–52, Papers of Harry S. Truman, WHCF: Confidential File, Box 42, Truman Library; and Lytle, *The Origins of the Iranian-American Alliance*, p. 200.

54. Dept. of State Incoming Telegram, Harriman to Sec. of State, July 19, 1951, PSF, Subject File, Foreign Affairs File, Box 180, Greece-Iran, Papers of Harry S. Truman, Truman Library.

55. Notes on Cabinet Meeting, Sept. 14, 1951, Post-Presidential File, Jan. 2–Dec. 31, 1951, Papers of Matthew J. Connelly, Set I, Cabinet Meetings, Box 1, Truman Library.

56. Ferrier, "The Anglo-Iranian Oil Dispute," p. 187.

57. Summary of Telegrams, Sept. 27, 1951, Naval Aide Files, State Dept. Briefs, State Dept. Summary of Telegrams, Truman Library.

58. Louis, "Musaddiq and the Dilemmas of British Imperialism," pp. 232–233.

59. Lytle, *The Origins of the Iranian-American Alliance*, p. 192.

60. Louis, "Musaddiq and the Dilemmas of British Imperialism," p. 230.

61. *Parliamentary Debates*, Commons, 5th Series, vol. 489 (June 20, 1951), col. 522.

62. Louis, "Musaddiq and the Dilemmas of British Imperialism," p. 249.

63. Memo of Conversation, Aug. 11, 1952, Message from Mr. Eden to Mr. Acheson regarding Iran, Box 71, Acheson Papers, Truman Library.

64. Eden, *Full Circle*, p. 230.

65. Louis, "Musaddiq and the Dilemmas of British Imperialism," pp. 240–241, 245.

66. Heikal, *The Return of the Ayatollah*, p. 23.

67. Hourani, "Conclusion," p. 338.

68. Summary of Telegrams, July 29, 1952, Naval Aide Files, State Dept. Briefs, State Dept. Summary of Telegrams, Truman Library.

69. 132nd NSC Mtg., Feb. 18, 1953, Dwight D. Eisenhower (DDE) Papers as President, Ann C. Whitman File (AWF), NSC Series, Box 4, DDE Library.

70. Ambrose, *Eisenhower, The President*, pp. 110–111.

71. Rubin, *Paved with Good Intentions*, pp. 77–78.

72. Gasiorowski, *U.S. Foreign Policy and the Shah*, pp. 72–74; Hersh, *The Old Boys*, pp. 330–333; Rubin, *Paved with Good Intentions*, p. 78; Ambrose, *Ike's Spies*, pp. 200–201; Roosevelt, *Countercoup*, p. 1; and Ruehsen, "Operation 'Ajax' Revisited," pp.481–482.

73. Bill, *The Eagle and the Lion*, pp. 89–90; and Louis, "Musaddiq and the Dilemmas of British Imperialism," p. 253.

74. Woodhouse, *Something Ventured*; Katouzian, *Musaddiq and the Struggle for Power in Iran*, pp. 188–193; Rubin, *Paved with Good Intentions*, pp. 54–90; and Roosevelt, *Countercoup*.

75. The agreement gave U.S. oil companies a 40 percent share of Iran's oil production, U.K. companies 40 percent, French companies 6 percent, and Dutch companies 14 percent, although the British owned a large percentage of the Dutch companies.

76. Memo of Conversation, Blair House, meeting Truman, Mossadeq and Acheson, Oct. 23, 1951, Papers of Dean Acheson, Memos of Conversations, Aug.–Dec. 1951, Box 69, Truman Library.

77. *Parliamentary Debates*, Commons, 5th Series, vol. 491 (July 30, 1951) col. 998.

78. *Parliamentary Debates*, Commons, 5th Series, vol. 489 (June 19, 1951), col. 526, and vol. 489 (June 21, 1951), col. 773.

79. Oral History 11, DDE, July 20, 1967, p. 53; Louis, "Musaddiq and the Dilemmas of British Imperialism," p. 243; and Ambrose, *Ike's Spies*, p. 200.

80. Lytle, *The Origins of the Iranian-American Alliance*, pp. 205–206.

81. Remarks at the Governors' Conference, Seattle, Washington, Aug. 4, 1953, *The Public Papers of the Presidents of the United States: Dwight D. Eisenhower, 1953*, item 156, pp. 536–544. Also see The President's News Conference of Aug. 11, 1954, ibid., item 192, pp. 696–705; and Address at the Illinois State Fair at Springfield, Aug. 19, 1955, ibid., item 203, pp. 729–733.

82. Memo of Conversation, April 27, 1951, Papers of Dean Acheson, Memos of Conversations, March–July 1951, Box 68, Memos of Conversations, Truman Library.

83. Macmillan, *Tides of Fortune*, pp. 341–342.

84. Attlee to Truman, June 5, 1951, Folder: Iran, PSF Subject File, Foreign Affairs File: Iran, Truman Library.

85. Daily Brief, Nov. 8, 1951, Naval Aide Files, State Dept. Briefs, State Dept. Daily Briefs, Truman Library.

86. Truman to Attlee, May 31, 1951, PSF Subject File, Foreign Affairs File, Iran, Truman Library.

5

A Madman Brandishing an Axe: Suez

Historical information retrieved by analogical reasoning significantly influenced British policy during the Suez crisis. The 1930's analogy dominated both Eden and British decision making. The crisis began on July 26, 1956, when President Gamal Abdel Nasser of Egypt nationalized the assets of the Suez Canal Company. Prime Minister Eden, Foreign Secretary Lloyd, and Chancellor of the Exchequer Macmillan, as well as President Eisenhower and Secretary of State Dulles,[1] all stated that they viewed the use of military force as a "last resort," yet the British used force while the United States did not even consider using force. Eisenhower and Dulles viewed force as a last resort in terms of time, especially until after the November elections,[2] and in terms of the attractiveness of options, to be used after all other means, such as negotiation and economic sanctions, had been tried and failed. For Eden and his cabinet, force was not a last resort in terms of attractiveness of options or in terms of time. Military force was the option of first resort.

Despite compelling evidence to the contrary, Eden and the British government repeatedly stated that force was a last resort. For example, the Commonwealth Office telegrammed its overseas offices: "We hope we may be able to attain this objective by bringing maximum political pressure to bear on Egypt. . . . But it may be that this will fail and that, in the last resort, force may have to be used to secure Egyptian agreement."[3] The British also repeatedly said that they favored a peaceful, negotiated solution.[4] However, such statements were part of a campaign to curry domestic and international support, especially from the United States.[5] On August 24 Lloyd and Foreign Minister Christian Pineau of France met to plan the "Development of

Favorable World Opinion for Necessary Measures," meaning the use of military force. The plan included publicly stating that force was a last resort, even though Eden and his cabinet had decided early in the crisis that military force would be used against Egypt unless Nasser capitulated to every British demand.[6]

The difference in the meaning of "last resort" as used by the British and the Americans rests, to a significant degree, on the use of lessons from history compared to reliance on current information. For the British, historical information overrode current information, while the Americans relied more on current information than on lessons from history. The British retrieved a historical analogy because the Suez crisis was dramatic, novel, and a surprise event. Eden's personality also inclined him to use historical analogies, while the personalities of Eisenhower and Dulles contributed to their reliance on current information rather than historical analogies. The Suez crisis was also less dramatic and had lower stakes for the Americans than for the British, which further decreased the probability that the Americans would use historical analogies to retrieve information from history to frame the crisis, to prescribe, or to justify policy.

From the outset of the crisis, as soon as the British framed the nationalization in terms of the 1930s and the Americans relied on current information, their perceptions of the crisis varied significantly. Although other variables influenced the differences, the 1930s was a significant factor in the different American and British perceptions of the Suez crisis. The 1930's analogy significantly influenced British beliefs about time, the stakes, and about Nasser, as well as their goals and preferred policy response. The British, on the basis of the 1930's analogy, believed that time was against them, the stakes were extremely high, and that Nasser was irrational and, therefore, could not be negotiated with and, even if an agreement was reached, that he could not be trusted to fulfill its terms. Therefore, the British believed that Nasser's nationalization justified prompt military intervention.[7] Eden only negotiated to gain time as Britain gathered forces to intervene militarily. The deployed forces also composed a compellence strategy to put pressure on Nasser. The British and the Americans viewed the same process, yet came to diametrically opposed conclusions about where the process was headed. Eisenhower and Dulles perceived that the compellence strategy, combined with negotiation, was not only succeeding, but was succeeding to the extent that their suggestions for conferences in London, a Suez Canal Users Association (SCUA), and U.N.–sponsored talks avoided a British use of force.[8] However, Eden, believing that time was against Britain and that Nasser was irrational, felt that the compellence strategy[9] and negotiations would fail. Eden assumed and, in fact, wanted, to use military force from the beginning of the crisis. Once the British and the Americans framed the crisis differently—the British using the 1930's analogy and the Americans using current information—Eisenhower and Eden would never again perceive the crisis in the same away.

This chapter discusses Eden's comparison of Nasser to Mussolini and then why Eden relied on historical information at the expense of current information so extensively during the Suez crisis. Because Suez is such a clear case of the influence of historical information on policy, the process by which lessons are drawn from a historical event is then analyzed, as well as the effects of historical analogies on foreign policy. The British decision to use force, as well as the American attempt to convince the British not to use force are then discussed. The final sections of the chapter analyze the types of historical analogies mentioned during the crisis, as well as the lessons retrieved from history by analogical reasoning. The conclusion summarizes the major points of the chapter.

WAS NASSER ANOTHER MUSSOLINI?

Ironically, during the Suez crisis, American and British goals were similar. Both sought a form of international control of, and free navigation through, the Suez Canal for the ships of all nations. They also wanted to minimize Soviet, while maintaining Western, influence in the region. The British also sought fair treatment for the Suez Canal Company's employees and shareholders.[10] The crucial difference between the British and Americans, however, was that the British also wanted "to secure the downfall of Colonel Nasser's regime in Egypt"[11] or, at a minimum, to "cut Nasser down to size."[12] Although Eisenhower and Dulles wanted to limit Nasser's power, they did not want to overthrow him, at least not on the basis of the nationalization issue. The Americans also wanted to avoid being identified with British and French imperialism, or the Israelis, for fear that the Soviets would gain influence in the region as the defender of the Arabs against "the imperialistic West and the Zionist state."[13]

The difference in goals accounts for part of the difference in policy between the Americans and British. However, Eden's retrieval and use of the 1930's analogy to frame the crisis, as well as to prescribe and justify policy, helps to explain why Eden's beliefs, perceptions, policy choices, and goals, especially that of deposing Nasser, differed so greatly from Eisenhower's beliefs, perceptions, policies, and goals. For Eden, the 1930's analogy became a set of interlocking beliefs about the use of force, Nasser, time, goals, and the stakes. These beliefs proved resistant to change by current information or by other methods of analysis.

During the Suez crisis, Eden heavily used the 1930's analogy and viewed Nasser as another Benito Mussolini, the Italian dictator. In public and in private, Eden mentioned the 1930s, Mussolini, and Hitler most often, rarely mentioning other analogies. This finding supports the argument that the public use of historical analogies for justification is an indicator that historical analogies have been used privately to diagnose crises and to prescribe policy. For example, Eden referred to Nasser as a "Moslem Mussolini" and said, "I have never thought Nasser a Hitler; he has no warlike people behind him. But the parallel with Mussolini is close."[14] On September 6 Eden wrote Eisenhower, "In the nineteen-thirties Hitler established his position by a series of carefully planned movements. . . . Similarly the seizure of the Suez Canal is, we are convinced, the opening gambit in a planned campaign designed by Nasser to expel all Western influence and interests from Arab countries."[15] In an October 1 letter to Eisenhower, Eden wrote, "Nasser . . . is now effectively in Russian hands, just as Mussolini was in Hitler's."[16] Eden's beliefs were reinforced by Macmillan, who called Nasser "an Asiatic Mussolini."[17] From the beginning, Eden, supported by Macmillan, viewed the Suez crisis through the distorted mirror of the 1930s.

The 1930s were a master analogy, with well-known and broadly accepted lessons. Eden did not need to explain extensively the lessons of the 1930s because Eden's colleagues, as well as Eisenhower and Dulles, already knew them. Although both the British and the Americans mentioned the 1930s, the British mentioned it far more often and, in so doing, broke the 1930's analogy down into more parts than Eisenhower and Dulles. For example, the British mentioned Fascist governments (cannot negotiate with such governments and military force must be used promptly, which supported the prompt use of force against Nasser, another dictator), Mussolini (a lackey of Hitler, just as Nasser, they argued, was under the control of the Soviet Union), and a cluster of analogies, including the 1930s generally, Hitler's remilitarization of the Rhineland, the 1934–35 Italian invasion of Abyssinia, the 1938 negotiations over the Sudetenland and subsequent German invasion of Czechoslovakia, and the 1939 Italian invasion of Albania, all of which prescribed the prompt use of force in response to aggressive dictators. The British also mentioned a possible "Werewolf" problem after their planned occupation of Egypt (Werewolf was the name of commandos Hitler planned to organize after the fall of the Third Reich to harass occupation forces); and Anschluss (letting a dictator expand his power, even diplomatically, only leads to more risky and more costly crises).[18] These events and lessons formed the master analogy of the 1930s.

It is difficult, however, to determine the relationship between Eden's beliefs and the 1930's analogy. The 1930's analogy reinforced beliefs Eden already held about how to respond to aggressive dictators. In the 1930s, Eden was a critic of Chamberlain's appeasement policy and, although he supported Attlee's conciliatory policy toward the Soviets after World War II, took a firmer line beginning in late 1948.[19] It would be preferable to determine which came first, the analogy or the beliefs. However, the most that can be said is that Eden held some general, basic beliefs before Suez, such as to use force against aggressive dictators, which he learned during the 1930s, and his hatred of Nasser, which predated the Suez crisis. For example, in March 1956, after Glubb Pasha was removed from power in Jordan, Eden said, "I want Nasser destroyed, not removed, destroyed."[20] However, the 1930s had far greater influence on Eden than just reinforcing beliefs he already held. Eden's beliefs that were specific to the Suez crisis, about time, the stakes, policy options, and goals, were developed at the beginning of the crisis and were significantly, if not predominantly, influenced by the 1930's analogy.

Historical information was not, of course, the only factor that accounted for the difference in American and British policies. The British had a far greater stake, historically, politically, and strategically, in Egypt than the United States. The British had protected the canal through two world wars. The British also wanted to prove they were still a world power, as well as to maintain access to Middle East oil and to India. Eden's gall bladder problems may also have contributed to an aggressive British policy, as did the emotional British reaction to what they called the "theft" of the canal. American policy was influenced by a stated support for the rule of law over the rule of force. However, far more important for the Americans was the goal of developing new ties with the Arab states and the Non-Aligned Movement, even while keeping old ties to the British and French. Moreover, Eisenhower wanted to be seen as a man of peace in the 1956 election. He hoped to continue the spirit of the Geneva summit of 1956 with the Soviets. The Americans also opposed imperialism and saw the British as the prime colonial power in the Middle East. Anglo-American relations were further soured by Macmillan's lies about the mood in Washington and the mutual dislike between Eden and Dulles, as well as Eden's selective listening to American messages. Although all of these factors influenced British and American policies, the role of historical information and lessons from history played a significant role, especially on the British side, in influencing goals, perceptions, and policy choices.

WHY DID EDEN RELY ON HISTORY?

A crucial question is why Eden relied so heavily on historical information during the Suez crisis while Eisenhower did not, even though both leaders faced the same event. Factors including complexity, novelty, the level of surprise, the personality of the policy makers, time pressures, level of drama, and the perceived stakes help to explain why Eden relied heavily on historical analogies while Eisenhower relied on current information.

Analogical reasoning is used to solve complex problems. The Suez crisis was complex enough to lead to the use of analogical reasoning. It involved a private company, with stock owned by the British and French governments, and a major international waterway enmeshed in multiple treaties. Therefore, the crisis did not yield easy or routine answers. The complexity

of the crisis contributes to an explanation of why Eden used historical analogies to frame the crisis. It does not, however, explain why Eden relied on
historical information while Eisenhower relied on current information. Both
viewed the same complex crisis, yet used different methods to analyze the
situation.

Analogical reasoning is also usually used to solve novel, but not unique,
problems. The Suez crisis was not common enough to have led to the creation of standard operating procedures, which would have negated the need
to use historical analogies to diagnose the crisis and to prescribe policy. It
was also not unique, which would have led policy makers to decide that
there were no valid historical analogies for the crisis. The British had dealt
with nationalization before—in Iran in 1951. The Americans had also faced
it once before in Mexico in 1938. However, nationalization of foreign companies, while not unique, was not a common occurrence by 1956. Furthermore, the Americans and British had both faced nationalistic leaders, like
Nasser, such as Mossadegh, Ramon Magsaysay in the Philippines, and Josip
Tito in Yugoslavia. Even the Suez Canal itself was not unique. Objectively,
it was similar to the Panama Canal, although the Americans vigorously denied the validity of the analogy.[21] However, this again only explains why
Eden relied on historical analogies to analyze the Suez crisis, but not why
Eisenhower did not turn to history as a cognitive shortcut to frame the crisis.

Events that are a surprise also lead to the use of historical analogies. Nasser's nationalization of the Suez Canal Company was a surprise to the British
and the Americans, which meant that they should have been inclined to use
historical analogies. However, because complexity, novelty, and surprise
were the same for the British and the Americans, these variables, while explaining why the British used historical analogies, cannot explain why the
British used historical analogies while the Americans relied on current information.

The level of stakes and of drama can explain the differences in British and
American reliance on historical information as opposed to current information. Historical analogies tend to be used for dramatic, high-stakes issues,
especially in the field of national security. Leaders rarely use historical analogies for routine policy decisions that lack high levels of drama and have
low stakes. Eden viewed the Suez crisis as dramatic, with extremely high
stakes involving national security and the potential use of force. Therefore,
he used historical analogies. Eisenhower, however, believed that Eden's view
of the stakes and the gravity of the crisis were "severely distorted" and "too
dark."[22] Furthermore, the American president, who did not even consider
the use of military force, did not perceive the nationalization of the canal
to be a national security issue nearly as much as Eden considered it to be
for Britain. Eisenhower may not have considered it a national security issue
at all. Objectively, the stakes were also higher for the British, who had
greater economic, strategic, and political interests in the canal and the com-

pany, than the Americans. The Americans lacked the same economic stake in the canal and, in 1956, were much less involved in the Middle East politically, economically, and strategically than the British. Therefore, Eden, dealing with high stakes, high drama, and a national security issue, should have been more likely to use historical analogies than Eisenhower, who was facing a crisis with lower stakes, lower drama, and of much less national security importance to the United States than to Britain. This was, in fact, what occurred: Eden relied heavily upon historical analogies, while Eisenhower relied primarily on current information.

Personality also contributes to an explanation of why Eden used historical analogies more than Eisenhower. Throughout his career, Eden used historical analogies more often than Eisenhower or Dulles, both of whom rarely used historical analogies.[23] Eden's greater inclination to use historical analogies was also influenced by Macmillan, a key cabinet member during the Suez crisis. Macmillan used historical analogies the most often in his career of any of the principal policy makers analyzed in this book. Therefore, the personalities of Eden and Macmillan made them more inclined to use historical information than their American counterparts.

Historical analogies are also more likely to be used as a shortcut in reasoning when actors perceive that time is limited. Eisenhower thought that time was working against Nasser or, at a minimum, that time could provide an opportunity to find a peaceful settlement. Eisenhower also believed there was sufficient time to analyze the issue without using shortcuts, such as historical analogies, and did not use the 1930's analogy or any other historical analogies, such as the Iranian oil nationalization crisis, to frame the Suez crisis or to prescribe policy. With ample time for analysis, Eisenhower ordered the Joint Chiefs of Staff (JCS), the National Security Council (NSC), and his advisors to study the canal issue. Eden, who was under intense domestic political pressure to react swiftly, believed that over time the position of Britain would weaken and Nasser's would strengthen. Therefore, he felt intense time pressures, which increased his inclination to use historical analogies as a cognitive shortcut to diagnose rapidly the crisis and to prescribe policy.

Another reason why Eden relied on the 1930's analogy while Eisenhower did not is because people are most likely to retrieve historical analogies from time periods in which they were involved personally, especially if the period involved traumatic events. Eden was involved personally in many of the major international crises of the 1930s: as foreign under-secretary (1931–34), Lord Privy Seal with responsibility for League of Nations Affairs (1934–35) and foreign secretary (1935–38). The 1930s also marked a traumatic period in Eden's life: the low point in February 1938, when he resigned from the government because he opposed the appeasement policy toward Italy over Abyssinia and the high point when he became foreign secretary. The 1930s was "a time when reputations were either made or savagely destroyed. Anthony Eden was that rare exception of a figure who made his reputation."[24] This level of involvement and trauma increased the probability that Eden would retrieve the 1930's analogy to frame the Suez crisis. Unlike Eden, Eisenhower was not personally involved in the major events of the 1930s. For Eisenhower, the 1930s were a dreary period of staff work first in Washington and then in the Philippines. It was only after Pearl Harbor that Eisenhower's career took off. The 1930s was less traumatic and important to Eisenhower than to Eden, which meant the president was less likely to retrieve the 1930s as a historical analogy to frame Suez than the prime minister. Furthermore, although age is a poor indicator of reliance on historical analogies, Eden, Macmillan, and Lloyd were between six and sixteen years younger than Eisenhower and Dulles, who were less influenced by the 1930's analogy during Suez. If older people are more experienced and, therefore, less influenced by the most recent, serious, and dramatic crisis, then this may explain why the younger British leaders were more influenced by this analogy than the older American leaders.

The complexity, novelty, and the level of surprise in the Suez crisis should have made both Eisenhower and Eden inclined to use historical analogies. However, their different personalities and beliefs about time, the level of drama, the stakes, and whether the issue involved national security, meant that Eden relied on analogical reasoning to frame the crisis in terms of the 1930s and to prescribe and legitimize policy, while Eisenhower did not rely on any historical analogies and focused on current information to frame the crisis and to formulate policy.

THE PROCESS OF DRAWING LESSONS FROM HISTORY

Once Eden decided, consciously or, more likely, subconsciously, to use analogical reasoning to retrieve historical information, what was the process by which he used such information? The common model, of an actor asserting the similarity of a historical analogy and the current case, explaining the similarity, and then describing the current case in terms of the analogy, does not reflect what occurs in a group of foreign policy decision makers. During the Suez crisis, an actor usually suggested, or implied, merely by mentioning a historical case, that the current case was similar to a historical analogy. Then, in many cases, another actor mentioned one difference and that was enough to scuttle the perceived validity of the analogy. For example, at an August 9 NSC meeting, "Secretary [of Defense] Wilson wondered whether the British and French, if they moved into the Canal area, would establish arrangements similar to those in Gibraltar. Mr. Allen Dulles pointed out that the Treaty of 1888 recognized the Canal as an integral part of Egypt,"[25] unlike Gibraltar, which was not recognized by treaty as part of Spain. This single difference invalidated the analogy, and neither

Wilson nor any other top policy maker raised the analogy again. Another example occurred on August 27 at a British cabinet meeting, when an analogy to Cyprus was invalidated by the mention of one difference: "Cyprus is not a true analogy. For the issue over self-determination did not involve the use of force."[26] In another example, in a July 31 draft of a letter to Eden, Eisenhower wrote, "It took your nation some eighteen years to put the original Napoleon in his proper place, but you did it. You have dealt more rapidly with his modern imitators."[27] Dulles "questioned the paragraph about Napoleon and his successors on the ground that they had been dealt with by force and it might be inappropriate to suggest that analogy. The president laughed and said he guessed I [Dulles] was right and struck out the paragraph."[28]

During the Suez crisis, there was almost never any debate about the interpretation of history in American and British policy-making meetings. Extended discussion of the similarities and differences between the current case and the analogy, or about the validity of the historical analogy for the current crisis, were extremely rare, if not nonexistent. Policy makers often mentioned two or three historical analogies in an attempt to find one that was valid for the current case. This process is similar to brainstorming, which is a technique of solving problems by stimulating creative thinking and developing new ideas by unrestrained and spontaneous participation. Once one policy maker suggested a historical analogy, others were more likely to think analogically, in a snowball effect: If someone in a group mentioned a historical analogy, other group members mentioned other analogies. For this reason, analogies often appear in clusters in the minutes of meetings. For example, at an August 9 NSC meeting, the Philippine independence agreement with the United States, British nationalizations, and arrangements similar to those in Gibraltar were mentioned as analogies to the Suez Crisis.[29] The process of using historical analogies tended to be in the form of brainstorming, with discussion swiftly moving from analogy to analogy, with most rejected on the basis of only one, often superficial, difference.

Another aspect of the process of analogical reasoning and of drawing lessons from history is that once an analogy is retrieved, individuals vary in their acceptance of the validity of the analogy to the current crisis. For example, Eden acted as a satisficer, meaning that he accepted that, because the first analogy he retrieved (that of the 1930s), was superficially similar to Suez: that the 1930s was a valid analogy. Eisenhower acted as a perfectionist and, unlike psychological laboratory studies, which have found that subjects tend to accept either all or none of an analogy, he accepted the superficial, surface similarities, but rejected the less similar causal elements, as well as the policy prescriptions between Suez and the 1930's analogy. Eisenhower and Dulles accepted that Nasser, like Hitler, was an aggressive dictator. They believed that Nasser had outlined his plans in *The Philosophy of the Revolution*, just as Hitler had outlined his plans in *Mein Kampf.* Eisenhower said,

"Nasser had indicated dangerous tendencies that needed to be curbed,"[30] and Dulles said that Nasser's action "was not an erratic or an isolated action but an integral part of a long-term program" to increase Arab power at the expense of the West.[31] However, Eisenhower and Dulles rejected key parts of the mapping between the Suez crisis and the 1930s that Eden accepted: that Nasser was as dangerous or as powerful as Hitler or even Mussolini; that the proper response was military force; and that if force was not used that the results would be disastrous. Eisenhower outlined his differences with Eden's views in a September 8 letter to Eden: "We have a grave problem confronting us in Nasser's reckless adventure with the Canal, and I do *not* differ from you in your estimate of his intentions and purposes. The place where we apparently do not agree is on the probable effects in the Arab world of the various possible reactions by the Western World . . . the result that you and I both want can best be assured by slower and less dramatic processes than military force."[32] In foreign policy, unlike psychology experiments, leaders may accept some parts of the lessons drawn from a historical analogy while rejecting others. However, one caveat to consider is that Eisenhower, throughout his career, was especially good at analyzing historical analogies and selecting both parts to use and parts to reject. Unlike Eden, Eisenhower was never dominated by a historical analogy to the extent that his objectivity and willingness to change his policy in reaction to new information was seriously impaired. Eisenhower was not as influenced by history and the 1930's analogy as Truman and Attlee had been during the Korean crisis or as Macmillan was to be during the Lebanon/Jordan crisis in 1958.

Sometimes, especially if a prime minister or president mentions a historical analogy and then pursues the validity of the analogy, then that analogy will often dominate the discussion. The leader does not even need to discuss the validity of the analogy; merely applying the lessons of the analogy to the current crisis usually leads to general acceptance of the validity of the analogy by the cabinet. This acceptance of an analogy verges on a form of "groupthink" and can stifle rival framings of the crisis, as well as other possible policies.

THE EFFECT OF THE 1930s

Once lessons from the 1930s had been integrated into the British decision-making process, they had a significant effect on British perceptions and policy making. The 1930s influenced Eden's perceptions of his own role, policy options, goals, time, stakes, and risks, as well as his policy choices and views regarding Nasser.

Eden drew the lesson from the 1930s that he must not be another Chamberlain and must not repeat Chamberlain's policy of appeasement and negotiating to buy time to rearm. Negotiations with Nasser would fail. Eden discussed whether to attend talks in Geneva in mid-October and made reference to the 1930s:

I could not return from Geneva with a piece of paper and commend it to the House of Commons, when I knew it had no real value. . . . I had been through so much of this before. I had not been willing to commend to Parliament an agreement with Mussolini which I had not believed would be fulfilled. Having resigned rather than do this twenty years ago, in the lesser responsibility of a Foreign Secretary, I was not prepared to reach and proclaim another agreement as a step to peace, when I did not believe that it was any such thing.[33]

Eden concluded from the 1930s that force must be used promptly against Nasser. In an October 1 letter to Eisenhower, Eden wrote, "It would be as ineffective to show weakness to Nasser now in order to placate him as it was to show weakness to Mussolini."[34] In his memoirs Eden wrote in a section about Nasser that "It is important to reduce the stature of the megalomaniacal dictator at an early stage. A check to Hitler when he moved to reoccupy the Rhineland would not have destroyed him, but it would have made him pause."[35] Based on this lesson from the 1930s, Eden and his cabinet decided early in the Suez crisis not to appease Nasser but instead to use force promptly.

Also based on their belief that Nasser was another Mussolini, the British viewed the Egyptian leader as irrational, expansionist, unreasonable, and unreliable. They therefore concluded that a reasonable, negotiated settlement was impossible.[36] Sir Humphrey Trevelyan, the British ambassador in Cairo, wrote to Lloyd on September 5 and said Nasser was an "irresponsible dictator lashing out in a tantrum."[37] Dulles said the British and French believed "that Nasser is a wild man brandishing an axe and that they do not have to wait for the blow to fall."[38] Eden said, "He [Nasser] has shown that he is not a man who can be trusted to keep an agreement."[39] The British delegation to the United Nations feared that Nasser would start negotiations, drag them out, and then break them off, leaving Britain in the same position as when the talks started.[40] Having concluded that Nasser was irrational and that a negotiated settlement was impossible, Eden preferred to use force promptly. Because he believed Nasser could not be trusted to keep a negotiated settlement even if one were reached, Eden preferred the use of force to a peacefully negotiated settlement unless Egypt capitulated to every British demand.

Eisenhower, who did not rely on the 1930's analogy and did not perceive Nasser to be another Mussolini, disagreed with the British and believed that the Egyptian leader was rational and amenable to negotiation. On July 31 Eisenhower wrote Eden that a conference of maritime nations should bring enough pressure to bear on Nasser to ensure the efficient operation of the canal.[41] On September 2 Eisenhower again wrote Eden, "If the diplomatic front we present is united and is backed by the overwhelming sentiment of our several peoples, the chances should be greater that Nasser will give way without the need for any resort to force."[42]

The British, on the basis of the 1930's analogy, when time favored Hitler and Mussolini, also viewed time as being against them and the situation as deteriorating. The longer dictators were in power, the more diplomatic successes they achieved, and the more difficult it was to weaken or overthrow them. Eden and his cabinet applied this lesson to Nasser, who was seen as a threat to his neighbors, as Hitler and Mussolini had been. The threat would increase unless the British promptly used force. This concern with time was reflected in British military planning. At first, the plan, based on the military's need for time to prepare, was to intervene in Egypt within six weeks, although U.S.–supported diplomatic plans and a lack of British military capabilities led to delays.[43] Time pressures, significantly influenced by the 1930's analogy, weighed heavily on British minds. On September 8 the British Foreign Office, via the British ambassador in Washington, Sir Roger Makins, told Dulles that with each day Nasser tightened his hold on the canal and further threatened friendly regimes in the area.[44] On October 5 Lloyd said the British position was "rapidly deteriorating. . . . We [the British] were therefore convinced that matters could not be allowed to drift and although we saw all the disadvantages we believed that in the last resort force would be the lesser evil. Time, however, was short." Force would have to be used soon because, the British feared, Egypt was planning a coup in Libya and was threatening governments in Saudi Arabia, Jordan, and Syria.[45]

Their view of time, based upon the 1930's analogy, led the British to conclude that they should use force promptly. This meant that they did not allow enough time for means other than military force to succeed. Lloyd said, "One course might be to apply economic pressure. If this would produce results in a week or two, it might be the best way. The indications, however, were that economic measures would injure us at least as much as Egypt and that their effects would be slow."[46] In September Lloyd noted that if the Suez Committee, the mini–British cabinet that handled the crisis, did not produce results in a week, further steps would have to be immediately considered and that "military measures cannot be postponed indefinitely."[47] Diplomacy and economic sanctions invariably take much longer than "a week or two" to produce results. Because of the belief that time was working against them, the British were not willing to give nonmilitary means adequate time to be effective. They would instead decide to use force promptly, just as Eden believed Chamberlain should have done during the 1930s. The British believed that time would only allow the dictator to prepare and grow stronger and even more threatening.

Relying on current information far more than on lessons from the past, the Americans had a very different view of time and of the situation than did the British. Eisenhower and Dulles believed that time was against Nasser, not the British, and that adequate time was needed to find a peaceful settlement. In early October, "He [Dulles] declared that he was with Britain on every point, except the use of force . . . he felt that to employ force in the immediate future would be a mistake, since in his view Nasser's position was deteriorating. [Eden believed] There were no grounds for this last estimate."[48] To the Americans, there was no rush to act. Egypt was operating the canal effectively and there appeared to be no threat of the canal being closed. In a September 8 letter to Eden, Eisenhower counseled patience and said it took the British eighteen years to topple Napoleon. Eisenhower said the West should explore all possible peaceful means, "regardless of the time consumed," before the British even considered using force.[49] Therefore, Eisenhower and Dulles, in contrast to Eden and his cabinet, believed, based on current information and not the 1930's analogy, that Egypt was effectively operating the canal and that there was time for negotiation and diplomacy. The use of force could wait. Nasser would weaken over time.

The 1930's analogy also influenced the British cabinet's views of the stakes in the crisis. Chamberlain's government had fallen because it failed to deal effectively with the rise of the Axis powers. Eden believed his government was also at stake. This, as time proved, was indeed true. The 1930s led to a world war, and Eden believed Suez was an equally grave crisis. For example, on July 28 Eden said that Nasser would control "the oil supplies of the free world . . . and Commonwealth communications and trade will be gravely jeopardized"[50] if the British did not act firmly. Macmillan said "that a success by Nasser would mean the end of Great Britain,"[51] while Eden wrote, "the seizure of the Suez Canal is, we are convinced, the opening gambit in a planned campaign designed by Nasser to expel all Western influence and interests from Arab countries."[52]

Because they believed, on the basis of the 1930's analogy, that the stakes were high, Eden and his cabinet were aware of, and willing to accept, the grave risks resulting from the use of military force. For example, Eden said there was a "serious risk" of the Arab world uniting against his country if the British used force.[53] On October 5 Lloyd said, "We did not want to employ this method [force] and were well aware of the dangers. There was the question of how we could get out once we had gone in and we also realized the need to justify the use of force to public opinion . . . although we saw all the disadvantages we believed that in the last resort force would be the lesser evil."[54] The British cabinet realized that the canal might be sabotaged and closed for as long as three months, resulting in serious financial and trade losses, and that, unless the intervention was swift, there would probably be "a run on sterling. This consequence might have to be accepted if the alternative was slow economic strangulation as Egypt extended her control over the Arab world and the oil-producing countries."[55] The cabinet also knew that the use of force would garner little, if any, international support, as well as damage Anglo-American[56] and Anglo-

Canadian relations. On August 15 the High Commissioner in Canada telegrammed the secretary of state for Commonwealth Relations that Canada would not support the use of force.[57] The risk of the rise of another Mussolini or Hitler, however, overrode any British fears about the risks and costs of using force.

Furthermore, the British use of the 1930's analogy blocked the generation of, and diverted attention from, other options and information that contradicted the 1930's Suez comparison. Even as Egypt showed signs of accommodation and willingness to negotiate, Eden and his cabinet continued with their plan to use force. In early October Egypt agreed to U.N.–sponsored negotiations with Britain and France, which resulted in general guidelines (the Six Principles) that were designed to resolve the crisis. The talks also led to an agreement to further negotiations between the British, French, and Egyptians in Geneva in late October. Egypt continued to keep the canal open and even to improve its efficiency. The canal, however, was closed when Israel attacked Egypt on October 29, 1956. A triumph of the idee fixe. The British would not give the Egyptians an opportunity to show that they could be reasonable.

The 1930's analogy influenced not only the type of British response, but also their goals and how they used force. The 1930's analogy caused the British to use military force in an extreme fashion with extreme goals in a manner, in many ways, out of proportion to the provocation caused by the nationalization of the canal. The British options at the start of the crisis were, broadly speaking, diplomacy, economic sanctions, covert operations, and the threat, or use of, military force. The 1930's analogy framed the Suez crisis in terms of a possible world war. The British believed that extreme measures had to be taken to avert such an outcome. They therefore chose the most extreme option: the use of military force. Within the category of military force, the British had a range of possible operations, including, among many other options: sending a warship through the canal; bombing selected targets; occupying only the canal; and attempting to depose Nasser with military force. The British chose an extreme operation and an extreme goal: an air attack followed by airborne and amphibious landings to occupy the canal and then an advance on Cairo, followed by the overthrow of Nasser and installation of a new government.

Eden and his cabinet also used the 1930's analogy to legitimize policy, which reflected their reliance on the analogy to frame the Suez crisis and to prescribe policy. For example, in a broadcast, Eden said, "We all know this is how Fascist governments behave and we all remember, all too well, what the cost can be in giving in to Fascism."[58] In Parliament, Eden compared the Suez crisis to the 1930s and raised the specter of appeasement. Eden quoted himself from 1938, when he resigned, and said, "I do not believe that we can make progress in European appeasement . . . if we allow the impression to gain currency abroad that we yield to constant pressure," and then said, "I do not think that that is menacing language in the temper of the situation in which we are now [Suez] . . . But we have, I believe, all of us in all parties learned our lesson since then. Do not let us, I implore the House and I implore the country, unlearn that lesson now."[59] The 1930s dominated the British justification for their use of force. Furthermore, because he disagreed with the prescriptions of the 1930's analogy, Eisenhower may have been more opposed to the British use of force than if Eden had justified the decision to use force on the basis of another analogy or on some other, entirely different, basis.

If the 1930s had such an influence on British decision makers, then other analogies should have led to different policies if the British had instead used them to frame the Suez crisis. The Algerian war and the conflict in Indo-China, for example, would have warned, contrary to the 1930's analogy, against the use of force in regional contingencies. Other historical analogies also prescribed policies other than the use of force. For example, the situation of Gibraltar and the aftermath of Filipino independence suggested that it was possible to negotiate agreements to retain control of land or bases in other states, even when nationalist feelings were running high. The Iranian oil nationalization was probably the most valid alternative historical analogy. It offered a case where a nationalistic leader appeared to be irrational and prescribed the use of covert action (Operation Ajax/Boot), instead of military force. Iran also suggested that if a crisis dragged on for months, or even years, the passage of time might not work against Britain and the West. The British spent years dealing with the Iran case, yet succeeded in overthrowing Mossadegh and retaining some control, albeit a reduced share, of Iranian oil. Iran and Suez were similar superficially. Both were Middle Eastern crises involving the nationalization of an asset by a popular, nationalistic leader. Both involved British national interests, with the United States playing a significant role in the crisis. Iran also had attributes that should have increased the chance that British policy makers would retrieve it as an analogy for Suez. The Iran crisis was recent and Eden was involved in it personally. There is no evidence, however, that Iran significantly influenced, if it had any influence at all on, Eden's thinking about Suez. Why? A master analogy, the 1930s, overrode the Iran analogy. Eden was also more involved in the 1930s, a period of his life more traumatic and important than the Iran crisis. Furthermore, in 1956 Operation Ajax/Boot was perceived as a success and policy makers usually draw on foreign policy failures as analogies. Eisenhower also could have used the Iran analogy. However, he also discounted it. At a July 27 meeting Eisenhower said nationalizing the canal was not like nationalizing an oil well, "since the latter exhausts a nation's resources and the Canal is more like a public utility, building them up."[60] At an August 9 NSC meeting, "Secretary Humphrey said that, ostensibly, Nasser wants to build a dam. Perhaps an Iran-style settlement would enable him to get the money to build the dam. The President said this solution would make Canal tolls too high."[61] Again, one criticism invalidated the analogy. The success of Ajax also decreased the probability that Eisenhower would use it as a historical analogy for the Suez crisis. Furthermore, U.S. participation in Ajax/Boot was still secret in 1956, and Eisenhower would not have wanted to make his involvement in the coup public. Eisenhower was also only involved in the later part of the Iran crisis and it was not a major event in his life or for the United States. This decreased the chance that Eisenhower would retrieve the Iran case during the Suez crisis.

To summarize, because of his reliance on the 1930s to frame the Suez crisis and to prescribe policy, Eden believed that the passage of time would hurt Britain, and that Nasser was irrational. Therefore, a reasonable, nego-tiated settlement was not possible and force would have to be used promptly. Also on the basis of the 1930s, Eden believed that the stakes were extremely high. These high stakes justified running the high risks associated with the use of force to achieve an extreme goal: the overthrow of Nasser by intervening with a significant military force. The Americans, relying on current information, as well as having less interest in, and prestige tied to, the canal, believed that the stakes were far lower. Eisenhower also believed that time was against Nasser and that Nasser was rational. These beliefs justified a search for a negotiated settlement, even if it took a long time. With a belief that the stakes were lower and that Egypt was running the canal effectively, the Americans did not believe that Britain's use of force was justified. Although Britain and the United States had different degrees of interest in the canal, much of the difference between British and American perceptions of the situation rested on their differing reliance on historical as compared to current information.

FORCE: THE PREFERRED OPTION

The day after Nasser nationalized the canal, at a July 27 meeting, under public and media pressure to take a firm stand,[62] the British cabinet already agreed that military force was the preferred response. The cabinet advised the Joint Chiefs to prepare a study as soon as possible "of what forces would be required to seize the Canal and how they would be disposed if military action became necessary."[63] Eden ruled out economic sanctions as the pri-mary British response because they would take too long[64] and would prob-ably not topple Nasser from power. The British did not even want a U.N. resolution to support economic sanctions. On August 27 Lloyd said, "It would not be possible to get, even if we wanted it, a [U.N.] resolution in favor of economic sanctions passed by a satisfactory majority, if at all."[65] As early as the July 27 meeting, Lloyd said he was already moving toward the conclusion that a Western consortium would have to take over the canal and run it, if need be, by force.[66] Eden agreed, and wrote in a July 27 letter to Eisenhower, "As we see it we are unlikely to attain our objectives by economic pressures alone. . . . My colleagues and I are convinced that we must be ready, in the last resort, to use force to bring Nasser to his senses. For our part we are prepared to do so."[67]

The cabinet, however, had one maverick, who thought he might be able to pursue his own policy. Early in the crisis, Macmillan believed that he might be able to convince the Americans that they had to pressure Nasser to capitulate to avoid prompt British military intervention. When Eisenhower sent Robert Murphy to London on July 28, Macmillan frightened Eisenhower's envoy so much with the prospect of a prompt British use of force that Dulles arrived on July 31 with a letter from Eisenhower urging the British to not even contemplate military intervention.[68] However, there is no evidence Eden or other cabinet members supported such a strategy. They all, including Macmillan after his failed attempt to provoke U.S. pressure on Nasser to back down, strongly supported Eden's decision to use force unless Nasser capitulated to British demands, which was unlikely given the secret British goal to overthrow Nasser.

At first, the British cabinet masked their military buildup and their decision to use force behind the façade of a compellence strategy,[69] which seeks to exert pressure on an adversary through the threat of using military force to alter a situation. The British "Foreign Secretary [Lloyd] said political and economic pressure was unlikely to have any effect on Nasser unless he knew that there were military sanctions in [the] background. . . . United Kingdom policy therefore was to proceed with precautionary military preparations."[70] British military preparations could have supported a compellence strategy or the actual use of force. However, the British believed that their compellence strategy would fail. They concluded that Nasser was unlikely to capitulate to Egypt's hated, former imperial master, Britain, on such an important source of Egyptian prestige as the Suez Canal, let alone step down as Egyptian leader. This belief was reinforced by an accurate reading of Egyptian nationalist sentiments. Therefore, the British were unlikely to achieve their goal of overthrowing Nasser using a compellence strategy; force would instead have to be used. Since the British assumed that Nasser would not capitulate, they were inclined to use force to overthrow the Egyptian leader from the beginning of the crisis. Compellence was designed to mask both British preparations to attack, as well as to appease U.S. demands that Britain seek a negotiated settlement and postpone, if not abandon entirely, plans to intervene militarily.

Powerful support can be found for the argument that the British sought Nasser's removal, instead of a compromise agreement, from the beginning of the crisis. At a July 31 meeting Eisenhower said the British planned "to initiate hostilities at an early date for this purpose [to break Nasser]."[71] On July 31 Eisenhower wrote Eden about the British decision to use force, "I realize that the messages from both you and Harold [Macmillan] stressed that the decision taken [to use force] was already approved by the government and was firm and irrevocable."[72] A few days later, on August 2, having allowed almost no time for negotiation to succeed, the British cabinet, in a crucial decision, agreed to intervene militarily if a negotiated settlement was not achieved.[73] On August 28 the Foreign Office telegrammed Dulles; "As you know, it is our intention to proceed with our plans [to use force] unless Nasser can be seen clearly and decisively to have given in."[74] Furthermore, the British wanted the Menzies mission, which met Nasser in Cairo starting on September 3, to fail, unless Nasser accepted the negotiating proposals without change. The British and French wanted the proposals dictated to the Egyptian leader without authorizing Prime Minister Robert Menzies of Australia to negotiate with Nasser. Most of the nations attending the London conference wanted, at a minimum, to have the proposals explained to Nasser, but Britain opposed even an explanation.[75] These restrictions doomed the Menzies mission to failure. In November the Anglo-French ultimatum to Egypt and Israel, blatantly tilted against Egypt, illustrated the British position. Eden said that if Egypt complied with the ultimatum it would undermine Nasser's prestige fatally, and if Egypt did not comply "there would be ample justification for Anglo-French military action."[76] Either Nasser would capitulate or the British would use military force.

On the basis of the 1930's analogy, Eden and his cabinet decided that military force was not the least, but instead the most, attractive option. Eden believed that in the 1930s too much reliance had been placed on diplomacy and negotiation and too little on military preparation and the use of force. He was determined not to make the same mistake. On September 7 "Eden said that the Arabs will interpret any other course short of military intervention as a sign of weakness."[77] On September 19 U.S. ambassador to Paris, Douglas Dillon, wrote, "both Macmillan and Salisbury still regard military action as the only satisfactory solution to the Suez problem."[78] Furthermore, although the British cabinet decided on September 6 that "Military action must remain subject to political decision,"[79] the need to justify and maintain the viability of the military option, the preferred option, quickly took precedence over diplomacy. As early as August 8, Eden told Dulles that any long delay in the negotiations was unacceptable because Britain could not keep its "military precautionary measures in a high state of readiness for any protracted period."[80] Whether this was an excuse or a genuine consideration, it shows that Eden was either placing military considerations above diplomacy or was using false military considerations to place a time limit on diplomacy and, therefore, decreasing the chance of a negotiated settlement. The decision to take the Suez crisis to the United Nations was also driven by considerations of justifying, and keeping viable, the use of force. On August 24 Lloyd and Pineau agreed to take the issue to the United Nations so they could not be criticized for not having tried to settle the crisis peacefully.[81] If the Soviets vetoed a U.N. resolution, it would put Britain and France in a better position to use force before world and, especially, American opinion, which tended to oppose military intervention, since it would look like the Soviets had blocked British and French attempts to settle the crisis.[82] On September 6 the cabinet agreed that "it was desirable that we should be seen to have made the fullest possible use of all available international machinery in our search for a peaceful settlement of the dispute."[83] Lloyd later reported that the U.N. process had turned out well because the Security Council had neither limited Britain's freedom of action nor appointed a mediator or a negotiating body.[84] In late October the British and French secretly met in Sevres, a Paris suburb, and agreed to use force against Egypt.

Force continued to be the preferred British option throughout the crisis. The British used force even as Anglo-French-Egyptian talks were planned for Geneva on October 29. Many believed the Geneva talks would lead to a settlement. In early October, Dulles thought an agreement was possible "in principle" and Under Secretary Herbert Hoover Jr. thought Britain and Egypt were "very close to agreement."[85] U.N. Secretary General Dag Hammarskjold thought the crisis "was all over" when he arranged the Geneva meeting.[86] The Egyptian Foreign Minister, Mahmoud Fawzi, later said "significant developments towards a solution had been made"[87] by the time of the Anglo-French military intervention. Even though an agreement may have been close, albeit in the eyes of those who eagerly sought a peaceful settlement, the British and French governments preferred the use of force to a peacefully negotiated settlement.

Nasser did not capitulate to British demands and the British, in league with the French and Israelis, used military force against Egypt. Anglo-French forces staged air raids on Egyptian airfields on October 31 and landed airborne and amphibious forces in Egypt on November 5–6, 1956. The British cabinet assumed that the operation would be a military intervention. There would be some opposition. "A Declaration of War is undesirable, but there will certainly be a condition of 'hostilities.' "[88] However, the British believed casualties would be light and that the operation would be brief. The minutes of the British Egypt Committee, which handled the crisis, on August 20 state, "We might hope to stay in Cairo no more than a day or two."[89] The British also believed that fighting would not spread. Although there would be threats against British nationals and property in the Middle East, such threats would not spread to the British Isles,[90] all of which fit the military intervention definition. The operation, however, had a total war objective: the overthrow of Nasser's government.[91]

Eden also used limited, proportional force to intervene in Egypt, even though his military commander favored using larger forces. The original British plan, "Musketeer," as devised by the military, envisioned using overwhelming force. Although constrained by a shortage of landing craft and a small number of British paratroopers, Musketeer envisioned an amphibious assault supported by an airborne landing by the British Parachute Brigade Group and 2,000 French paratroopers. The buildup after the landing would include a division from Germany, an armored division from Libya, and a

French light armored division.[92] However, the Allied commander-in-chief, General Sir Charles Keightley, bowing to political considerations, scaled down the plan and proposed Musketeer Revised. Eden wrote in his diary that Musketeer Revised was being pursued more for its political, than military, advantages.[93] The British would use limited and proportional, not overwhelming, force. Musketeer Revised shifted the focus from an air- and sea-landing to a concentrated air and naval bombardment of Port Faud and Port Said, as well as military targets around Cairo. The Chiefs of Staff said the plan was "based on the assumption that the air offensive will break the Egyptian will to resist and bring about the disintegration of the army."[94] The military buildup after the landing was also reduced greatly. 2 Infantry Division, based in Germany and originally designated to participate in Musketeer, was left out of Musketeer Revised. 3 Infantry Division, based in England and originally slated to participate early in the invasion, would not embark until after the operation had begun.[95] British civilian policy makers believed that the forces involved were limited and proportional to their goals and to the expected resistance. British cabinet minutes state: "the degree of force used could match the extent of the opposition encountered."[96] Military officers, however, preferring overwhelming force, criticized Musketeer Revised as lacking sufficient force to seize the Suez Canal and march on Cairo to overthrow Nasser.[97] The Anglo-French force consisted of about 80,000 troops, 150 warships, 7 carriers, 40 submarines, 80 merchant ships, and 20,000 vehicles.[98] A very large force. However, the gradual application of the forces, first air strikes and then, days later, an amphibious landing, dissipated the force of the blow. The goals of the operation, seizing Cairo and deposing Nasser, were also ambitious, even for the forces involved. Political considerations, especially appeasing the Americans, who wanted Britain to negotiate, combined with the principle of proportionality, and not the principle of overwhelming force, drove the new plan.

THE TERRIBLE PROBLEM: U.S. OPPOSITION TO THE USE OF FORCE

Suez provides an example of a leader using historical information that distorted reality and led to a flawed foreign policy. Eden's use of the 1930's analogy distorted his perception of current information and led him to pursue a fatally flawed policy during the Suez crisis. Eisenhower, whose perceptions were clearer than Eden's because he did not rely on the 1930's analogy, perceived current information more objectively and pursued a more effective policy. Eisenhower's view of policy options was different from Eden's because they disagreed on the validity of the 1930's analogy as applied to the Suez case. This disagreement led to their different views of the stakes, time, risks, and of policy options. When Eisenhower said force was a last resort, he meant that force was the least attractive option and that it should not be used until all other means of settling the crisis had been exhausted. Because he was free to rely on current information instead of current information that had been distorted through the lens of the 1930s, Eisenhower was able to make the distinction between guaranteeing an open, free canal and overthrowing Nasser, a distinction the British did not choose to make. From the British standpoint: if Nasser was another Mussolini, then he must be overthrown. This distinction led Eisenhower to focus on peaceful tactics that would settle the canal issue, but would not achieve the British goal of overthrowing Nasser.[99] Eisenhower wrote Eden on July 31 that for the United States to use force "there would have to be a showing that every peaceful means of resolving the difficulty had previously been exhausted."[100] In a September 8 letter to Eden, Eisenhower outlined other "peaceful means," including an international organization (SCUA) to operate the canal, economic measures, exploiting Arab rivalries, and building new tankers and pipelines, that should be tried before force.[101] Some of the suggestions were absurd, such as building new tankers and pipelines. They would take years to construct and would not address the central issue of Egyptian nationalization of the canal. However, they showed that Eisenhower wanted to pursue all other possible options before condoning the use of force. On August 12 Eisenhower "re-emphasized the need for exploring every peaceful means for settlement."[102] At an October 5 meeting with Pineau and Lloyd, Dulles said, "The position of the United States Government was that a peaceful solution should be sought by all possible means and that war would be a disaster."[103] And even if an alternative plan failed, such as SCUA, Eisenhower said, the United States would not "shoot our way" through the canal.[104]

Eisenhower's chosen policy, resting on current information and lacking the distortion of the 1930's analogy lens, was opposed to the British use of force. From almost the beginning of the crisis on July 26 until Anglo-French forces landed in Egypt, Eisenhower and Dulles, in what Eisenhower called a "terrible problem,"[105] tried to convince Eden not to use force.[106] At first, Eisenhower worried whether canal operations would deteriorate. On July 28 he said, "The problem arises that, lacking intervention now, the Canal operations may gradually deteriorate without giving a specific occasion for intervention at any later time."[107] Eisenhower also wondered if Egypt would attack U.S. citizens or interfere with the movement of oil,[108] which might require the use of force. By July 31, however, Eisenhower had decided force should not be used by Britain, France, or the United States. He wrote Eden, "I have given you my personal conviction, as well as that of my associates, as to the unwisdom even of contemplating the use of military force at this moment."[109] Eisenhower even opposed the use of clandestine force, such as he had supported against Mossadegh, to topple Nasser.[110]

Eisenhower and Dulles also opposed the use of force, in part, because of a consideration based upon their evaluation of current information: They deemed public support essential for any use of force and did not believe public opinion would tolerate the seizure of the canal as justifying military intervention.[111] Eisenhower wrote Eden on September 2, "I must tell you frankly that American public opinion flatly rejects the thought of using force."[112] On October 30 Eisenhower said, "the French and the British do not have an adequate cause for war. Egyptian action in nationalizing the Canal was not enough to justify this."[113] On November 9 Eisenhower told the British ambassador to Washington, Sir Harold Caccia, that, from the perspective of world public opinion, he "felt from the beginning of the Suez crisis that this was a difficult ground to choose for bringing Nasser down."[114]

The Americans also opposed intervention for another reason based upon their interpretations of current information. They wondered how the British would disengage from Egypt[115] and knew that Britain lacked the financial resources to sustain an occupation indefinitely.[116] On July 31 Eisenhower wrote Eden; "Moreover, initial military successes might be easy, but the eventual price might become far too heavy."[117] On July 31 Dulles said a British military intervention would lead to unceasing Egyptian terrorist attacks and 90,000 British troops guarding the canal.[118] Dulles said that he and Eisenhower "saw no end to the consequences of military intervention. It would be possible to occupy key points, but in the President's view there were not enough troops and resources to put out all the fires that would be started."[119] Dulles's primary fear was an Arab backlash to Western intervention that would result in the Arab world aligning with the Soviets against the West. On September 2 Eisenhower wrote Eden that a British military intervention would set the Third World against the West for a generation, as well as giving the Soviets a chance to make "mischief."[120]

Despite all their efforts, the Americans failed to dissuade the British from using force. A significant cause of this failure was the strength of Eden's belief, based on the 1930's analogy, about the need to use force promptly. However, another significant cause was that Dulles's messages and statements to the British about the American position on the use of force were not as adamant as those of Eisenhower. For example, Dulles's statement that Nasser must be made "to disgorge what he was attempting to swallow," muddied the clarity of the U.S. message that Britain must not use force.[121] Macmillan further obscured Eisenhower's messages to Eden. From Washington, Macmillan cabled Eden that "Ike [*sic*] is really determined, somehow or other, to bring Nasser down." The message was a lie concocted by Macmillan.[122] Macmillan also told Eden that Eisenhower's letters did not rule out the use of military force, even though this was blatantly false.[123] Eden accepted Macmillan's lies and misinterpretations of the American position because he believed that Nasser must be brought down: a lesson he drew largely from the 1930's analogy.

Also contributing to the U.S. failure to dissuade the British was that, by stressing the potential costs of a military intervention, Eisenhower and Dulles selected the wrong tactic to convince Eden not to use force. Eden was aware of, and accepted, the costs and risks of military intervention that Eisenhower raised. However, Eden believed that the intervention would probably succeed, thus avoiding many of the costs raised by Eisenhower. At worst, Eden believed, if military intervention failed, then the situation would be no worse than the current one. The 1930s provided the lesson that it was less risky to use force promptly against an aggressor than to wait, when the risks, and the costs of stopping the aggressor, increase. Eisenhower's focus on current issues and information caused his arguments and policy choices to exist in a different perceptual world than Eden's 1930's oriented world.

TYPES OF HISTORICAL ANALOGIES

Although the British relied heavily on the 1930's analogy, they, as well as the Americans, mentioned many other historical analogies during the Suez crisis. The same historical analogies were mentioned privately as well as publicly, which supports the argument that the public use of analogies for justification mirrors the private use of historical analogies to frame a crisis and to prescribe policy. The large number of historical analogies mentioned during the Suez crisis also supports the argument that the use of historical analogies tends to snowball: if one policy makers uses a historical analogy other policy makers mention other historical analogies.

Even though Eisenhower and Dulles were not inclined personally to use historical analogies, they and their advisors publicly and/or privately mentioned many historical analogies. Analogies they mentioned more than twice[124] include the following (with their lessons briefly outlined in parentheses):[125] World War I and II (Britain and France dragged the United States into a war, as Dulles feared would occur over Suez); Napoleon (it took Britain years to depose a dictator and, therefore, the British should be patient in attempts to overthrow Nasser); 1930s/Hitler/Mussolini (use force promptly against an aggressive dictator, which supported Eden's argument to use force promptly against Nasser); and the Iranian oil crisis settlement (recognize nationalization and form an international consortium to run the nationalized industry, although in the Iran case, the consortium deal only succeeded after Mossadegh was overthrown in an Anglo-American–backed coup. The lesson could be to overthrow Nasser in a coup and make a deal with his successor). The Americans also mentioned the following analogies, but only once or twice: the French colonial war in Algeria (a militarily, politically, and financially costly failed use of force); Admiral Darlan's deal with Eisenhower in World War II (Eisenhower made an unpopular deal with Darlan to retain Darlan in power in North Africa and President Roosevelt and Prime Minister Churchill supported his unpopular decision); Egypt 1952[126] (riots against British forces in Egypt, which argued against any long-term British intervention in Suez); Gibraltar (British base arrangement, which suggested a Suez settlement where the British controlled a strip of territory on either side of the canal); Hitler in 1945 (a desperate, cornered dictator is unpredictable, as Nasser might be if he was attacked); Indo-China in 1954 (Eden did not want to aid the French in 1954, even though the Americans pressed the British to intervene with them in Indo-China,[127] which implied that U.S. lack of support for the British in Suez was payback for the British lack of support of the Americans in Indo-China); Philippine independence (an agreement recognizing Philippine independence and sovereignty, while the United States retained bases in the Philippines, which suggested a similar British base agreement along the Suez Canal); the decline of Portugal and the Netherlands (if Britain did not forcefully defend its interests in the Middle East, Britain would decline just as Portugal and the Netherlands had); and British acts of nationalization at home (the British should not be outraged at Nasser's nationalization of the canal, since the British had nationalized some of their own industries).

British policy makers raised even more historical analogies than U.S. policy makers. The British mentioned, more than twice, the following historical analogies: the Iranian oil deal; the 1948 Berlin Blockade (respond promptly and aggressively to a dictator's brinkmanship); Egypt 1952; Guatemala (the United States used force to restore order and protect American lives and property, which, the British argued, they were trying to do the same for British nationals in Egypt); and the 1947 agreement over Trieste (the peace treaty with Italy created a free territory of Trieste occupied by the United States and Britain in the north, and Yugoslavia in the south, which suggested a possible deal over Suez, with continued British occupation of the canal). The British also mentioned the following historical analogies once or twice: the Buraimi oasis dispute, Cyprus and the settlement over Indo-China (the policy maker who mentioned these analogies did not explain the related lessons or policy prescriptions); Korea (a U.N. police action, which, the British argued, was a model for an international force to operate the Suez Canal); a settlement like Korea (the status quo was restored, which suggested a return to British control of the Suez Canal); Chinese volunteers intervening in Korea (the British feared Soviet volunteers fighting for Egypt in the case of a British intervention); Prime Minister Mossadegh of Iran (unreasonable, like Nasser, who should be removed, as Mossadegh was, through covert action); Russian tactics 1945–56 (aggressive diplomatic acts); and World War I (keep pace with events, which, Eden argued, suggested that the British must act promptly before the crisis spun out of control with possibly dire consequences, such as world war).

The British and the Americans tended to mention historical analogies with similar characteristics. In the Suez crisis, Eden, Macmillan, Lloyd, Eisenhower, and Dulles drew most of their historical analogies from their personal experiences from their time in government or events they had observed as adults. Personally experienced or observed events, in the form of the 1930's analogy, had the greatest impact on British policy. Eden was involved in, while Macmillan, Lloyd, Eisenhower, and Dulles observed, most of the 1930's crises. Learned analogies from history were, by far, the least common type of analogy and had the least impact on policy. Furthermore, most of the learned historical analogies had current referents, such as ongoing wars, treaties, or arrangements, such as the Algerian war, and the treaty between Spain and Britain over Gibraltar, which was still in effect in 1956.[128] Only Eisenhower's use of Napoleon as an analogy for Nasser and the U.S. recognition of Philippine independence were clearly historical analogies which had no continuing referent to the present situation over the canal. The less common an event, the more likely leaders will use learned history to find an analogy, since it is less likely that an analogous event will have occurred during their lifetimes. Suez was not unique, since Iran had nationalized its oil industry in 1951, as had Mexico in 1938. There had also existed previously other nationalistic, Third World leaders. Therefore, Eden and most of the other policy makers in the Suez crisis were able to find analogies to Suez in their own experiences or in observed history, the first places leaders look for analogies, and did not have to delve back into learned history for analogies.

Actors are also likely to retrieve recent historical analogies. Many of the historical analogies mentioned by the British and the Americans, such as the Algerian, Indo-Chinese, and Korean wars, were very recent, or even current, events, that had occurred within the past five or ten years and the decade of the 1930s was only some twenty years in the past. Decision makers also retrieved historical analogies involving their own states roughly two-to-one over analogies where their own state was not directly involved in the historical events.

The generational hypothesis is not a strong indicator of which historical analogies policy makers will use. Neither British nor American policy makers, as the generational theory would predict, used historical analogies from when they were in their twenties. This period occurred, for most of them, during World War I. The two British leaders, Eden (born 1897) and Macmillan (born 1894), who were in their late thirties and early forties during the 1930s, used the 1930's analogy, not a World War I analogy, as the generational hypothesis would predict. The strongest case for the generational hypothesis is Lloyd (born 1904), who turned thirty in 1934 and used the 1930's analogy to frame the Suez crisis. Although Eisenhower (born 1890) and Dulles (born 1888) were both in their twenties during World War I and their late forties during the 1930's crises, neither drew heavily on World War I or the 1930s as analogous to Suez. The generational model is flawed because it assumes that major events will occur when a future leader is in his twenties. However, major events destined to become master analogies, such as World War I, the 1930s/World War II, or Vietnam, occur at irregular intervals and dominate several generations. If leaders are old enough to be aware of major events when the events occur, they are likely to draw upon them as historical analogies later in life, regardless of whether the events occurred when they were in their late teens, twenties, thirties, forties or even later.

Actors usually retrieve historical analogies that share surface similarities with the current case. The most commonly used historical analogy in the Suez crisis, events from the 1930s, such as the remilitarization of the Rhineland and the invasion of Abyssinia, shared surface similarities with the Suez crisis. Both cases involved crises where Britain and France allied against a dictatorial regime that had broken international conventions and used aggressive diplomacy. Both cases also involved debates about whether and when to use military force. International organizations (the League of Nations and the United Nations) were also involved to varying degrees in both crises, which were both seen as concerning Britain's vital interests.

Despite surface similarities, however, the more policy makers think about deeper, causal links, the more differences between the analogy and the current case they will notice. The 1930s and Suez had vast causal differences. Nazi Germany and Mussolini's Italy were a threat because Germany and, to a lesser extent, Italy were industrialized, modern states. Nasser's Egypt was a Third World state that did not pose nearly as much of a conventional military threat against its neighbors or Britain as did the Germany and Italy of the 1930s. Unlike Nazi Germany, Egypt in 1956 posed an economic threat, that of controlling the canal and Britain's oil that flowed through the waterway. Britain, however, would have had far more support for a military operation to reopen the canal, if Egypt had blocked it, than Britain did when it intervened at a time when the canal was open and operating normally. Morally, Nasser's Egypt was not Nazi Germany, nor even Mussolini's Italy. Eisenhower was not Franklin Roosevelt. Eden was not Chamberlain, or Churchill, and the League of Nations was not the United Nations. However, no analogy is exactly the same as a current case and the more developed the analysis of any historical analogy, the greater the number and degree of differences that will be found. Decision makers who seek an exact historical analogy are seeking a mythical holy grail.

Decision makers are also more likely to retrieve foreign policy failures than successes. Eden and many of his colleagues believed the 1930s was a failure of British foreign policy. Similarly, Dulles, when he mentioned Korea as an analogy, raised a U.S. failure when he mentioned that the United States did not clearly state U.S. intentions in regard to a possible North Korean invasion. "On this subject the Secretary [Dulles] observed that in . . . Korea a clearer indication of our position and our intentions might have operated as a deterrent to the outbreak of hostilities."[129] Eisenhower also mentioned Algeria, referring to the costly French war, which, in 1956, appeared to be dragging on without end and appeared to be another foreign policy failure.

Eisenhower wrote Eden on October 31, "Indeed I have difficulty seeing any end whatsoever if all the Arabs should begin reacting somewhat as the North Africans have been operating against the French."[130]

Although events and people are linked, whether the current case is an event, such as the North Korean invasion of South Korea, or is dominated by an individual, such as Nasser's nationalization of the Suez Canal, has a strong influence on the type of historical analogies (event or person) that are selected. Not surprisingly, given that individuals map analogous cases, current events lead to the retrieval of historical events and current people lead to the retrieval of historical figures. When policy makers mentioned the nationalization of the Suez Canal, an event, they mentioned as analogies historical events, such as the invasions of Manchuria, Abyssinia, and Poland. However, when Nasser, an individual, was mentioned, the more commonly mentioned analogies were historical figures, such as Mussolini and Hitler.

Almost all the types of events and people retrieved as historical analogies were dramatic, vivid, and emotional events or historical figures with an emphasis on national security, war, or the threat of war. To Eden, the Suez crisis was a high-stakes, dramatic event, and he retrieved the 1930s, which was a series of high-stakes, dramatic events involving national security. Eisenhower, although he did not believe the Suez crisis was as dramatic as Eden, still retrieved vivid, emotional, and dramatic events as historical analogies, such as the world wars, the Algerian war, and the long struggle to topple Napoleon. The historical analogies were also well known, which supports the argument that historical analogies are a cognitive shortcut to avoid in-depth analysis and to simplify issues. If an actor had to explain an obscure historical analogy, it would defeat its purpose.

Policy makers in the Suez case retrieved historical analogies from recent personal experience or observation that involved their own states in major foreign policy failures that were superficially similar to the Suez case. The events also tended to be dramatic, vivid, emotional, and to involve national security issues. The generational model was not supported in a narrow sense. However, regardless of their ages at the time when the events occurred, policy makers retrieved major, traumatic, history-changing events, which were often master analogies, as analogous to current crises.

LESSONS

In the Suez case, the lessons from historical analogies fell into two categories: macro and micro. Macroanalogies, such as the 1930s, which was also a master analogy, and the Korean War, have broad, multifaceted meanings and refer to a cluster of events, acts, and phenomena tied to an interrelated set of lessons. Macroanalogies have a longer life because they support general principles, such as the 1930's lesson to use force promptly against aggressive dictators. This allows a range of actors to support the general lesson of the analogy yet disagree on specific tactics. When should force be used? What degree of force should be used? Was appeasement a total failure? Should any negotiation be conducted? Would the United States support the use of force by Britain? What role did the Soviet Union play? Microanalogies, such as Philippine independence or the British treaty for Gibraltar, refer to a specific crisis, treaty, or event and lead to narrow and specific lessons. Microanalogies have little, if any, room for interpretation to allow actors with slightly different views to support the same analogy. Also, given that microanalogies are specific, they are more likely to be rejected as invalid on the basis of small differences between the current crisis and the historical analogy than a more general analogy, which can gloss over small differences and focus on general similarities. For example, Eisenhower's comment that the Iranian oil crisis dealt with an extractive industry, oil, which decreased Iran's wealth, whereas the Suez Canal could only increase Egypt's wealth, was enough to scuttle any further mention of the Iran settlement in American policy-making meetings.[131]

Any historical analogy can provide a range of lessons. For example, the 1930s can provide the lesson that force must be used promptly to stop aggressive dictators, that Britain needed U.S. and Soviet aid to defeat a dictator, that time bought through negotiation can be used to arm and to ensure eventual victory, or a range of other possible, credible lessons. Some lessons were clearly inapplicable to Suez. For example, there was no question of enlisting Soviet military aid against Nasser. However, even after ruling out inapplicable lessons, there are still too many possible, credible lessons to predict which lessons actors will draw from a given historical analogy. However, if an analogy has a simple, commonly accepted interpretation, decision makers will usually use lessons based on that interpretation. For example, in 1956, the commonly accepted, British conservative interpretation of the 1930s was that appeasement was a failure and that if force had been used earlier against the Axis, then the Second World War would have been averted. This simple, broadly known and widely accepted interpretation formed the basis of Eden and his colleagues' decision that force should be used promptly against Nasser.

CONCLUSION

Historical analogies are used when policy makers are surprised by a dramatic, high-stakes event and must formulate policy under intense time pressures. Historical analogies serve as cognitive shortcuts to simplify complex issues. Policy makers tend to retrieve recent, dramatic, personally experienced or observed historical analogies that involved their own state in a foreign policy failure. These situational variables led to the use of historical analogies by British and American policy makers during the Suez crisis. Certain policy makers, however, are more likely, due to foreign policy experience, interest in history, personality, and leadership style, to use historical analogies. Eden, steeped in the Churchillian tradition of great oratory and the importance of history, was far more inclined to use historical analogies than Eisenhower, who was trained in military staff work. Furthermore, for Eden, the 1930s were an important and traumatic period in his life. Individual variables, such as the importance of the 1930s in Eden's life, explain why lessons from the 1930s dominated Eden's beliefs, perceptions, and policies during the Suez crisis, while Eisenhower and Dulles were not dominated by lessons from history. Situational variables caused Eisenhower and Dulles to use historical analogies during Suez, while individual variables ensured that they would not be dominated by these historical analogies.

The 1930's historical analogy had a significant influence on Eden and British perceptions of the crisis, including perceptions about the stakes, time, Nasser, goals, and policy options. Suez illustrates the power of historical analogies to blind policy makers to contrary evidence and to notice information selectively that supports their analogy-based beliefs. Eden decided to use force on the basis of the 1930's analogy and would not change his mind, even as current information, especially Eisenhower's opposition to the use of force and Egypt's willingness to negotiate and ability to operate the canal effectively, became clear. Eden's beliefs, firmly grounded on the lessons of the 1930s, still pointed toward the prompt use of force. Eden's belief that Nasser was irrational reinforced this tendency to use force promptly. Furthermore, the 1930s suggested that the United States would support a British military intervention, just as the Americans had, after a period of neutrality, supported the British in the 1930s and early 1940s. However, in part because he did not accept the 1930's analogy, Eisenhower did not support Eden's policy, which was based on, and justified by, the 1930's analogy. If Eden had justified his policy using other means, Eisenhower may have been more likely to support the British use of force. The British decision to intervene and the American decision not to use force also supports the argument that decisions about whether or not to use force are made early in a crisis and are rarely, if ever, changed.

NOTES

1. For simplicity's sake, J. F. Dulles will be referred to as Dulles, while Allen Dulles will be referred to by his full name.

2. Michael Fry suggested that if war erupted in the Middle East it would have confirmed Eisenhower's election. Who better to lead the United States during a war than General Eisenhower?

3. Outward Telegram from Commonwealth Relations Office, Eden to the Prime Ministers of Canada and South Africa, July 28, 1956, Nos. 1332 and 1333. Prime Minister Office (PREM) 11/1094 (116320). Also see Foreign Office to Washington, Sept. 8, 1956, Telegram No. 4102, PREM 11/1100 (116444); and Washington to Foreign Office, Sept. 9, 1956, No. 1838, PREM 11/1100 (116444).

4. Cabinet Minutes (C.M.) (56) 70th Conclusions, Minute 6, Suez Canal, PREM 11/1103 (116671); and Summary of Developments in Suez Situation, Sept.

20, 1956, State Dept., Summaries of Suez Crisis Situation, Sept.–Nov. 1956, DDE Library.

5. The CIA concluded the same thing. See Special National Intelligence Estimate, Number 30–5-56, "The Likelihood of a British-French Resort to Military Action Against Egypt in the Suez Crisis," Sept. 19, 1956, CIA, Intelligence Estimates, Sept.–Nov. 1956, DDE Library.

6. Record of a conversation between the (UK) Secretary of State and M. Pineau on August 24, 1956, PREM 11/1100 (116444).

7. The Conservatives had never supported nationalization at home and, in part, because of this history, reacted differently than Attlee's cabinet to the Iranian nationalization of their oil industry in 1951.

8. SCUA, which Dulles proposed at the Second London Conference, was to be a staff that would manage the canal's operation, collect fees and work with the Egyptians on behalf of states that used the canal. Kyle, *Suez*, pp. 242–255.

9. Eden argued that the lack of U.S. support for Britain's compellence strategy doomed the policy. Eisenhower and Dulles undercut the strategy publicly by stating that the United States did not support the use of force. Publicly removing the threat of U.S. support for British intervention, Eden believed, weakened the pressure on Nasser. However, the United States did not doom the compellence strategy. Nasser and Eden had diametrically opposed goals: Eden wanted to establish international control of the canal and to topple Nasser; Nasser wanted Egyptian control of the canal and, of course, to remain in power. Nasser would not be compelled to capitulate, even though he believed the British might use force, and Eden would not accept a compromise.

10. Outward Telegram from Commonwealth Relations Office, No. 304, July 31, 1956, PREM 11/1094 (116320).

11. C.M. 73 (56), Suez Canal, PREM 11/1103 (116671).

12. Minutes of the 295th Meeting of the NSC, Aug. 31, 1956, DDE Papers as President, AWF, NSC Series, Box 8: 295th Meeting, DDE Library.

13. Eisenhower to Nehru, Nov. 6, 1956, Communications with Prime Minister Nehru (Sept. 1956–Jan. 1957), DDE Papers as President, AWF, International Series: Nehru, DDE Library; and Memorandum of Conference with the President, Nov. 20, 1956 (dated Nov. 21, 1956), by Andrew J. Goodpaster, DDE Papers as President, AWF, DDE Diaries, Box 16: Staff Memos, DDE Library.

14. Eden to Eisenhower, Aug. 5, 1956, DDE Papers as President, AWF, International Series: Suez, DDE Library; and Eden to Eisenhower, Nov. 5, 1956, DDE Papers as President, AWF, International Series: Suez, DDE Library.

15. Eden, *Full Circle*, pp. 519–520.

16. Ibid., p. 556.

17. Horne, *Harold Macmillan*, Vol. I, p. 396.

18. Calvocoressi, "Egyptian Outlook," p. 35; Eden, *Full Circle*, pp. 519–520, 556, 578; Thornton, "The Trouble with Cousins," pp. 281–286; Andrew J. Goodpaster, Memo of Conference with the President, July 31, 1956, DDE Papers as President, AWF, DDE Diaries, Box 16, DDE Library; Khong, *Analogies at War*, p. 7; and Macmillan, *Riding the Storm*, p. 156.

19. Rothwell, *Anthony Eden*, p. 96.

20. Horne, *Harold Macmillan*, Vol. I, p. 396.

21. For example, Eisenhower wrote in his diary on August 8, that the Panama

Canal was "built as a national undertaking by the United States in terms of a bilateral treaty with Panama, the Suez Canal was built by an international group." Aug. 8, 1956, DDE Papers as President, AWF, DDE Diaries, Box 16, DDE Library. Also see Bi-Partisan Meeting, Aug. 12, 1956, DDE Papers as President, AWF, Legislative Meeting Series, Box 2: Legislative Leaders Meeting, 1956–57, DDE Library; "The President's News Conference of Aug. 1, 1956," *The Public Papers of the President's of the United States: Dwight D. Eisenhower, 1956*, p. 627; JFD, Memo of Conversation, Aug. 14 (dated Aug. 15) 1956, JFD Papers, White House Memoranda Series, Box 4: Meetings with the President, Aug.–Dec. 1956 (8), DDE Library; and PREM 11/1100 (116444), Washington to UK Foreign Office, Sept. 7, 1956, No. 1823.

22. Eisenhower to Eden, Sept. 8, 1956, DDE Papers as President, AWF, International Series: Box 19: Eden, July 18, 1956–Nov. 7, 1956, DDE Library.

23. Orbovich, "The Influence of Cognitive Style on National Security Decision Making," p. 9.

24. Aster, *Anthony Eden*, pp. 23, 50–54.

25. 292nd Meeting of the NSC, Aug. 9, 1956, Minutes, DDE Papers as President, AWF, NSC Series, Box 8: 292nd Meeting, DDE Library.

26. PREM 11/1100 (116444), "The U.N. and Suez," Note by the Foreign Secretary (Salisbury), Aug. 27, 1956, p. 285.

27. Draft Letter from Eisenhower to Eden, July 31, 1956, DDE Papers as President, AWF International Series: Box 19: Eden, July 18, 1956–Nov. 7, 1956, DDE Library.

28. Memo of Conversation with the President, Sept. 8, 1956, JFD Papers, White House Memo Series, Box 4: Meetings with the President, Aug.–Dec. 1956, Dept. of State, DDE Library.

29. "The Vice President said . . . The Philippine situation had once been confused by nationalistic attitudes on sovereignty, and we had made a deal recognizing Philippine sovereignty and our use of Philippine bases. Perhaps something similar could be worked out in the case of the Canal if old concepts were re-examined." "Sec. Wilson said nationalization was too familiar to cause excitement. The British had engaged in nationalization." "Sec. Wilson wondered whether the British and French, if they moved into the Canal area, would establish arrangements similar to those in Gibraltar." See Minutes of the 292nd meeting of the NSC, Aug. 9, 1956, DDE Papers as President, AWF, NSC Series, Box 8, DDE Library.

30. Memo of Conversation with the President, Oct. 2, 1956, Subject: Suez Canal, JFD Papers, White House Memo Series, Box 4: Meetings with the President, Aug.–Dec. 1956, (5), DDE Library. Also see Andrew J. Goodpaster, Memo of Conference with the President, July 31, 1956, DDE Papers as President, AWF, DDE Diaries, Box 16: July 1956, DDE Library.

31. Minutes of the 292nd Meeting of the NSC, August 9, 1956, DDE Papers as President, AWF, NSC Series, Box 8: 292nd Meeting, DDE Library. Also see Memorandum of Conversation with Sir Anthony Eden, Sept. 21, 1956, JFD Papers, Subject Series, Box 11: Misc. Papers, UK (1), DDE Library.

32. Eisenhower to Eden, Sept. 8, 1956, DDE Papers as President, AWF, International Series, Box 19: Eden, July 18, 1956–Nov. 7, 1956, DDE Library. Also see Washington to Foreign Office, Sept. 9, 1956, No. 1838, PREM 11/1100 (116444) (Sir R. Makins); Eisenhower to Captain E. E. Hazlett, No date, probably early November 1956, DDE Papers as President, AWF, DDE Diaries, Box 20: Nov. 1956,

Misc., DDE Library; and Eisenhower to Secretary of State, Dec. 12, 1956, Folder: President Eisenhower, Communications with J. F. Dulles, Dec. 1956, DDE Library.

33. Eden, *Full Circle*, p. 568.

34. Ibid., p. 556.

35. Ibid., pp. 480–481.

36. The French held similar views of Nasser. See Dept. of State Telegram from Paris (Dillon) to Sec. State, July 27, 1956, DDE Papers as President, AWF, Dulles-Herter Series, Box 5: J. F. Dulles, July 1956, DDE Library.

37. Trevelyan to Lloyd, Suez Canal: Egyptian Motives, Sept. 5, 1956, PREM 11/1100 (116444).

38. Bi-Partisan Meeting, Aug. 12, 1956, DDE Papers as President, AWF, Legislative Meetings Series, Box 2: Legislative Leaders Meetings 1956–57, DDE Library.

39. Calvocoressi, "Egyptian Outlook," p. 35.

40. Washington to Foreign Office, Sept. 8, 1956, No. 1829, PREM 11/1100 (116444).

41. Eisenhower to Anthony Eden, July 31, 1956, DDE Papers as President, AWF, International Series, Box 19: Eden, July 18, 1956–Nov. 7, 1956, DDE Library.

42. Eisenhower to Eden, reprinted in Dwight D. Eisenhower, *The White House Years, Waging Peace, 1956–1961*, Appendix C, pp. 666–668. The State Department supported Eisenhower's belief that Nasser could be negotiated with. See Summary of Developments in Suez Situation, Oct. 2 and 12, 1956, State Dept., Summaries of Suez Crisis Situation, Sept.–Nov. 1956, DDE Library. For Dulles's views, see Bi-Partisan Meeting, Aug. 12, 1956, DDE Papers as President, AWF, Legislative Meetings Series, Box 2: Legislative Leaders Meetings, 1956–57, DDE Library.

43. Andrew J. Goodpaster, Memo of Conference with the President, July 31, 1956, DDE Papers as President, AWF, DDE Diaries, Box 16: July 1956, DDE Library; and Dept. of State Telegram, Sept. 1, 1956 from London (Barbour) to Sec. of State, DDE Papers as President, AWF, Dulles-Herter Series, Box 6: J. F. Dulles, Sept. 1956 (2), DDE Library.

44. Foreign Office to Washington, Addressed to Washington, Telegram No. 4102 of Sept. 8, 1956, PREM 11/1100 (116444).

45. Pineau added that there was an Egyptian threat to Algeria, Morocco, and Tunisia. Record of Conversation between the Sec. of State, Mr. Dulles and M. Pineau in Mr. Dulles's apartment on Oct. 5, 1956, at 10:15 A.M. in New York, PREM 11/1102 (116639); and Outward Telegram from Commonwealth Relations Office to Commonwealth High Commissioners, Nov. 1, 1956, No. 435, PREM 11/1096 (116320).

46. Record of Conversation between the Sec. of State, Mr. Dulles and M. Pineau in Mr. Dulles's apartment on Oct. 5, 1956, at 10:15 A.M. in New York, PREM 11/1102 (116639). For Eden's views of time, see Eden, *Full Circle*, pp. 508–509, 517, 531.

47. Summary of Developments in Suez Situation, Sept. 4, 1956, State Dept., Summaries of Suez Crisis Situation, Sept.–Nov. 1956, DDE Library.

48. Eden, *Full Circle*, p. 561. Also see Record of Conversation between the Sec. of State, Mr. Dulles and M. Pineau in Mr. Dulles's apartment on Oct. 5, 1956, at 10:15 A.M. in New York, PREM 11/1102 (116639); and Minutes of the 292nd

Meeting of the NSC, Aug. 9, 1956, DDE Papers as President, AWF, NSC Series, Box 8: 292nd Meeting, DDE Library.

49. Eisenhower to Eden, Sept. 8, 1956, DDE Papers as President, AWF, International Series, Box 19: Eden, July 18, 1956–Nov. 7, 1956, DDE Library. Also see Bi-Partisan Legislative Meeting, Nov. 9, 1956, DDE Papers, AWF, Legislative Meeting Series, Box 2: Legislative Leaders Meetings, 1956–57, DDE Library.

50. Telegram from Commonwealth Relations Office, Eden to P.M. [Prime Minister of] Canada and South Africa, July 28, 1956, Nos. 1333 and 1332, PREM 11/1094 (116320).

51. Memorandum for the Secretary from Amb. Dillon, Sept. 19, 1956, "Estimate of Objective Sought by Macmillan and Salisbury," Folder: Memoranda prepared for the Sec. of State, July 1956–March 1957, JFD Papers, Subject Series, Box 7: Suez Problem, July–Nov. 1956–Feb.–March 1957 (6), DDE Library. Also see Memo of Conversation, Sept. 6, 1956, JFD Papers, Subject Series, Box 7: Suez Problem, July–Nov. 1956–Feb.–March 1957 (7), DDE Library.

52. Eden, *Fill Circle*, pp. 519–520. Also see Macmillan, *Riding the Storm*, p. 156.

53. C.M. 73 (56), Suez Canal, PREM 11/1103 (116671). Also see Memo of Conversation with Sir Anthony Eden, Sept. 21, 1956, JFD Papers, Subject Series, Box 11: Misc. Papers, UK (1), DDE Library.

54. Record of Conversation between the Sec. of State, Mr. Dulles and M. Pineau in Mr. Dulles's apartment on Oct. 5, 1956, at 10:15 A.M. in New York, PREM 11/1102 (116639).

55. Cabinet, confidential annex, C.M. (56) 63rd Conclusions, 6 Sept. 1956, PREM 11/1100 (116444).

56. C.M. 74 (56), Suez Canal, PREM 11/1103 (116671); Letter, Eisenhower to Eden, July 31, 1956, DDE Papers as President, AWF, International Series, Box 19: Eden, July 18, 1956–Nov. 7, 1956, DDE Library; and Letter from Eisenhower to Eden, Sept. 8, 1956, DDE Papers as President, AWF, International Series, Box 19: Eden, July 18, 1956–Nov. 7, 1956, DDE Library.

57. Record of Conversation between the Sec. of State for Commonwealth Relations and the Canadian High Commissioner, 15th August, 1956, PREM 11/1094 (116320).

58. Calvocoressi, "Egyptian Outlook," p. 35. Stated in a broadcast while he was prime minister, although no date is given for the broadcast.

59. *Parliamentary Debates*, Commons, 5th Series, vol. 558, (Sept. 13, 1956), cols. 298–299. Also see *Parliamentary Debates*, Commons, 5th Series, vol. 558 (Sept. 13, 1956), cols. 162, 279, 298–299.

60. DDE Papers as President, AWF, DDE Diaries, Box 16: July 1956, Andrew J. Goodpaster: Memo of Conference with the President, July 27, 1956, DDE Library.

61. 292nd meeting of the NSC, Aug. 9, 1956, Minutes, DDE Papers as President, AWF, NSC Series, Box 8: 292nd Meeting, p. 18, DDE Library.

62. Fisher, *Harold Macmillan*, p. 161.

63. Dept. of State Telegram from Paris (Dillon) to Sec. State, July 27, 1956, DDE Papers as President, AWF, Dulles-Herter Series, Box 5: J. F. Dulles, July 1956, DDE Library. Also see Dept. of State Telegram, July 27, 1956, from London (Fos-

ter) to Sec. of State, DDE Papers as President, AWF, Dulles-Herter Series, Box 5: J. F. Dulles, July 1956, DDE Library; and Memo for the Record, Dec. 12, 1956, JFD Papers, General Correspondence and Memoranda Series, Box 1: Memos of Conversations, General L-M (2), DDE Library.

64. Summary of Developments in Suez Situation, Sept. 11, 1956, State Dept., Summaries of Suez Crisis Situation, Sept.–Nov. 1956, DDE Library. For discussion of economic sanctions, see Record of a Conversation between the (UK) Secretary of State and M. Pineau on August 24, 1956, PREM 11/1100 (116444).

65. The United Nations and Suez, note by the Foreign Secretary, Britain, August 27, 1956, PREM 11/1100 (116444).

66. Dept. of State Telegram, July 27, 1956 from London (Foster) to Sec. State, DDE Papers as President, AWF, Dulles-Herter Series, Box 5: J. F. Dulles, July 1956, DDE Library; Memo for the Record, Dec. 12, 1956, JFD Papers, General Correspondence and Memoranda Series, Box 1: Memos of Conversations, General L-M (2), DDE Library; and Bi-Partisan Meeting, Aug. 12, 1956, DDE Papers as President, AWF, Legislative Meetings Series, Box 2: Legislative Leaders Meetings, 1956–57, DDE Library.

67. Eden, *Full Circle*, p. 477.

68. Lyon, *Eisenhower*, p. 695; Fisher, *Harold Macmillan*, pp. 162–163; and Horne, *Harold Macmillan*, Vol. I, pp. 398, 415.

69. C.M. 74 (56), Suez Canal, PREM 11/1103 (116671). Objectively, a compellence strategy should have been effective. In 1956, the British knew they could defeat Egypt on the battlefield and Egypt knew it too. However, compellence failed.

70. Outward Telegram from Commonwealth Relations Office, No. 304, July 31, 1956, PREM 11/1094 (116320).

71. Andrew J. Goodpaster, Memo of Conference with the President, July 31, 1956, DDE Papers as President, AWF, DDE Diaries, Box 16: July 1956, DDE Library. Also see Dept. of State Telegram, Sept. 1, 1956 from London (Barbour) to Sec. of State, DDE Papers as President, AWF, Dulles-Herter Series, Box 6: J. F. Dulles, Sept. 1956 (2), DDE Library.

72. Eisenhower to Eden, July 31, 1956, DDE Papers as President, AWF, International Series, Box 19: Eden, July 18, 1956–Nov. 7. 1956, DDE Library.

73. Horne, *Harold Macmillan*, p. 399; and Fisher, *Harold Macmillan*, p. 163.

74. From Foreign Office to Washington, No. 3931, Aug. 28, 1956, no name to Dulles, PREM 11/1100 (116444).

75. Minutes of the 295th Meeting of the NSC, Aug. 31, 1956, DDE Papers as President, AWF, NSC Series, Box 8: 295th Meeting, DDE Library.

76. C.M. 74 (56), Suez Canal, PREM 11/1103 (116671).

77. Summary of Developments in Suez Situation, Sept. 7, 1956, State Dept., Summaries of Suez Crisis Situation, Sept.–Nov. 1956, DDE Library.

78. Memorandum for the Secretary from Amb. Dillon, Sept. 19, 1956, "Estimate of Objective Sought by Macmillan and Salisbury," Folder: Memoranda prepared for the Sec. of State, July 1956–March 1957, JFD Papers, Subject Series, Box 7: Suez Problem, July—Nov. 1956—Feb.—March 1957 (6), DDE Library.

Like the British, the French position was that "Nasser must be made to yield—and in such a way as not to save his face in any substantial degree." See Summary of Developments in Suez Situation, Sept. 4, 1956, State Dept., Summaries of Suez Crisis Situation, Sept.–Nov. 1956, DDE Library.

79. Cabinet, confidential annex, C.M. (56) 63rd Conclusions, Sept. 6, 1956, PREM 11/1100 (116444).

80. "International Conference," E.C. (56) 21st Meeting, Minute 1, Aug. 24, 1956, PREM 11/1100 (116444).

81. The U.N. episode had an important side effect: it soured relations between Dulles and the British. Dulles, who favored the SCUA plan, was furious that Eden and Lloyd had taken the issue to the United Nations.

82. Record of a conversation between the (UK) Secretary of State and M. Pineau on Aug. 24, 1956, PREM 11/1100 (116444). Also see From Foreign Office (Eden) to New York, U.K. Delegation to United Nations, Pct. 13, 1956, No. 1172, PREM 11/1102, Subject File; Record of Conversation between the Sec. of State, Mr. Dulles and M. Pineau in Mr. Dulles's apartment on Oct. 5, 1956, at 10:15 A.M. in New York, PREM 11/1102, (116639); The United Nations and Suez, note by the Foreign Secretary, Britain, Aug. 27, 1956, PREM 11/1100 (116444); From Foreign Office to Washington, No. 3931, Aug. 28, 1956, no name to Dulles, PREM 11/1100 (116444); and Record of the Decisions taken at a meeting held on the evening of Sept. 5, 1956, between the (UK) Sec. of State, M. Mollet and M. Pineau, by Lloyd, PREM 11/1100 (116444).

83. Cabinet, confidential annex, C.M. (56) 63rd Conclusions, Sept. 6, 1956, PREM 11/1100 (116444).

84. C.M. (56) 70th Conclusions, Minute 6, Suez Canal, PREM 11/1103 (116671). Also see Summary of Developments in Suez Situation, Oct. 3, 1956, State Dept., Summaries of Suez Crisis Situation, Sept.–Nov. 1956, DDE Library; and From New York to Foreign Office, U.K. Delegation to the United Nations, Sir P. Dixon, Sept. 8, 1956, No. 650, PREM 11/1100 (116444).

85. Memo, Discussion at the 300th Meeting of the NSC, Oct. 12, 1956, DDE Papers as President, AWF, NSC Series, Box 8: 300th Meeting NSC, DDE Library.

86. Heikal, *The Cairo Documents*, pp. 168–169.

87. Mr. Fawzi (Egypt), 600th Meeting, Nov. 28, 1956, United Nations, *Official Records of the General Assembly 11th Session, Plenary Meetings*, vol. 1, p. 395, paragraph 51, 1956–1957 (NY).

88. Cabinet, Egypt Committee, Egypt: Military Planning, Memo by the Foreign Secretary, E.C. (56) 28, Aug. 20, 1956, PREM 11/1100 (116444).

89. Ibid.

90. C.M. 73 (56), Suez Canal, PREM 11/1103 (116671).

91. Cabinet, Egypt Committee, Egypt: Military Planning, Memo by the Foreign Secretary, E.C. (56) 28, Aug. 20, 1956, PREM 11/1100 (116444).

92. Kyle, *Suez*, p. 177.

93. Ibid., pp. 236, 238.

94. Ibid., p. 236.

95. Ibid., p. 235.

96. C.M. 74 (56), Suez Canal, PREM 11/1103 (116671).

97. Kyle, *Suez*, chapter 13.

98. Wyllie, *The Influence of British Arms*, p. 34.

99. Eisenhower to Eden, in Eisenhower, *The White House Years, Waging Peace 1956–1961*, Appendix C, pp. 666–668.

100. Eisenhower to Eden, July 31, 1956, DDE Papers as President, AWF, International Series, Box 19: Eden, July 18, 1956–Nov. 7, 1956, DDE Library.

101. Eisenhower to Eden, Sept. 8, 1956, DDE Papers as President, AWF, International Series, Box 19: DDE Diary, DDE Library; Cablegram to the Secretary of State, from DDE, Dec. 12, 1956, Folder: President Eisenhower, Communications

with J. F. Dulles (Dec. 1956), DDE Library; and State Dept., Intelligence Report, re: Sanctions against Egypt, 8–10–56, OSANSA, Special Assistant Series, Subject Subseries, Box 9: Suez Canal (Aug. 1956), DDE Library.

102. Bi-Partisan Meeting, Aug. 12, 1956, DDE Papers as President, AWF, Legislative Meetings Series, Box 2: Legislative Leaders Meetings, 1956–57, DDE Library. Also see Department of State Telegram, Hoover to U.S. Embassies in London, Paris and Middle East States, Sept. 2, 1956, Folder: Dept. of State, Telegrams from Sec. of State to various U.S. Embassies, (Sept.–Nov. 1956), JFD Papers, Chronological Series, DDE Library; DDE to Nehru, Sept. 15, 1956, DDE Papers as President, AWF, International Series: Nehru Communications with Prime Minister Nehru (Sept. 1956–Jan. 1957), DDE Library; and Eisenhower to King Saud, Sept. 18, 1956, Folder: President Eisenhower, Communications with King Saud (Sept. 1956–May 1957), DDE Library.

103. Record of Conversation between the Sec. of State, Mr. Dulles and M. Pineau in Mr. Dulles's apartment on Oct. 5, 1956, at 10:15 A.M. in New York, PREM 11/1102 (116639).

104. Memo of Conversation, Jan. 30, 1957, JFD Papers, General Correspondence and Memoranda Series, Box 1: Memos of Conversations, General, S (1), DDE Library.

105. Dec. 19, 1956, Communications with Prime Minister Nehru (Sept. 1956–Jan. 1957), DDE Papers as President, AWF, International Series: Nehru, DDE Library.

106. Andrew J. Goodpaster, Oral History, 1967, Interview 2 of 3, p. 81, DDE Library.

107. Andrew J. Goodpaster, Notes on Conversation with the President, July 28, 1956, DDE Papers as President, AWF, DDE Diaries, Box 16: July 1956, DDE Library.

108. Andrew J. Goodpaster, Memo of Conference with the President, July 30, 1956, DDE Papers as President, AWF, DDE Diaries, Box 16: July 1956, DDE Library. Makins reported on September 8 that "If Nasser obstructed the Canal and used force, they (the United States) would use it too." From Washington to Foreign Office, Sept. 9, 1956, No. 1838, PREM 11/1100 (116444).

109. Eisenhower to Anthony Eden, July 31, 1956, DDE Papers as President, AWF, International Series, Box 19: Eden, July 18, 1956–Nov. 7, 1956, DDE Library. Also see James Haggerty, Oral History, 1968, OH-91, p. 216, DDE Library; and Memo of Telephone Conversation with Amb. Lodge, Oct. 23, 1956, JFD Papers, Telephone Calls Series, Box 5: Memos of Telephone Conversations, General, Oct. 1–Dec. 29, 1956 (4), DDE Library.

110. JFD Papers, Chronological Series, Oct. 1956 (2), DDE Library; Memo of Conversation with the President, Oct. 2, 1956, Subject: Suez Canal, JFD Papers, White House Memo Series, Box 4: Meetings with the President, Aug.–Dec. 1956, (5), DDE Library; and Andrew J. Goodpaster, Memo of Conference with the President, Oct. 8, 1956, Memos of Conferences with the President, March 1956–April 1957, DDE Library.

111. Bi-Partisan Meeting, Aug. 12, 1956, DDE Papers as President, AWF, Legislative Meetings Series, Box 2: Legislative Leaders Meetings, 1956–57, DDE Library.

112. Eisenhower to Eden, in Eisenhower, *The White House Years, Waging Peace, 1956–1961*, Appendix C, pp. 666–668.

113. Memo of Conference with the President, Oct. 30, 1956, JFD Papers, White House Memo Series, Box 4: Meetings with the President, Aug.–Dec. 1956 (3), DDE Library.

114. From Washington to Foreign Office, Sir. H. Caccia, Nov. 9, 1956, No. 2277. PREM 11/1106 (116444).

115. Andrew J. Goodpaster, Oral History, 1967, Interview 2 of 3, p. 81, DDE Library.

116. Andrew J. Goodpaster, Oral History, OH-378, Jan. 16, 1978, Interview 4, pp. 111–112, DDE Library.

117. Eisenhower to Eden, July 31, 1956, DDE Papers as President, AWF, International Series, Box 19: Eden, July 18, 1956–Nov. 7, 1956, DDE Library. Also see Bi-Partisan Meeting, Aug. 12, 1956, DDE Papers as President, AWF, Legislative Meetings Series, Box 2: Legislative Leaders Meetings, 1956–57, DDE Library.

118. Andrew J. Goodpaster, Memo of Conference with the President, July 31, 1956, DDE Papers as President, AWF, DDE Diaries, Box 16: July 1956, DDE Library.

119. Sir Roger Makins, Washington to Foreign Office, Sept. 9, 1956, No. 1838, PREM 11/1100 (116444).

120. Eisenhower to Eden, in Eisenhower, *The White House Years, Waging Peace, 1956–1961*, Appendix C, pp. 666–668.

121. Kyle, *Suez*, pp. 159–160; and Fisher, *Harold Macmillan*, p. 163.

122. Ashton, "Macmillan and the Middle East," p. 41.

123. Horne, *Harold Macmillan*, Vol. I, pp. 399, 418, 425.

124. The use of an analogy more than twice is a critical threshold because if an analogy is only mentioned once, or once by an actor and then repeated by another actor to rebut the analogy's application to the current case, the analogy probably did not influence policy. However, if an analogy was mentioned more than twice, it usually influenced policy making.

125. It is sometimes difficult to determine the lesson an individual derived from a historical analogy. In many cases a historical analogy is mentioned with no statement of its relevance to the current case nor to what lesson the actor drew from the analogy.

126. In January 1952, the British ordered the surrender of an Egyptian police barracks at Ismailia. The police did not surrender and, on the orders of the Egyptian minister of the interior, the Egyptian police fought the British. The Egyptians surrendered after losing forty-six dead. Mobs took to the streets the next day, attacking Britons and other foreigners, and their property, killing twenty people, including eleven Britons. Kyle, *Suez*, pp. 40–41.

127. Rothwell, *Anthony Eden*, p. 141; and Lyon, *Eisenhower*, p. 606.

128. Imperialism and colonialism were also mentioned often. However, they are extrapolations from past Anglo-French behavior. The decline of Portugal and the Netherlands are coded as historical analogies, because by 1956 their decline from imperial greatness was largely in the past, although Portugal still held colonies.

129. Memo for the Record, Conversation Monday Aug. 6, 1956 in the President's Office, re: Egypt, Suez, OSANSA File, Special Assistant Series, Chronological Subseries, Box 4: Aug. 1956 (1), DDE Library.

130. Eisenhower to Eden, Oct. 31, 1956, DDE Papers as President, AWF, International Series, Box 19: Eden, July 18, 1956–Nov. 7, 1956, (6), DDE Library.

131. Andrew J. Goodpaster: Memo of Conference with the President, July 27, 1956, DDE Papers as President, AWF, DDE Diaries, Box 16: July 1956, DDE Library.

6

Indirect Aggression:
Lebanon and Jordan

In 1958, when the British intervened militarily in Jordan and the Americans intervened militarily in Lebanon, historical information significantly influenced their policy decisions. The Suez analogy cast a pall over British decision making, while historical analogies clustered around incidents of indirect aggression strongly influenced American decision making. Historical information affected perceptions of time, the stakes, policy options, and the perceived rationality of adversaries, as well as serving to justify the use of force.

Macmillan, Eisenhower, and their colleagues believed that the pro-Nasser forces, who they credited with the 1958 Iraqi coup, and believed were now threatening Lebanon and Jordan, were irrational. Therefore, Macmillan and Eisenhower decided early in the crisis to use force. Unlike the British and Americans in Korea, or the British in Suez, however, they used force only as a last resort in Jordan and Lebanon, after other means had been tried and failed. The decision was made early, but it was only implemented two months later.

The first section of this chapter outlines the major events leading to the British and American military interventions, as well as the goals of the two intervening states. The next section discusses the influence historical analogies and information had on British and American policy decisions and is followed by a discussion of the types of historical analogies used during the crisis and the conditions that led to their use. Then the lessons British and American decision makers draw from history are analyzed. The conclusion summarizes the major points raised in the chapter.

THREE CRISES AND AMERICAN AND BRITISH GOALS

The Lebanon/Jordan case can be divided into three crises during May, June, and July 1958. If viewed as a set—the American and to a lesser degree the British responses to these crises—support an escalation model. The only difference between an escalation model and what actually occurred was that the decision to use military force, if required, was made early in the crisis, in May, and was never changed.

Civil war erupted in Lebanon in May 1958. On May 13 President Camille Chamoun of Lebanon separately asked the ambassadors from the United States, Britain, and France how their states would reply if he requested military intervention. Eisenhower, Dulles, Prime Minister Macmillan, and Foreign Secretary Lloyd quickly decided that Lebanon was worth the use of force, but only as a last resort after other means had failed. There was no escalation in their thinking during the remainder of the crisis. During the following months, when the threat appeared to increase, on June 15 and July 14, the British and Americans prepared to intervene. When the perceived threat receded, other means were pursued, although the initial May decision to use force if required remained the foundation of British and American policy. As the May crisis passed, Eisenhower and Macmillan preferred to use economic and military aid and to let regional (such as the Arab League) or international (such as the United Nations) organizations attempt to devise a settlement, rather than use force. However, force was always reserved as a last resort if other means failed.

In June the crisis again flared and Chamoun asked the same question of the three ambassadors as he had asked in May. Again, all three said their countries would intervene and, again, the crisis rapidly passed. On July 14 suspected pan-Arab, pro-Nasser army officers overthrew King Faisal and the government of Iraq. Lebanon asked for immediate American, British, and French military intervention. Jordan first asked for U.S. intervention and then, on July 16, asked the British to intervene militarily. The United States and Britain responded quickly; they implemented their May decision, that force had become the preferred option because other means had failed. Lebanon, Jordan, and the Middle East appeared to be on the brink of falling to pro-Nasser forces. The United States intervened militarily in Lebanon, and the British sent forces to Jordan.

The Americans and British pursued consistent goals throughout the three crises of 1958. Although both nations wanted to protect the lives of their citizens, the primary U.S. goal was for Chamoun to complete his term and then step down in accordance with the Lebanese constitution, which forbade a president succeeding himself. The United States also sought to maintain an independent and stable Lebanon against the threat posed by the rebels in the civil war, as well as against the perceived threat from pro-Nasser forces, primarily aided by the United Arab Republic (UAR–Syria and Egypt), in the region. The British wanted to bolster their credibility in the Middle East by aiding their ally, Jordan, and to preserve Jordan's territorial integrity against internal threats, which might lead to the dismemberment of their client state by Syria and by Israel, who, the British and Americans feared, might seize the West Bank. The British also wanted to ensure Jordan's political independence from pro-Nasser factions in the region.

THE MAY DECISION

On May 13 Chamoun asked the British, American, and French ambassadors how their states would reply if he requested military intervention within forty-eight hours. Although the official records that are available at the Eisenhower Library are incomplete, due to the deletion of classified portions, there is evidence that for the first twenty-four hours of the May crisis the United States and Britain planned to use military force in Lebanon. At a May 13 meeting just after Chamoun made his request, Eisenhower and Dulles discussed military intervention and, while Dulles focused on the difficulties of intervention, Eisenhower leaned toward using force.

The Secretary [Dulles] and the President discussed generally the problems involved in United States intervention. . . . The President thought it would be a great mistake if the French would participate in such a military intervention. . . . The President observed that it was well to consider such problems [of intervention], but that we also had to take into account the apparently much larger problems which would arise if the Lebanese needed our intervention and we did not respond. The Secretary [Dulles] agreed, and said he had been giving thought to the mission of any forces which might be sent in.

Dulles said, "Perhaps our dispatch [of troops] should be on the basis of protecting, at the request of the Lebanese Government, lives and property of United States citizens, and of assisting the Lebanese Government in connection with its military program." Dulles, however, argued that the Eisenhower Doctrine could not be invoked, "since it would entail a finding that the United Arab Republic had attacked Lebanon and that the United Arab Republic was under the control of international communism." After discussion of these factors, Eisenhower still leaned toward the use of force and asked how U.S. military interventions in Central America had been justified in the days of so-called "gun-boat" diplomacy. Dulles, still focused on the negative aspects of using force, responded, "that this policy in the world today no longer represented an acceptable alternative, unless the forces went in at the invitation of the host government." Dulles then outlined the difficulties of intervening, including: the difficulty of withdrawal; the creation of "a wave of anti-Western feeling in the Arab world comparable to that associated with the British and French military operation against Egypt [Suez]"; oil pipelines might be cut; the canal might be closed; and the possible collapse of friendly governments in Jordan and Iraq.

While Dulles focused on the possible costs of intervention, Eisenhower was thinking of using force. Eisenhower said that if the United States used force, he would have U.S. ambassadors in the area stress that "we had no intent other than helping a friendly government to maintain its sovereignty and independence." Eisenhower assumed the United States would use force if invited to do so and if the situation deteriorated. He observed, "it was difficult to see how we could afford not to respond to a properly worded request by President Chamoun and the Lebanese Government if circumstances clearly showed that our aid was essential for the preservation of Lebanese independence." Eisenhower also confined the discussion at the May 13 meeting to the use of force and did not discuss other methods, such as diplomacy and economic or military aid. Eisenhower wanted to be ready to use force, and he concluded "by saying that he thought it was right to let the Lebanese know that we would help them in case it should become necessary. He thought the military should immediately issue a warning order to our forces and put them on the alert."[1] Eisenhower was not just talking. By May 15 the U.S. Navy had doubled its amphibious forces in the Mediterranean and airborne units were alerted.[2] The Americans were ready to use force in Lebanon.

The British Cabinet also met on May 13 to discuss Chamoun's request and agreed to use military force, if required. The British believed that if Lebanon fell, Iraq and Jordan would probably follow.[3] "The [British] Cabinet had decided that the United Kingdom should respond favorably, if the United States agreed . . . although they assumed that the major responsibility would be America [sic]."[4] Illustrating their resolve to use force, on the same day as Chamoun's request, May 13, Eisenhower and Macmillan agreed to joint talks to plan an Anglo-American military intervention in Lebanon. As early as October 1957 the British and American militaries had outlined the forces available for intervention in Lebanon and/or Jordan. The United States, however, was unwilling to commit itself to detailed planning for intervention until the May crisis, when, having decided to use force, American policy makers began to make concrete plans with the British.[5] On May 22 British and American officers met on Cyprus to develop a joint plan to intervene in Lebanon, which was the basis of the plan used in the July 15 intervention.[6]

The planning was supported by American and British military action. On May 15 "the President indicated agreement that the Marines should start moving eastward. . . . Secretary Dulles suggested that U.S forces could operate with two missions—the protection of life and property, and the provision of assistance to the Lebanese Army. . . . The President thought we should send out warning orders to our forces, including the three battle groups in Europe, the Marines and the carriers so as to get them into better positions."[7] The British also moved forces to prepare to intervene. This Anglo-American planning and the movement of forces in May shows that the Americans and British seriously considered using military force in Lebanon if the situation worsened. The planning was for intervention, not deterrence. Neither the British nor the Americans discussed the military preparations as part of a deterrent strategy against anti-Western forces in the Middle East. Military forces would be ready to use, if required.

WHY MILITARY FORCE?

In terms of a cost-benefit analysis, for the British and the Americans, the Lebanon/Jordan crisis offered an opportunity to intervene militarily with minimal cost and risk while supporting allies and appearing forceful and resolute. In 1958 the United States and Britain were concerned with the spread of Arab nationalism, Nasserism, and of Soviet influence in the Middle East. The British and Americans were also invited to intervene by legal governments with which they had well-established political and economic ties. The U.S. embassy in Beirut was the largest in the Middle East. The Lebanese government had also been the only government in the region to support the Eisenhower Doctrine, which pledged U.S. aid to Middle Eastern governments fighting Communist forces who were receiving foreign support. The British had held a mandate over Transjordan after the First World War and still had strong political, social, and economic ties with Jordan. Furthermore, Pakistan, Turkey, Iran, Iraq, and Jordan all wanted the United States and Britain to intervene. In addition, assuming that the Soviets would not counterintervene, which seemed a remote possibility, military intervention would show nationalistic Arabs that the Soviets would not fight for them. British and American credibility, therefore, rested on supporting Lebanon and Jordan. The British also hoped that the intervention would be part of a general program, conducted in tandem with the United States, to buttress Western influence in the region. Eisenhower, however, later dashed their hopes.[8]

Even though all of these factors influenced British and American decision making, historical information also influenced their decision making significantly, although it was balanced with current information far more than during British decision making about Suez, or U.S. and U.K. decision making about Korea. No one knew what would happen if Lebanon and Jordan were left to deal with their own crises without British and American intervention. Eisenhower, Macmillan, and their advisors, however, used historical analogies, primarily the 1930s, Suez, and a cluster of analogies around indirect aggression, to clarify and to frame the crisis, prescribe policy, and to go beyond the information available to forecast what might happen if they used force or if they did not use force. Lebanon was threatened by ill-defined forces that the Americans and British had difficulty identifying. Historical analogies simplified and clarified the crisis.

During the May 1958 Lebanon crisis, but also during the crises in June and July, American and British policy makers mentioned the same historical analogies in private as in public, further supporting the argument that public use of historical information reflects its private use. American policy makers, especially Eisenhower, repeatedly mentioned historical analogies clustered around cases of indirect aggression (civil wars fueled by support from outside the state), which were superficially similar to the 1958 Lebanon crisis. On July 15, for example, Eisenhower mentioned that Lebanon and Jordan were similar to the "pattern of conquest" of 1945–50: "This involves taking over a nation by means of indirect aggression; that is, under the cover of a fomented civil strife the purpose is to put into domestic control those whose real loyalty is to the aggressor."[9] American decision makers also mentioned Greece 1947 (Yugoslavia aided the rebels, the United States and Britain aided the government), Czechoslovakia 1948 (Soviet-backed coup), China 1949 (civil war with the Soviets supplying the Communists and the United States, in a failed policy, aiding the Nationalists), Indo-China 1950 (French fought Soviet-supported rebels and were defeated), and Korea 1950 (U.S. intervention halted a Soviet-backed North Korean invasion).

Eisenhower and Dulles perceived the indirect aggression analogies as valid to frame Lebanon's civil war. The analogies influenced perceptions of the adversary, current information, costs, policy options, and the limits of the use of force. The indirect aggression analogies simplified the Lebanon crisis, especially by clarifying the actors involved. The rebels in Greece and China had been supplied by the Soviets, and Czechoslovakia had fallen to a Soviet-supported coup. The analogy was clear: the Iraqi coup was backed by the Soviets and by Nasser, and the rebels in Lebanon were supplied and supported from outside Lebanon, even though there was little evidence of UAR or Soviet infiltration of arms or men into Lebanon. Even so, the influence of the analogy was strong. On June 26 Dulles said, "In the case of Lebanon there was no doubt whatever as to the activities of the UAR."[10] On July 14 Dulles argued that the Iraqi coup "looks like a plot by Nasser to take over the whole thing [the whole Middle East]."[11] Both statements were incorrect, but in the confusion of the U.S. intelligence failure to foresee, let alone forecast, or even provide analysis of the Iraqi coup immediately after the fact, the Americans used historical analogies to make sense of the situation. This was a case where a historical analogy had an irrational, although not an entirely unjustified, influence on the decision-making process. As with Eden's use of the 1930's analogy during the Suez crisis, the indirect aggression analogies blinded Eisenhower and Dulles to contradictory, current information. Once a historical analogy is accepted it forms a comprehensive framework that is resistant to change even in the face of current information that contradicts the historically based framework. For example, the U.N.

Observer Group in Lebanon (UNOGIL) found little, if any, evidence of UAR infiltration of men or arms into Lebanon, yet UNOGIL's report did nothing to change the minds of U.S. decision makers about who they believed was causing the strife in Lebanon.[12]

The indirect aggression analogies that Eisenhower relied on highlighted the costs of losing an ally to indirect aggression. The loss of China had ignited a firestorm of domestic criticism of Truman and helped Eisenhower win the White House. The Czechoslovakian coup suggested that a state could be "lost" quickly through inaction. Korea, Greece, and Indo-China suggested that states of minor importance in the global balance of power could assume great significance in the Cold War. Lebanon may be just as important as Korea, Greece, and Indo-China were believed to have been.

Even while highlighting the costs of losing an ally, the indirect aggression analogies did not provide a single, clear policy prescription. Greece had been "saved" through economic and military aid, while Korea had been "saved" through the use of military force, although Eisenhower had been elected, in part, by promising to end the Korean War. China and Czechoslovakia had been "lost," even though China had received substantial U.S. military and economic aid. In the face of multiple policy prescriptions, some of which contradicted each other, Eisenhower used different historical analogies in succession during the crisis. In May and June 1958 Eisenhower, focusing on the Greece analogy, relied on economic and military aid to Lebanon, which fit the escalation model of a state providing economic and military aid before using force. In Greece, military and economic aid succeeded, which negated the need to use military force. However, when the Iraqi coup increased the perceived level of threat to Lebanon by the UAR, now unrestrained by Iraq, Eisenhower followed the Korean analogy and promptly used military force.

Although Eisenhower decided to use force, prudence, especially in relation to where, and to what degree, to use force were clearly etched in the historical analogies he selected. In the Korean analogy, the Americans invaded North Korea and paid the price when the Chinese intervened militarily. In the China analogy, a point was reached when it was time to abandon the mainland and concentrate on Taiwan. Eisenhower followed the lessons from Korea and China in the Lebanon/Jordan case. When the United States finally intervened militarily in Lebanon, he kept the intervention limited in size and did not intervene in Jordan, nor did he attempt to invade Iraq and restore the king. In June the Americans discussed the possibility of landing in Tripoli, as well as Beirut, but dropped the idea of expanding the operation because it would make withdrawal more difficult.[13] After the landing, on July 21, Eisenhower cancelled plans to embark the 101st Airborne and 2nd Marine Divisions for transport to Lebanon,[14] and on July 22 he overruled stationing troops throughout Lebanon.[15] Eisenhower and Dulles also limited the length of time the operation lasted. On

July 19, for example, Dulles said that he did not want a long-term operation.[16]

If the indirect aggression analogies influenced U.S. policy, the use of other
historical analogies should have led to different policies. The British offer
evidence that different historical analogies did in fact lead to different policies. The British, who did not draw upon the indirect aggression analogies
and the prudence they prescribed, were far more willing than the Americans
to consider a larger operation on a scale similar to Suez and the 1930s, cases
on which the British relied as analogies. In fact, Macmillan expanded the
original intervention from Lebanon to Jordan by convincing King Hussein
of Jordan to ask for British military intervention in the first place.[17] Macmillan also wanted to discuss contingency plans to intervene with the Americans in most of the Middle East. Eisenhower, however, relying on the Korea
and China analogies, refused to agree to any operations outside Lebanon.[18]
Unable to secure American participation in any interventions outside of Lebanon, the British would intervene alone in Jordan.

The Americans also mentioned the Suez analogy many times. The United
States had opposed Anglo-French intervention in 1956 and had reaped the
respect and gratitude of the Arabs for their stance. The Suez analogy supported those who warned against intervention because the use of force
might be a costly failure, as it had been for the British and French. The
Suez analogy contributed to U.S. caution in May and June, although the
July Iraqi coup overcame U.S. caution caused, in part, by the Suez analogy.
The indirect aggression analogies, however, predominated. Eisenhower
feared the spread of Nasserism and Soviet influence if the United States did
not intervene militarily. By July 1958 this fear overcame the caution prescribed by the Suez analogy. American policy makers also mentioned gun-
boat diplomacy (the use of force is outdated), Prohibition (an unpopular
policy that failed), Operation Torch 1942 (Anglo-American cooperation),
Hungary 1956 (the Soviets intervened militarily in an allied state and world
opinion condemned them), and Soviet aid to Syria (massive military and
economic aid to bolster an ally) only once or twice, with no apparent influence on policy.

Even though indirect aggression historical analogies and Suez influenced
U.S. policy, lessons from history had a greater influence on British decision
making than it had on American decision making during the Leba-
non/Jordan crises. The analogy to Suez dominated British policy making
about Lebanon and Jordan. Several questions, such as about the causes of
the Lebanese civil war, the source of the threat to Hussein, Nasser's role, if
any, and about the relative pros and cons of different methods of responding
to the crisis, were assumed to be obvious, on the basis of the Suez analogy,
or ignored, if the Suez analogy did not emphasize that issue. Nasser and
the Soviets were believed to be behind the Lebanese civil war and the threat
to King Hussein, just as Eden had believed that Nasser had been a Soviet

lackey. The British had believed that Nasser had been too irrational to negotiate with in 1956 and, the Suez analogy suggested, negotiation and diplomacy would be futile again in 1958; force would have to be used. The British also believed that the stakes were high in Jordan. Failure could lead to the fall of the British government, just as Eden's government had fallen after Suez, as well as financial catastrophe, as had loomed over Britain after Suez. Macmillan also drew from Suez that the longer the crisis dragged on, the weaker Britain's position would become. Delay had crippled the military operation against Egypt and Macmillan was determined not to make the same mistake as Eden had made. On the basis of the Suez analogy, Macmillan's cabinet also believed that Britain must not use force in the Middle East without U.S. support. Failure to secure American support, the British believed, had crippled the British military intervention in Suez. Macmillan focused on ensuring U.S. support and was upset when the Americans would not intervene with the British in Jordan. On July 14, in a telephone call with Eisenhower, Macmillan said that by intervening in Lebanon alone, Eisenhower was "pulling a Suez" on him by not supporting the British in Jordan.[19]

The British reliance on the Suez analogy also played a significant role in the parliamentary debate about policy toward Lebanon and Jordan. Macmillan spent much of his time publicly defending charges that his government was committing another Suez. On June 25 an Opposition MP asked in the House, "Can he [Duncan Sandys, the Minister of Defence] give a definite assurance that these troops . . . will not be used in another Suez venture in the [sic] Lebanon?" Lloyd was asked in the House, "Has the right hon. and learned Gentleman seen reports . . . that all the Western residents in the [sic] Lebanon are most anxious that there should be no intervention because they do not desire to share the fate of the British in Egypt eighteen months ago?"[20] The Labour opposition drew the lesson from Suez that Britain must not use force in the Middle East, even if the prime minister offered assurances that the United States supported British intervention. During Suez, Eden had assured Parliament that he had U.S. support, yet, when he intervened in Egypt, U.S. opposition was fierce. Labour, drawing on the Suez analogy, feared Macmillan might be another Eden. However, Macmillan masterfully turned the use of the Suez analogy against his domestic opponents by arguing for the need for U.S. support and, once he secured U.S. support to intervene militarily in Jordan, argued, on the basis of the Suez analogy, that the intervention would succeed. The flaw in Suez had been fixed: U.S. support was assured.

The Spanish Civil War (the British did not aid either side and should not aid either side in the Lebanese conflict) and Hungary 1956 (Soviets intervened against an ally and were condemned) were also mentioned as analogous to Lebanon and Jordan, although far less often than Suez and with no apparent influence on British policy.

The British and the Americans mentioned the 1930's analogy during the Lebanon/Jordan crisis many times. They compared Lebanon/Jordan to the September 1938 Munich Conference, as well as to Chamberlain, Hitler, and to pan-Germanism, which was compared to Nasser's pan-Arabism, with both seen as threats to Western interests. For example, Sir Harold Caccia said Nasser was following in Hitler's footsteps.[21] Dulles said, "Nasser, like Hitler before him, has the power to excite emotions and enthusiasm."[22] At a July 1 meeting, "The Secretary [Dulles] compared Nasser and his pan-Arabism with Hitler's pan-Germanism. Nasser saw an opportunity for advancing the grandeur of Egypt and of setting himself up as the Arab 'hero' with the West in his clutches."[23] The 1930's analogy highlighted the gravity and high stakes of the Lebanon/Jordan crisis, since the 1930s led to a world war.

The analogy also suggested that time was against the West in Lebanon/Jordan. In the 1930s, as time passed, the Axis powers increased their diplomatic, economic, and military strength through territorial expansion, and the British and the Americans feared that as time passed Nasser's forces would also grow stronger, most likely by gaining support in other Arab states. For example, Eisenhower said, "In the 1930s the members of the League of Nations became indifferent to direct and indirect aggression in Europe, Asia and Africa. The result was to strengthen and stimulate aggressive forces that made World War II inevitable. The United States is determined that that history shall not now be repeated."[24]

The British and Americans viewed Hitler as irrational, untrustworthy, and someone who understood only the use of force. They, therefore, believed that Nasser, who they said was behind the Iraqi coup and the threat against Jordan and Lebanon, was just as ruthless and willing to use force as Hitler had been. The Suez analogy reinforced this lesson. If the West did not use force, Nasser's forces would only grow stronger. Nasser had triumphed at Suez and now, two years later, he appeared to have toppled the king of Iraq and to be threatening Lebanon and Jordan. On July 15 Eisenhower said, "We share with the Government of Lebanon the view that these events in Iraq demonstrate a ruthlessness of aggressive purpose which tiny Lebanon cannot combat without further evidence of support from other friendly nations."[25] Later research and analysis would find that the claim that the coup in Iraq posed a threat to Lebanon was false. However, partly based upon this view of the lack of rationality of their adversaries, the Americans and British decided that negotiation and diplomacy could not succeed and that force would instead have to be used.

However, just as in the Suez case, Eisenhower separated the 1930's analogy into two parts. Eisenhower accepted that Nasser, through his allies in Lebanon, Jordan, and Iraq, was a threat similar to Mussolini or Hitler, just as he had in 1956. Similarly as he had done in 1956, Eisenhower rejected the prescription that force would have to be used promptly. In May, he decided to use force, but only if economic and military aid, coupled with diplomacy, failed. In June, these other means again staved off the need to intervene militarily, and it was not until the July crisis that Eisenhower concluded that nonmilitary means had failed and military force would have to be used. Macmillan, on the other hand, accepted the entire 1930's analogy and favored the prescribed policy option: the prompt use of military force. He therefore favored intervening in May, June, and July.

On the basis of the Suez and the 1930's analogies, as well as the cluster of analogies around indirect aggression, U.S. and U.K. policy makers perceived the stakes in Lebanon and Jordan as being very high. Macmillan and Eisenhower were therefore willing to accept the potential costs and risks of intervening militarily in Lebanon and Jordan. The Americans were concerned enough about the potential effects of an American and/or British military intervention that both Eisenhower and Dulles said they had serious reservations about the need for the operation and its desirability. In a July 16 telephone call, Macmillan and Dulles "agreed the whole thing is terrible."[26] Macmillan said, "There are dangers in this action. If there were not dangers, it would not have been so difficult to make this decision."[27] Eisenhower thought intervention might worsen violence in Lebanon and confirm the charges of Arab nationalists who alleged U.S. interference in Arab domestic affairs. At a July 21 meeting Eisenhower said, "if we started pushing around too much we would shortly have the whole Arab world against us."[28] Dulles telegrammed the U.S. ambassador in Beirut, "Moreover, intervention could and probably would lead to solidification of opposition throughout [the] Muslim world not only to Christians in Lebanon but to the West in general. We have also noted growing indication that allied military intervention would be viewed with repugnance even by many Lebanese Christians."[29] On June 18 Dulles said, "If we go in it will turn Arab sentiment against us."[30] Concern about the Arab reaction provided a strong argument to keep the French and British, with their imperial pasts, out of Lebanon. "Foster Dulles felt that if we should send troops into Lebanon there would be a major adverse reaction in the Middle East," pipelines across Syria would probably be blown up, the Suez Canal might be blocked, and it might make it impossible for the governments of Iraq and Jordan to cooperate with the West.[31] The Americans also were concerned about how their forces would withdraw. "While we will probably be able through the presence of our forces to hold Lebanon's independence, we would be drawn into the area and it is not clear how we would withdraw."[32] These were the same worries they had expressed to the British during Suez. Dulles said, "We don't want to get bogged down like the British in Suez and have to pull out."[33] However, neither Eisenhower nor Macmillan allowed these risks to deter them from intervening because they believed, based on the indirect aggression analogies, as well as the 1930's and Suez analogies, that the stakes were high enough in Lebanon and Jordan to merit the risks.

Even though historical analogies pointed to the potential costs of military intervention, they also highlighted the costs of not intervening. China had been "lost" to indirect aggression, which ignited a firestorm of criticism of Truman. The 1930's analogy suggested that if the West had acted forcefully early in the rise of the Axis powers, then world war would have been averted. By blaming the Suez failure on a lack of U.S. support, the British could still believe that force had been the correct policy, but had just been wrongly employed. On the basis of these analogies, the Americans and British intervened to avoid what they believed would be an even less favorable situation if they did not use force. On July 1, "he [Eisenhower] and the Secretary [Dulles] considered that even though intervention would involve great problems, that course would be a better one to follow than to do nothing and permit Lebanon to fall. This was, he said, the lesser of two evils."[34] Furthermore, the domino theory,[35] embedded in the indirect aggression analogies, exaggerated the perceptions policy makers had of the consequences of not intervening. For example, during the May crisis Dulles said, "If we did nothing, we would have to accept heavy losses not only in Lebanon but elsewhere."[36] During the June crisis, Dulles said, "If we go in[,] it will turn Arab sentiment against us. If we don't all the Arab countries which have pro-Western governments will be overthrown," including Turkey, Iran, Ethiopia, Sudan, and Libya.[37] "The Secretary [Dulles] then pointed out that if Chamoun calls on us and we do not respond, that will be the end of every pro-Western government in the area. This leaves us with little or no choice, even though every alternative is 'wrong.' " Eisenhower agreed,[38] even though it was a gross exaggeration to argue that not intervening would lead to the loss of every pro-Western government in the Middle East.

The Americans held the same beliefs during the July crisis as they had during June. At a July 14 meeting attended by Eisenhower, Dulles, Allen Dulles, Twining, and other U.S. policy makers, "There was general agreement that the effects of the United States doing nothing would be: 1. Nasser would take over the whole area; 2. The United States would lose influence not only in the Arab states of the Middle East but in the area generally . . .; 3. The dependability of United States commitments for assistance in the event of need would be brought into question throughout the world."[39] "On balance, the Secretary [Dulles] was inclined to feel that the losses from doing nothing would be worse than the losses from action—and that consequently we should send out [sic] troops into Lebanon."[40] In a dilemma imposed by their exaggerated view of the crisis, in large part on the basis of the indirect aggression analogies and the 1930's analogy, as well as growing fear of Soviet and Nasserite expansion, U.S. policy makers believed that whether or not the United States intervened pro-Western Arab governments might fall. On July 14 Dulles said, "If we go in we must expect very threatening gestures, particularly affecting Turkey and Iran. . . . If we do not respond to the call from Chamoun, we will suffer the decline and indeed the elimination of our influence—from Indonesia to Morocco. . . . The President said it was clear in his mind that we must act, or get out of the Middle East entirely."[41]

The British felt similarly about Jordan. Suez cast a pall over the British decision-making process, highlighting both the potential costs of intervening, as well as the costs of delaying intervention.[42] Macmillan believed that delay and indecisiveness had crippled the Suez operation. He would not waiver in his decision to use force promptly in Jordan. On July 16 at a cabinet meeting, the case against intervening in Jordan was made, including the arguments that only limited objectives could be secured because British forces were ill-equipped for heavy fighting and that military intervention would spread disaffection in Jordan's army. However, on July 17, in Parliament, Macmillan compared the danger of not doing anything to the danger of intervening militarily. He said that if the British did not intervene, the British position in the whole Middle East would suffer, and Nasser's prestige and power would increase. Macmillan said, "I am well aware of them: dangers to our own position; dangers to the future developments in the Middle East, and, perhaps, all over the world."[43] Although Macmillan favored intervention, he also feared using force, based on the Suez analogy. He said military intervention would be a "quixotic undertaking."[44] The Suez analogy also may have increased Macmillan's preference for intervention: he was prime minister in part because Cabinet Minister Rab Butler had opposed military intervention in Suez.[45] Therefore, Macmillan's support for military intervention in Suez had, in part, brought him to Number 10 Downing Street. Military intervention in Lebanon and Jordan similarly might raise Macmillan's stature, as well as his place in history. However, Suez was a double-edged sword since it also suggested that a failed military intervention could cause a government to fall. Macmillan believed that Suez prescribed the prompt use of military force with U.S. support. If done correctly, military intervention did not necessarily destroy a government, as it had Eden's in 1956; it could instead make a government, as had happened when military exploits had created the Churchill legend in the 1940s.

Although lessons from history reinforced growing fears of Soviet expansion and the spread of Nasserism in the Middle East, historical lessons also had significant independent effects. British and American policy makers relied on analogies drawn from the 1930s, Suez, and cases of indirect aggression to go beyond the information available. The analogies influenced their views of the stakes, risks, time, Nasser, and policy options, as well as how they justified their decisions to use force. The British drew from the Suez analogy the belief that they required American support to intervene militarily. The British took from the 1930's and Suez analogies that Nasser was irrational, that the stakes and risks were high, that their adversaries grew stronger over time while the West grew weaker, and that the best policy was the prompt use of military force in Lebanon and Jordan. The Americans drew from Korea the lesson that the stakes were high and that force might have to be used. Korea also suggested that crises could occur suddenly and that the United States had to be prepared to accept significant, long-term military and economic commitments on the basis of rapid decision making. Korea also prescribed prudence in the use of military force. In Korea, the United States had led the way into North Korea only to be counterattacked by the Chinese. In Lebanon, Eisenhower limited the intervention and refused British urging to intervene also in Jordan. Greece taught the importance of military and economic aid, while China suggested the limits of such aid. Massive aid to the Nationalist government of China had failed to avoid the "loss" of China. Lessons from history also reinforced growing fears of Soviet expansion and the spread of Nasserism in the Middle East.

THE MAY CRISIS SUBSIDES

The British and American decisions to use military force in May were negated for the moment as Lebanese government forces took control of Beirut. Having decided that they would use force only as a last resort, the British and Americans now sought to ensure that if they intervened, it would be a last resort on their terms—not on Chamoun's. Other means must be tried first. The Americans, relying on the Greece analogy, provided military and economic aid to Lebanon's government in an attempt to avoid having to use force. The British, relying on the Suez and 1930's analogies, not Greece, favored the early use of military force with much less of an emphasis on military and economic aid. On May 17 the United States responded favorably to Lebanon's May 13 request about the possibility of intervening militarily, but with conditions. These conditions were first raised by Eisenhower on May 15, two days after the meeting where Eisenhower favored the use of force and, most significantly, after the crisis had eased. On May 15 Eisenhower said he wanted "to put a price" on U.S. intervention, that would compel Lebanon to pursue other avenues to settle the civil war.[46] The conditions would ensure that Chamoun did not use the threat of U.S. intervention to avoid a reasonable, negotiated settlement: Lebanon must take the issue of the Lebanese civil war to the Arab League and to the United Nations; at least two Arab states must support Lebanon's request for U.S. military intervention ("if the Arab countries think we should intervene, they must join in requesting us to do so"); and the U.S. mission would be "to protect American life and property." Furthermore, the Americans said, "we could send in military elements to engage in military assistance to the Government of Lebanon, in order to help them preserve their independence and integrity," but, "Secretary Dulles said he did not feel we should back a second term for President Chamoun. The President agreed we must ask Chamoun for what purpose he is seeking help."[47] On June 15 Dulles emphasized these points when he said that force was a last resort and reported that for the United States to use force, "the situation [must] be desperate . . . that there be some concurrent support from one or more Arab countries . . . that such intervention have at least the moral support of some international organization."[48]

Besides adding conditions to any U.S. use of force, Eisenhower pursued other means to decrease the chance that intervention would be necessary. On May 15, as a memorandum of a meeting reports, "There was next some discussion concerning the activity of Radio Cairo in inciting disorder [in Lebanon]. The President said we should have some stations in other countries friendly to us for broadcasting or jamming purposes."[49] The United States also airlifted tear gas and small arms ammunition for the Lebanese police[50] and on May 17 shipped tanks to Lebanon, which had been requested months before.[51]

Although Eisenhower imposed conditions on the use of force and pursued other forms of aid to Lebanon, he had decided to use military force unless the situation improved. Eisenhower and Macmillan both focused on the military option to the exclusion of other policy responses as long as the crisis remained grave. Conditions and alternatives were not even mentioned in British decision meetings and were mentioned in American policy meetings only after the crisis in Lebanon began to calm on the afternoon of May 14, as the Lebanese army reasserted control of Beirut and the need for intervention had passed. No conditions or alternatives to military intervention were discussed on May 13 or 14 when the situation in Lebanon appeared grim. Historical analogies influenced American and British decision making. Eisenhower, relying on the Greece analogy, decided to give other means a chance to remedy the crisis. If the crisis continued or worsened, however, then, as the United States had done in Korea, he had decided that force would have to be used. The 1930s, Korea, and Suez prescribed the prompt use of military force, especially when a situation deteriorated. The British believed that hesitation had led to disaster in Suez and the Americans and British believed that only a rapid response had saved South Korea. The 1930's analogy also prescribed the prompt use of military force before dictators grew stronger and the costs of stopping them increased.

Although almost all military intervention decisions are unanimous, there are variations in decisions to intervene.[52] There are emphatic, broadly supported decisions to intervene, such as Truman's in Korea. There are decisions not even to consider intervening, as was the case with Truman in Iran and Eisenhower in Suez. However, there are also decisions to use force, which are made reluctantly, such as the British decision to use force in Korea and Eisenhower's decision in May to intervene in Lebanon, if required. There are also variations in decisions not to intervene. For example, the British decision not to intervene in Iran was made reluctantly by a divided cabinet under U.S. pressure.

Because of his reliance on the Suez and 1930's analogies, which warned against delay, Macmillan, even more than Eisenhower, favored prompt military intervention from the beginning of the crisis. Unlike the Americans, the British attached no conditions, except U.S. support, to British intervention in Lebanon even as the May crisis eased.

THE JUNE CRISIS

On June 15 the situation in Lebanon again worsened and Chamoun asked whether the United States would intervene "at once," if asked.[53] The British, relying on lessons from Suez, were again ready to intervene promptly, but, as in May, and as the Suez analogy prescribed, only if the Americans also intervened. Eisenhower, on the basis of the Korea and 1930's analogies, again prepared to use force. Lebanon had technically, if not in spirit, met the U.S. conditions for military intervention set down in May. Lebanon's foreign minister, Jacob Malik, appealed to the Arab League on May 21. On June 5 the league suggested sending a committee to Lebanon to study, and attempt to calm, the situation, even though Chamoun rejected the proposal as Nasser-inspired. Malik also presented Lebanon's case to the U.N. Security Council on May 27 and welcomed UNOGIL, only to reject the UNOGIL report, which found no significant UAR infiltration into Lebanon. On May 23 the Lebanese government also stated it would not change the constitution to allow Chamoun to stand for reelection. Last, Jordan and Iraq promised political support for a U.S. intervention. Eisenhower could have argued that the Lebanese had not given the Arab League or the United Nations a chance to settle the conflict because of Lebanon's rejection of the proposals by the Arab League and of the UNOGIL report. However, Eisenhower did not do so, which highlighted his growing, although reluctant, belief that his May decision would have to be implemented and force would have to be used as prescribed by the Korean analogy. On June 15 Eisenhower said, "the United States had made a commitment which it should fulfill if the United Nations cannot solve the problem."[54] This response suggested that Eisenhower, reflecting his May decision, believed that the crisis required the use of military force as the Korean and the 1930's analogies suggested, and not just negotiation or military aid, as the Greece analogy prescribed. On June 15 Eisenhower said, "that a limited intervention in port cities might have a tremendously effective morale value, [and] that the JCS [Joint Chief's of Staff] should be giving attention to what would be the most effective way to help." Dulles said such a study was already under way.[55] Eisenhower was not just talking. He had military forces ready if intervention was required. On June 14 the Defense Department reported that U.S. forces were ready to intervene,[56] and Dulles said U.S. armed forces were in a state of "instant readiness."[57] However, reflecting Eisenhower's ambivalence, on June 15, the same day he said an intervention might have tremendous morale value, "The President said he had little, if any, enthusiasm for our intervening at this time."[58] This ambivalence reflected Eisenhower's use of two historical analogies, Greece and Korea, which suggested different prescriptions: military and economic aid versus the prompt use of military force.

Luckily for Eisenhower, he did not have to decide whether to intervene militarily in June because the crisis quickly passed. The Americans and, to a limited degree, the British then returned to searching for other means to settle the Lebanon issue and to ensure that if force was used, it would be a last resort. This change showed that the Greece analogy had again moved to the fore, as the Korea and 1930's analogies faded in U.S. decision-making circles. On June 19 Dulles cabled his reservations about intervening to the U.S. ambassador in Beirut, including possible Arab nationalist backlash, the probability that Lebanon would only remain stable as long as foreign troops were present, and the possibility of an intervention adding to Nasser's prestige. Dulles then cabled, "For these reasons we take this occasion to urge Chamoun to do everything in his power to avoid a situation in which a request for intervention might be required. He should know that he will have our full backing in his efforts to safeguard Lebanese independence and integrity by other means."[59] Eisenhower "urged President Chamoun to do everything in his power to solve the problem with his own forces."[60] The Americans would also not act while UNOGIL was operating nor until it had been given a chance to succeed. In his June 19 cable to the U.S. ambassador in Beirut, Dulles said, "US would find it very awkward to act militarily while it was still uncertain UN action would be inadequate and where responsibility of collapse of UN effort would be generally attributed to US."[61] The British agreed. Lloyd cabled and said, "the focus should be on further UN activity."[62] "The President also felt that we should examine the possibility of supplying massive military aid and technicians, as the Soviets did in Syria, as an alternative to military intervention."[63] Eisenhower approved sending 3 LCMs (landing craft) and 8,000 rounds of 75 mm ammunition to Lebanon.[64] He was also exasperated by the Lebanese army's lack of initiative in fighting the rebels, which he blamed on Chamoun and the commander of the Lebanese army, General Fuad Chehab. Eisenhower asked, "How can you save a country from its own leaders?" He was even willing to jettison Chamoun and support another Lebanese leader to avoid intervention, as long as Lebanon remained pro-Western. Dulles also wanted to pursue further what Iraq and Jordan could do to settle the Lebanon conflict.[65] The Greece analogy had taken its place in the forefront of the minds of Eisenhower and Dulles, as Korea receded.

THE JULY CRISIS

The July 14 Iraqi coup drastically changed the Lebanon situation, making it appear to the British and Americans that the Middle East was on the brink of chaos. The coup frightened pro-Western governments in Lebanon, Jordan, Iran, Turkey, the Sudan, Kuwait, and Saudi Arabia. The coup in Iraq, which had served as a Western-oriented balance to Syria and its UAR partner, Egypt, and a protector of Jordan, appeared to remove the balance to Syria and increase the UAR–threat posed to Jordan and Lebanon. Chamoun, fearful of a Nasser-backed coup and taking the opportunity of the crisis atmosphere in London and Washington after the Iraqi coup to try to quash the rebellion with outside help, asked Britain, the United States, and France to intervene within forty-eight hours.[66] The British and American decisions, made in May, to use force if the situation was dire and the Lebanese government appeared to be about to fall to pro-Nasser forces, were swiftly implemented. In an environment of confusion and uncertainty, after other means appeared to have failed, Macmillan and a reluctant Eisenhower believed that the last resort had been reached. The Americans and British now followed the policy prescriptions of Suez, the 1930s, and Korea; Greece was forgotten.

Eisenhower implemented the May policy and decided within hours to intervene with military forces. Korea prescribed the prompt use of force, as did the 1930s, and Eisenhower did not hesitate. The historical analogies were cognitive shortcuts, negating the need for lengthy analysis. The National Security Council (NSC) met at 9:45 A.M. on July 14, soon after news of the coup reached Washington. Eisenhower had already decided to use force: "Because of my long study of the problem, this was one meeting in which my mind was practically made up regarding the general line of action we should take, even before we met." At the meeting he said, "a decision must be made . . . within the next hour or two."[67] Eisenhower said, "If the Iraq coup succeeds it seems almost inevitable that it will set up a chain reaction which will doom the pro-West governments of Lebanon and Jordan and Saudi Arabia, and raise grave problems for Turkey and Iran."[68] When congressional leaders met with Eisenhower at 2:30 P.M. on July 14 he had already decided to use force and said the meeting was "only explanatory."[69] Eisenhower then met with his advisors and at 4:30 P.M. ordered the Marines to land the next day at 3 P.M. Lebanon time (9 A.M. EDT). Eisenhower pursued diplomatic means at the same time as using force, just as Truman did during the Korean crisis. The United States called an emergency meeting of the U.N. Security Council the same morning as the landing. However, force was the preferred response to the Iraqi coup. Diplomacy was only used to gain support for the use of force, as in Korea, and to search for a long-term solution.

Historical analogies help to explain why the Americans responded to a coup in Iraq by intervening in Lebanon, not in Iraq. The U.S. response to the invasion of South Korea and to the cases of indirect aggression pointed to a response that focused, to varying degrees, on neighboring states. The successful response to the Greek civil war in 1947 included aid to neighboring Turkey, as well as to Greece. The 1948 Czechoslovakian coup contributed to the establishment of NATO the following year, composed of some of Czechoslovakia's neighbors. The fall of China to the Soviets led to support for the Nationalists on Taiwan and the French in Vietnam. The invasion of South Korea sparked a NATO military buildup and tighter American alliances with Japan and the Philippines. In each case, the United States responded to a crisis by bolstering states near the state that had "fallen." In the Iraqi case, the response was clear: aid friendly states located near Iraq— Lebanon and Jordan.

Macmillan, supported unanimously by his cabinet and also on the basis of the May decision, decided as quickly as Eisenhower to intervene militarily in Lebanon. Macmillan's decision was influenced significantly by Suez and the 1930's analogies: to use force promptly with U.S. support. The 1930s reinforced the lesson of Suez: the British had achieved victory in World War II only with massive American aid and intervention. However, Eisenhower, seeking to avoid association with Britain's imperial past, opposed British participation in Lebanon. Dulles reported that the British "would want to know if we can help and support them. The President said that it might be better to put our troops into Lebanon unilaterally. Mr. Dulles recalled that we had been working closely with the British on this whole matter. . . . The President said he thought we could give them logistical support, but did not see how we could commit ourselves quickly to do more."[70] American opposition blocked British military intervention in Lebanon. On the day of the coup, July 14, in a telephone call with Eisenhower, Macmillan agreed to keep British troops in reserve. Dulles had told the British, "if it is militarily feasible for the British to hold back from the initial operation as planned, that would be agreeable to us."[71] In fact, the U.K. cabinet saw advantages in letting the Americans intervene alone in Lebanon: It would keep British oil interests in the Lebanese city of Tripoli safer; it would be easier to dissuade the French from intervening; and there would be more time to get Commonwealth support if British troops intervened after the Americans had intervened.[72] The British use of force in Lebanon was postponed. Current information, in the form of U.S. opposition had prevented British action, although this current information was based on history, albeit extrapolation, not a historical analogy: Britain's imperial past. The reason the British were so concerned with U.S. approval and support, however, was a lesson drawn from the Suez analogy: do not intervene militarily without U.S. support, as well as the 1930's emphasis on the alliance with the United States.

The day of the Iraqi coup, Jordan's King Hussein also requested U.S. military intervention,[73] even as the king and Eisenhower received reports of a UAR–backed coup attempt in Jordan planned for the next day.[74] The Americans half-heartedly and briefly considered intervening in Jordan, but decided quickly not to do so. The Chinese counterintervention in Korea prescribed the limited use of force. The 1949 China analogy also suggested knowing when to cut your losses and, as the Greece, Korea, and Czechoslovakia analogies suggested, aiding states that neighbored the state that was "lost." On July 15 Eisenhower said he was "giving deep thought to finding a moral ground on which to"[75] intervene in Jordan, but the next day had decided not to intervene and said he "knew of no basis on which we could move in."[76] Besides the influence of the Korea, China, and indirect aggression analogies, Eisenhower and Dulles were also hesitant to intervene in Jordan because they believed, on the basis of current information, that Jordan was on the verge of collapse. Dulles said, "In Jordan, public support for the government is no greater—and possibly less—than Iraqi public support was for the deposed Iraqi regime." King Hussein has no roots in the country and Jordan is an "artificial creation resulting from World War I, with no history."[77] "[JCS Chairman] General Twining thought the British should get their forces in [to Jordan] at once, but Secretary Dulles said he had no enthusiasm for British forces going in. Lebanon has not been swept by pan-Arabism, but in Jordan and Iraq, pan-Arabism could sweep the country very quickly." However, sitting firmly on the fence, Dulles then said, given Britain's long relationship with Jordan, that "if any troops were sent in they should be British, although we might provide air logistical support."[78] Like Greece in 1947, the Americans would supply material support, but not troops. Prudence and the limited use of force, on the basis of the Korea and China analogies, won out.

The British cabinet, in a climate of confusion and uncertainty about the aims and future policies of the new Iraqi government and worried about the British position in the Middle East, decided to convince King Hussein also to ask the British to intervene. Suez and the 1930s prescribed the prompt use of force in the face of aggression. On July 16 Hussein again asked the United States to intervene and, for the first time, using a British-drafted request, asked Britain to intervene militarily. On the basis of information about the planned coup and acting on his decision in May to use force, as well as the Suez and 1930's analogies, Macmillan told Dulles the same day that the British were intervening militarily that same night. "Mr. Macmillan called [Dulles] at 8 p.m. EDT. [July 16] He said they were probably going in tonight; dared not risk a day's delay. . . . He said he would cable the final decision within an hour or two."[79]

Macmillan spent the entire crisis ensuring that the British would have U.S. support, first in a possible intervention in Lebanon and, later, for the Jordan intervention. If there is a commonly accepted lesson from a historical analogy, it will probably be used. Macmillan relied on a common lesson the British had drawn from Suez: ensure U.S. support before intervening militarily in the Middle East. The 1930's analogy reinforced this lesson. Eisenhower said, Macmillan "wanted my assurances that we were in this together, all the way. This I gave him."[80] Macmillan even sent Lloyd to Washington to urge that Jordan be a joint Anglo-American operation. Macmillan also wrote Eisenhower, hoping that both states would use force in Jordan.[81]

Even on the eve of the British intervention, Macmillan asked Dulles at 6:20 P.M. on July 16 to intervene together. Dulles said the United States would provide moral and logistical support and might "come along later,"[82] although, by then, there was no chance of that. Macmillan called again at 8 P.M. to talk with Dulles: "He [Macmillan] wanted to confirm that we would: 1) Give moral support, 2) Give support in UN, 3) Give, if needed, logistic support, 4) Would, in light of events and after Congressional consultation, consider what combat potentiality we would supply if needed. I confirmed the above." Eisenhower had agreed to a fly-over by U.S. aircraft over Jordan, but Dulles now tried to cancel even that limited support. "He [Macmillan] said that he thought our air display, planned for early tomorrow, should avoid Amman [the capital of Jordan] lest there be possible confusion in the two operations. I said we could call it off. He said no, only avoid Amman."[83] The Suez lesson, reinforced by the 1930s, cast its shadow over British policy making: Britain must have U.S. support, however limited, to intervene militarily.

On July 15, 1958, the United States intervened militarily in Lebanon[84] and on July 17 Britain intervened militarily in Jordan. The United States and Britain provided logistical, and other, limited, support for each other.[85] On July 17 at 9 A.M. Lebanon time fifty to one hundred U.S. aircraft flew over Jordan's West Bank in conjunction with the British,[86] while the British cruiser *Sheffield* and two destroyers steamed off the Lebanese city of Tripoli to evacuate British nationals, if needed. At the height of the intervention, about 13,000 U.S. soldiers and Marines, supported by about seventy warships were directly involved in Lebanon, while about 2,500 British paratroopers were in Jordan.

THE USE OF FORCE

The American and British operations in Lebanon and Jordan fit the definition of the use of force. Although Dulles said the intervention in Lebanon was "not a combat operation"[87] and Eisenhower later wrote that "The basic mission of United States forces in Lebanon was not primarily to fight,"[88] U.S. policy makers believed combat was a possibility. JCS Chairman General Twining did not believe there would be "heavy fighting,"[89] but did not rule out combat. On July 14 Dulles said he expected some "sniping."[90] Furthermore, Eisenhower emphasized that the landing must be a surprise to avoid possible armed opposition.[91] The location of the landing also provides evidence that the Americans thought there might be combat. U.S. troops landed on the beaches. It was easier to fight from the beaches than in a port and, even though Chamoun had invited them, the Americans did not know whether the rebels or the Lebanese army would oppose the Marines. The Lebanese army, instead of welcoming the Americans as allies, instead might view them as invaders.[92] The possibility of combat between the Marines and the Lebanese army was not insignificant. The day after the Marines landed, General Chehab ordered the Lebanese army to fire on the Marines if they advanced on Beirut. Combat was only avoided by negotiations on the road to Beirut between Chehab, U.S. special envoy Robert Murphy, and the Marine commander.

The British also believed there was a possibility of combat and casualties when they intervened in Jordan. The British were concerned that there might be fighting if the UAR invaded Jordan from Syria, if a pro–UAR faction toppled King Hussein, or if Hussein fell and Jordan descended into chaos, tempting Israel to seize the West Bank. In any of these scenarios, British troops might have to fight. The British cabinet favored prompt military intervention in Jordan in part because of a combat consideration: Amman's airfields were still under government control.[93] The British and American military interventions were not merely a peaceful troop movement to support a friendly government; combat was a possibility and they fit the definition of military intervention.

Unlike other leaders who used force, such as Truman and Attlee in Korea and Eden in Suez, Eisenhower, reflecting his military training, did not use limited and proportional force. Eisenhower followed the military dictum of using overwhelming force against whatever opposition, including rebels, the Syrians, or the Lebanese army that might arise in the confused Lebanese situation in 1958. Eisenhower wrote, "if you took action promptly, and showed that you meant business, that this would be more effective and would lead to less serious consequences, rather than the opposite; that if you sat around and temporized too long, others would get the idea that you were afraid to do something, and then you would have a different and worse situation."[94] Andrew J. Goodpaster said Eisenhower intervened in Lebanon "with very substantial resources, so that essentially the game was over before it ever started" and that Eisenhower intervened with "such a preponderance of force that there was no invitation to resist."[95]

Eisenhower marshaled overwhelming force for the landing in Lebanon. One marine battalion made the initial landing, followed by two more battalions within two days. Two army battle groups were ready to move from Germany, while two carrier groups were in the eastern Mediterranean[96] and two divisions in the United States were ready to load for transport.[97] The JCS even recommended an increased level of alert for the Strategic Air Command and moving air force tankers into forward positions. Eisenhower agreed and said such a move would show U.S. "readiness and determination."[98] This nuclear-backed force was facing what Anglo-American planners had projected would be, in a worst and exaggerated case, 6,000 to 9,000 insurgents and about 1,000 armed volunteers from Syria. If the Lebanese army opposed the invasion, it could only muster 9,000 lightly armed men and a gendarmerie of 2,500 men. An Anglo-American plan devised in May, which formed the basis of the U.S. landing, had envisioned intervention by

2,000 British and 3,000 American troops.[99] Eisenhower greatly exceeded this 5,000-man level proposed by his own generals and quickly committed about 13,000 troops. Although the number of troops was not large compared to the possible adversaries (13,000 U.S. troops versus either 10,000 rebels and Syrians or 11,500 Lebanese army troops and gendarmerie) it was overwhelming when combined with the supporting forces of seventy to seventy-five warships, hundreds of aircraft, and the divisions that were alerted to be ready for transport to Lebanon if needed.[100]

Macmillan, reflecting Britain's lack of logistical resources and military capabilities,[101] but also the fact that he was not a career soldier, committed only 2,500 troops to Jordan compared to Eisenhower's 13,000 in Lebanon. Macmillan followed the principle of proportional, not overwhelming, force. He called the airlift to Amman airport a "small force."[102] Although both the Americans and the British planned to secure limited objectives—the Americans, a beachhead and Beirut airport, the British, Amman's airport—Eisenhower used vastly greater forces than Macmillan. Eisenhower could have committed 2,500 instead of 13,000 troops to seize Beirut's airport, or Macmillan could have airlifted many more than 2,500 troops into Amman. The difference in size between seaborne and airborne operations does not explain the difference in size between the operations, especially the vast difference in the buildup after the initial interventions. Although the civil war in Lebanon subsided soon after the Marines landed, Eisenhower rapidly and significantly increased the size of the U.S. force, while in Jordan, where the crisis also passed quickly, Macmillan did not substantially increase British force levels. Eisenhower's military training and reliance on the principle of overwhelming force, and Macmillan's lack of military training and reliance on the principle of proportional force significantly influenced American and British levels of force when they intervened in Lebanon and Jordan.

HISTORICAL ANALOGIES

The vast majority of the historical analogies policy makers retrieved and used during the Lebanon/Jordan crises fell into two recent time periods: the 1930s and post-1945. Therefore, almost all of the historical analogies used were either observed or personally experienced by the policy makers and not based on learned history. As an army staff officer Eisenhower observed the events of the 1930s, was supreme allied commander in Europe during the post-1945, indirect aggression crises, and was president during Suez. Dulles was an international lawyer during most of the 1930s and, although involved in foreign policy during the late 1940s as a consultant, especially on the United Nations, was not directly involved in the crises of the late 1940s. Macmillan was in Parliament, but not in office, during the 1930s, and was chancellor of the exchequer during the 1956 Suez crisis.

Most of the historical analogies retrieved shared surface similarities with the Lebanon and Jordan crises. Lebanon and Jordan may have been cases of indirect aggression. Other states, especially the UAR through its propaganda broadcasts, aided rebels or factions within Lebanon and Jordan. The historical analogies also involved relatively weak allies threatened by what appeared to be powerful external threats. The British and Americans viewed the Lebanon and Jordan situations in a similar light. Apart from these superficial similarities, however, there were far more differences than similarities between Lebanon and Jordan in 1958 and Greece in 1947, Czechoslovakia in 1948, China in 1949, Indo-China in 1950, and Korea in 1950. They varied greatly in that Greece, China, Indo-China, and Lebanon were civil wars. Korea could be seen as a civil war, although neither the Czechoslovakian coup nor Jordan was a civil war. The amount of fighting in the cases that were civil wars also varied greatly with little actual combat in Lebanon. The underlying causes of the conflicts also varied greatly.

The most commonly mentioned British historical analogy, Suez, was also only superficially similar to Jordan in 1958. Both were in the Middle East and involved Nasser. However, Jordan invited the British to intervene, while Egypt did not. The British goal in Jordan was to support the government, while in Egypt the British sought to overthrow Nasser. In addition, compared to the 1930's Axis, Nasser's Egypt was far less of a threat than Nazi Germany or even Fascist Italy. If policy makers looked beyond surface similarities, the causal chains of all the historical analogies, whether Suez, the 1930s, or the cases of indirect aggression, varied greatly from the crises in Lebanon and Jordan.

The crises in Lebanon and Jordan were events and generally did not revolve around a specific person. Therefore, policy makers mainly retrieved historical events, such as China 1949, Suez 1956, and Korea 1950, instead of people as historical analogies. However, when Nasser was mentioned, Hitler, a historical person, was used as an analogy.

Most of the historical analogies retrieved were foreign policy failures for the United States and/or Britain, such as Czechoslovakia 1948 (an Anglo-American failure to keep Czechoslovakia neutral), China 1949 (a U.S. failure despite enormous U.S. aid to the Nationalists), and the 1930s (an Anglo-American failure to deal effectively with the Axis and avoid a world war). Suez in 1956, which both the Americans and British mentioned repeatedly, was a failure for the British, but was a success for the Americans. Suez, therefore, was, for the United States, an exception to the pattern of retrieving analogies of foreign policy failures, although the British mentioned it far more than the Americans. Other exceptions included Greece and, to a lesser extent, Korea, both of which could be seen as U.S. successes. For the British, the Suez analogy and many of the 1930's crises involved their own state. For the Americans, the indirect aggression cases, such as Greece 1947, Czechoslovakia 1948, China 1949, and Korea and Indo-China in 1950, involved their own state to varying degrees, from direct involvement in Korea to economic and military aid to Greece and China, and aid to France in the Indo-China case. The 1930's cases did not directly involve the United States and the Americans did not mention them nearly as often as did the British, nor as often as the indirect aggression cluster of historical analogies, in which the Americans were involved.

Because historical analogies are used to simplify crises, decision makers naturally focus on simple, easily noticeable, salient causes of the historical analogies they retrieve, especially causes directly related to their own behavior. For example, in the Suez analogy, the British focused on their failure to secure U.S. support to explain the disastrous results of the intervention. They ignored the role of the British-French-Israeli conspiracy to attack Egypt; the lack of public and U.N. support; and the delay, and lack of military capability, all of which contributed to the Suez failure. Similarly, Eisenhower focused on the salient causes, especially U.S. actions or lack of actions, that resulted in the U.S. failures in Czechoslovakia and China and successes in Korea and Greece. He ignored the numerous and varying internal causes that led to a coup in Czechoslovakia and conflicts in China, Greece, and Korea. Eisenhower focused on U.S. aid to China and Greece, as well as on the prompt U.S. military intervention in Korea. Delving into the complexities of an analogical case negates the simplifying role of a historical analogy by making the analogy and the mapping to the current case as complex as the current case. The maxim for using historical analogies is to keep it simple.

The generational hypothesis was not a strong indicator of which historical analogies policy makers used. Eisenhower (born 1890), Dulles (born 1888), and Macmillan (born 1894) were in their twenties during World War I. Under the generational hypothesis, they should have used World War I as an analogy, but did not mention it during the Lebanon/Jordan crisis. Furthermore, World War I was a major event in the lives of Macmillan, Eisenhower, and Dulles. Macmillan served in the trenches and many of his friends were killed in the war.[103] For Eisenhower, World War I was a period of intense frustration because he remained in the United States training men and missed seeing combat.[104] World War I was also crucial for Dulles. During the war he worked as a lawyer on many government contracts culminating in his role at the Versailles Peace Conference as an expert on reparations. Even though World War I was a major, traumatic event in their lives, neither Macmillan, Eisenhower, nor Dulles drew on World War I as an analogy to Lebanon. Lloyd (born 1904) provides some support for the generational hypothesis, since he was in his late twenties and early thirties during the 1930's crises, which he used as an analogy during the Lebanon/Jordan crisis. However, apart from Lloyd, the major policy makers were in their forties, fifties, and sixties during the 1930s and late 1940s–50s, when Korea, Greece, China, Czechoslovakia, and Suez occurred, which they mentioned as analogies to the Lebanon/Jordan crisis. The leaders were not in their twenties during the time periods when the historical analogies they retrieved occurred, as the generational hypothesis predicts.

Regardless of their age, however, World War II was a major event in the lives of the principal decision makers. The events leading up to World War II became a master analogy, which they used to frame the Lebanon/Jordan crisis. For Macmillan, World War II was his great opportunity; first as a junior minister in the Churchill government; and then, in 1942, as under-secretary of state for the colonies; and finally, most important, in December 1942, as minister of state in North Africa. World War II was also Eisenhower's great opportunity. In early 1942, he was a staff officer in Washington before commanding the landings in North Africa, Sicily, and then, in June 1944 in Normandy. Eisenhower's stature as supreme commander Allied Expeditionary Forces during the war led to his appointment as chief of staff (1945–47) and Supreme Headquarters Allied Powers Europe (SHAPE) NATO commander (1951–52) after the war. World War II was a major event in the lives of Macmillan and Eisenhower, regardless of their age when it occurred and contrary to the generational model, the 1930s became a master analogy and influenced their policy making during later crises, including Lebanon/Jordan. Similarly, the Suez analogy, which Macmillan relied on during the Lebanon/Jordan crisis, was crucial in his life; it resulted in him becoming prime minister after Eden's fall. Macmillan, however, was well past his twenties during Suez. Korea and China, which Eisenhower used as historical analogies during the Lebanon/Jordan crisis, were important to him to the extent that they were issues that contributed to his defeat of Truman. Even so, he was well past his twenties when they occurred. The generational theory should be expanded: Any major event can influence future policy decisions as long as the policy maker was aware of foreign affairs during the time period when the major event occurred.

The most commonly mentioned analogies, Suez, the 1930s, and the cases of indirect aggression, provided macrolessons, which allowed many people to support them, yet disagree about how specifically to implement the lessons. For example, for the British, the Suez crisis provided the general lesson that intervention in the Middle East without U.S. support was disastrous. The Suez crisis was such a macroanalogy that the Labour Party used it to argue that the British should not intervene under any circumstances, while the Conservative government used it to illustrate the need for U.S. support and, once having secured that support, to justify intervention.[105] The indirect aggression analogies suggested even more general lessons than Suez by prescribing multiple policies: use military force promptly (Korea); supply military and economic aid (Greece); and aid neighbors of state in conflict (China, Greece, and Czechoslovakia). Eisenhower could vary his policy choices as the situation in Lebanon changed. The American president did indeed switch from one analogy to another to adjust to the changing circumstances. The 1930's analogy also offered a macrolesson: to use military force promptly against aggressive dictators. Almost no historical analogies that provided narrow, microlessons were mentioned more than once by the leaders, and none had any apparent influence on British or American policy.

CONDITIONS THAT INFLUENCED THE USE OF HISTORICAL ANALOGIES

Personality variables, as well as the level of drama, time pressures, surprise, and high stakes led U.K. and U.S. policy makers to use historical analogies as a cognitive shortcut to diagnose the Lebanon/Jordan crisis. Personality helps to explain the use of lessons from history in the Lebanon/Jordan case. Macmillan, who often used historical analogies throughout his career, including during the Suez crisis, used them during the Lebanon/Jordan crisis. Eisenhower, who used historical analogies only occasionally in his career, used them less often than Macmillan in the Lebanon/Jordan crisis, although he did mention the 1930s, Suez, and the indirect aggression analogies. Eisenhower also had more control over his own use of historical analogies and their effect on him than did the other leaders. Lloyd and Dulles, who used historical analogies rarely in their careers, also used them rarely during the Lebanon/Jordan crisis, although they too mentioned Suez, the 1930s and the indirect aggression analogies. Although personality can begin to explain the use of historical analogies in the Lebanon/Jordan case, situational factors must also be analyzed to explain the use of historical analogies by those who rarely used historical information, especially Lloyd, Dulles, and Eisenhower.

Historical analogies are usually used in novel, complex situations. All international relations crises are complex enough to lead to the use of historical analogies. Lebanon/Jordan, which was no exception, may have been even more complex than most foreign policy crises. American and British policy makers were not sure who the key actors were, what the stakes were, the geographical scope of the crisis, and what would occur if they intervened or did not intervene. They were also unsure who was behind the coup in Iraq and what type and degree of threat those behind the coup posed to Lebanon and Jordan.[106] The crisis involved many states—Lebanon, Jordan, Egypt, Iraq, Syria, Israel, the United States, Britain, and France. At the same time, Lebanon was riven by civil war and there was a threatened coup in Jordan. Despite its complexity, however, the crisis was not novel. Civil war is as old as states, and foreign aid for rebels, such as the Americans and British believed Nasser was providing to the Lebanese rebels, was also not a new phenomenon. For example, rebels had received outside aid during the Greek civil war in the late 1940s, and, far earlier, the young United States had secured French aid during its war for independence. Eisenhower believed that the Lebanon situation was not new and was another case of indirect aggression, like Greece, Korea, China, and Czechoslovakia. Mac-

millan also believed that Lebanon/Jordan was just another Middle East crisis, similar to Suez. The complexity of the crisis should have led to the use
of historical analogies. However, the lack of novelty should have meant that
policy makers would not use historical analogies.

Time pressures can also lead to the use of historical analogies as cognitive
shortcuts. When the Iraqi coup occurred, American and British policy makers felt intense urgency to respond to what they believed was a rapidly
deteriorating situation.[107] Macmillan mentioned the "urgency of the moment"[108] and on July 16 Macmillan said Britain was intervening in Jordan
tonight and "dared not risk a day's delay."[109] Eisenhower also decided to
use force quickly, within hours.[110] Also contributing to the sense of urgency
and the tendency to use historical analogies was the fact that the coup in
Iraq was a vivid, dramatic event that surprised the British and Americans.
Western intelligence services, which had failed to forecast the coup, had no
idea who was behind it or what were the motives and goals of its leaders.[111]
The Americans and British felt the drama of the unknown at full force.
Similarly, during the May and June crises in Lebanon, the situation was
unclear and the crises, while not unexpected, were surprises.

High stakes also tend to lead to the use of historical analogies. After the
Iraqi coup, the British, and the Americans to a lesser degree, believed that
the whole Middle East was on the brink of chaos. The importance of oil
and the perceived Soviet threat, which appeared to be increasing in power
and scope, further heightened the perceived stakes. In the atmosphere of
uncertainty, overreaction was rampant and the Americans and British believed that the stakes were high. Besides Lebanon and Jordan, the United
States briefly considered a British proposal to intervene in Iraq, while Britain
sent troops to Kuwait and Libya, and U.S. Marines were moved to the
Persian Gulf. Trying to determine the implications of the Iraqi coup for
Lebanon, Jordan, and the Middle East, Eisenhower, Macmillan, Dulles, and
Lloyd, under intense time pressures and with what appeared to be a great
deal at stake, turned to historical analogies as cognitive shortcuts to simplify
and diagnose the crisis, as well as to prescribe and justify policy.

PROCESS OF ANALOGICAL REASONING

The model in the literature of analogical reasoning by a group, which
posits that an actor suggests an analogy and then describes it, which leads
to debate, is not supported by the Lebanon/Jordan case. There was almost
never any debate about a historical analogy, its interpretation, or its validity
for the current case. American policy makers, for example, never debated
the interpretation of the indirect aggression analogies or their validity as
analogies for the Lebanon/Jordan crisis. Nor was there any debate about
the validity of the Suez analogy in British policy making meetings. For example, at a May 13, 1958, meeting, Macmillan and his cabinet, relying on
the Suez analogy, agreed that Britain could intervene in Lebanon only with

U.S. support.[112] There was no debate in the cabinet about the validity of the Suez analogy for the Lebanon/Jordan crisis. There was, however, debate in Parliament about whether the lesson of Suez was not to intervene at all in the Middle East or only to intervene with U.S. support. Parliament debated the analogy because there was greater diversity of opinion and political beliefs in that body than in the cabinet. The cabinet members were all of the same party and shared similar basic beliefs, which made it more likely that they would agree on the lessons to be derived from a historical analogy.

There was little time or need for members of the small group involved in the American and British decisions about Lebanon/Jordan to brainstorm to search for other possible historical analogies or policy options, as had occurred during the Iran crisis.[113] If a president or prime minister raises a historical analogy there is little chance that there will be any debate about the validity of the analogy. During the first crisis, in May, Eisenhower and Macmillan decided, within hours, on the basis of Suez, Korean, and the 1930's analogies, to use military force, if required. Their advisors, therefore, had no need, and probably no opportunity, to search for other possible analogies, since Eisenhower had already retrieved the indirect aggression analogies and Macmillan had already retrieved the Suez analogy. Both leaders had also quickly selected a policy option: military force. Because there was no need to search for other possible analogies or policy options, there was also no snowball effect of an actor mentioning an analogy and others mentioning other analogies in a search for other possible valid analogies or policy options. Eisenhower had already decided to rely on the indirect aggression analogies to frame the crisis and to prescribe policy. His position as president cemented the validity of these historical analogies as a framework for the Lebanon crisis, although the 1930s and Suez were also mentioned, albeit with less effect on policy. Like the indirect aggression analogies for the Americans, Suez so dominated British discussions that there was also no need, or probably, opportunity, in British decision-making meetings to search for other possible historical analogies or policy options, especially once Macmillan championed the Suez analogy.

The usual process of analogical reasoning by a group was overridden by a dominant historical analogy, Suez, in the British case, and by the indirect aggression analogies, in the American case, which were championed by a prime minister and a president. This meant that in the Lebanon/Jordan case there was no brainstorming to find other possible analogies and no snowballing, as the mention of one analogy might have led to the mention of other historical analogies. Unlike other cases in this study, no one mentioned even one difference between the analogies that were used and the current case. With Eisenhower and Macmillan using certain analogies, it would have been difficult for other cabinet members or advisors to raise another analogy, especially given the time constraints of the Lebanon/Jordan crises in May, June, and July 1958.

LESSONS

The Suez case provided the British with a specific lesson for Jordan: ensure U.S. support before intervening militarily. Macmillan ensured U.S. support for the intervention in Jordan and thus achieved the immediate British goals. It is impossible to say, however, whether U.S. support made the difference between success and failure. British intervention might have succeeded on its own. Furthermore, Macmillan's unsuccessful attempts to convince the Americans to intervene elsewhere in the Middle East might have been more successful if he had based his arguments on the indirect aggression analogies, which Eisenhower used to frame the crises in Lebanon and Jordan, instead of Suez and the Nasser/Soviet threat, on which Macmillan focused. The lessons Eisenhower drew from the indirect aggression analogies also led to a policy that achieved the immediate U.S. goals in Lebanon. However, the lesson did not ensure success. The U.S. intervention could have led to battles with the rebels or the Lebanese army, if negotiations on the road to Beirut had failed to reach an agreement that the U.S. Marines would enter Beirut in convoy with Lebanese army units. Furthermore, international relations is too complex to predict accurately outcomes if other policies had been followed, especially if significantly different policies were pursued. Lebanon may have remained stable even without U.S. military intervention. Economic and military aid might have been enough to calm the civil war, which was, in any case, barely being waged.

If historical analogies influenced the policy decisions in July 1958, then different historical analogies should have led to different policies. For example, if Eisenhower had focused exclusively on the China analogy, he might have concluded that even large-scale aid to the Lebanese government would not prevent its demise. The United States provided billions of dollars in aid to the Chinese Nationalist government, yet it fell to the Communists in 1949. The Chinese analogy might have prescribed cutting your losses and abandoning Lebanon. Macmillan could also have drawn lessons from other recent analogies, which would have led to different policy choices. In July 1957 there was a revolt in Oman. Macmillan, without American support, dispatched troops, who successfully restored the sultan's authority.[114] Also in 1957, Macmillan sent troops to take the disputed Buraimi Oasis from the Saudis for the Trucial States. At the time, he said it was better not to consult the United States before intervening with force. The intervention was a success.[115] From these recent events, which Macmillan could have used as analogies to Jordan, he could have drawn the lesson that Britain should not even consult the United States before intervening, let alone seek U.S. approval. In contrast, by relying on the Suez case, Macmillan sought American support for multilateral intervention in Lebanon and Jordan. Macmillan's application of the lesson of Suez, about securing U.S. support for intervention, to certain crises and not others shows that Suez was a historical analogy, not a general lesson that Macmillan and the British had learned and applied to every later crisis. If Macmillan had drawn a general lesson from Suez, then he would not have intervened militarily without U.S. support in Oman or the Trucial States. Macmillan did not apply the Suez analogy to the Oman or the Trucial States cases and, therefore, he did not seek U.S. support. He did, however, retrieve Suez for the Lebanon/Jordan crises and did seek U.S. support for the intervention in Jordan.

A different historical analogy would have led to different policies. Retrieving the long and bloody Algerian war as an analogy would have prescribed avoiding military intervention in Lebanon or Jordan. Policy makers, however, usually retrieve foreign policy failures, not successes, that involved their own state as analogies. Algeria did not involve Britain or the United States. Therefore, the British and Americans did not retrieve it to frame the crises in Lebanon and Jordan. The British retrieved Suez more than other, more recent analogies, because it was a failure of British foreign policy, unlike the Oman and Buraimi analogies, which were successes. Suez was also a more dramatic event with higher stakes than the Oman and Buraimi cases, which made it more likely to be retrieved as an analogy. The more known an analogy is, the more explanatory it is to the public in framing a new, complex crisis. Macmillan, therefore, retrieved Suez, not another, less well-known historical analogy.

CONCLUSION

The Lebanon and Jordan case illustrates the significant influence of historical information retrieved by analogical reasoning on foreign policy decision making. Policy makers tended to retrieve recent, vivid, and dramatic historical analogies from their personal experience or observation. They were also likely to use historical analogies that shared superficial similarities with the Lebanon/Jordan crisis, and which also involved their own state in foreign policy failures. The exceptions to this tendency were Greece, Suez, and Korea, for the United States, which were U.S. foreign policy successes. British policy makers predominantly relied on the Suez analogy to frame the crisis, while the Americans relied on the cluster of analogies around indirect aggression, as well as the 1930's analogy and, to a lesser degree than the British, the Suez analogy. The British drew from the Suez analogy the need for U.S. support, as well as the need to intervene militarily without delay. Eisenhower displayed an uncommon ability to rely on several analogies to shift policy preferences as the crisis progressed between May and July 1958. The Americans drew from the indirect aggression analogies the belief that indirect aggression had to be met as resolutely as direct aggression. The Greece analogy prescribed aid to besieged governments, while Korea prescribed the prompt use of military force when a foreign policy crisis appeared bleak, such as when an ally is being overrun militarily. China and Korea also provided warnings about the limitations of using force, which led Eisenhower to limit the duration and scope of the U.S. military intervention. Korea, Greece, and China also prescribed aiding the neighbors of states that were "lost" to adversaries. Therefore, the Americans and British intervened and aided the neighbors of the state that had been "lost," Iraq. The 1930s warned of the danger of allowing a nationalistic, dictatorial leader, such as Nasser, to expand his power unchecked, which led to Anglo-American intervention in Lebanon and Jordan. The Lebanon/Jordan case also shows the broad impact of lessons based on analogies, including influencing beliefs about the importance of the stakes involved, an adversary's rationality, time, risks, and policy options. This case also supports the power of historical analogies to resist current, contradictory information, as occurred during the Suez case when Eden was enthralled by the 1930's analogy. Eisenhower and Dulles believed that Lebanon was a case of indirect aggression, similar to Greece, China, and Czechoslovakia, even though the United Nations found little, if any, evidence of foreign support for Lebanese rebels. It also shows that policy makers can, as Eisenhower did, accept part of a historical analogy and reject other parts. Eisenhower accepted Macmillan's characterization of Nasser as another Hitler, but did not support the policy prescription that force must be used promptly. Eisenhower would allow time for other measures to attempt to resolve the crisis in Lebanon, as the Greece analogy suggested. This is a rare use of historical analogies, as a cluster that allows a policy maker to shift policy and yet continue to use the set of analogies. Usually one historical analogy dominates the perceptions of a policy maker, such as the use of the 1930s by Attlee and Truman during the Korean crisis and Eden's reliance on the 1930s during Suez.

The Lebanon/Jordan case also supports the argument that those who believe their adversary is irrational will favor the use of force. Eisenhower and Macmillan believed, in part on the basis of the 1930's and Suez analogies, that Nasser was irrational. Since Eisenhower and Macmillan thought that Nasser was behind the Iraqi coup, they believed, also on the basis of the 1930's and Suez analogies, that force was the preferred policy response. They believed that the irrational Nasser would not be amenable to diplomacy, a negotiated settlement, or to economic sanctions. The British and the Americans also decided early in the crisis to use force, but only as a last resort. There was no change after the initial decision, even as events in Lebanon and Jordan ebbed and flowed. Force would be used if the situation deteriorated. When the situation appeared to deteriorate in July 1958 Eisenhower and Macmillan intervened with the U.S. Marines and the British Paras.

NOTES

1. Memo of Conversation, May 13, 1958, Subject: Lebanon, JFD Papers, White House Memo Series, Box 6, DDE Library; Eisenhower, *The White House Years, Waging Peace, 1956–1961*, pp. 265–267.

2. Memo for the Record, May 15, 1958, DDE Papers as President, AWF, DDE Diary Series, Box 32, DDE Library.

3. Ovendale, "Great Britain and the Anglo-American Invasion," p. 287. From May through July, the United States and Britain opposed French intervention in Lebanon. Lebanon had been a French mandate and the United States did not want the intervention to reek of colonialism. Even so, the French sent a warship to the Lebanese coast. See Memo of Conference with the President, dated June 16, 1958 but held June 15, 1958, DDE Papers as President, AWF, DDE Diary Series, Box 33, DDE Library; Memo of Conversation, Subject: Lebanese Crisis, May 13, 1958, JFD Papers, White House Memo Series, Box 6, DDE Library; Memo for the Record, May 15, 1958, DDE Papers as President, AWF, DDE Diary Series, Box 32, DDE Library; and Memo of Conversation, June 15, 1958, DDE Papers as President, AWF, DDE Diary Series, Box 33, DDE Library.

4. Memo of Conversation, Subject: Lebanese Crisis, May 13, 1958, JFD Papers, White House Memo Series, Box 6, DDE Library; Ovendale, "Great Britain and the Anglo-American Invasion," p. 288; and Horne, *Harold Macmillan*, Vol. II, p. 92.

5. Ovendale, "Great Britain and the Anglo-American Invasion," pp. 286–287.

6. There were two modifications to the plan: a U.S. Army battle group was substituted for British paratroopers; and the two U.S. Marine battalions did not land simultaneously, the second landed several hours after the first because it was farther away than planned. Report by the Joint Middle East Planning Group to the JCS, "Study of the Long Range Military Implications of U.S./U.K. Intervention in Lebanon," June 23, 1958, DDRS, (81), 311A, DDE Library; and Tillema, *Appeal to Force*, p. 79.

7. Memo for the Record, May 15, 1958, Staff Notes (2), Folder: May 1958, DDE Library.

8. Statement by the President on the Lebanese Government's Appeal for United States Forces, July 15, 1958, *The Public Papers of the Presidents of the United States: Dwight D. Eisenhower, 1958*, pp. 549–550; Memo of Conference with the President, July 14, 1958, 10:50 A.M., DDE Papers as President, AWF, DDE Diary Series, Box 38: Folder, Staff Memos, July 1958, DDE Library; JFD telephone Call to Amb. Lodge, July 17, 1958, JFD Papers, Telephone Series, Box 8, DDE Library; Fry, "The Uses of Intelligence," pp. 69–78; Murphy, *Diplomat Among Warriors*, pp. 442–443; Eisenhower, *The White House Years, Waging Peace, 1956–1961*, p. 266; *Parliamentary Debates*, Commons, vol. 592, 5th Series (Oct. 23, 1958), col. 1887; and vol. 591, (July 14, 1958), col. 1511; Qubain, *Crisis in Lebanon*, pp. 89, 126–129, 174; Ovendale, "Great Britain and the Anglo-American Invasion," p. 287; and Korbani, *U.S. Intervention in Lebanon*; Goria, *Sovereignty and Leadership*, p. 43; Carpenter, "Direct Military Intervention," pp. 136–138; and Meo, *Lebanon*, p. 188.

9. Eisenhower, *The White House Years, Waging Peace, 1956–1961*, pp. 274–275; and "Statement by the President Following the Landing of United States Ma-

rines at Beirut," July 15, 1958, *The Public Papers of the Presidents of the United States: Dwight D. Eisenhower, 1958*, pp. 553–557.

10. Memo of Conversation with Prime Minister Daud, June 26, 1958, JFD Papers, General Correspondence and Memo Series, Box 1, DDE Library.

11. Telephone call from Amb. Lodge, July 14, 1958, JFD Papers, Telephone Series, Box 8, DDE Library. Also see Murphy, *Diplomat Among Warriors*, p. 442.

12. However, shortly after UNOGIL issued its report in early July, the issue changed from infiltration into Lebanon to the consequences of the Iraqi coup.

13. JFD telephone call to Sec. Quarles, June 14, 1958, JFD Papers, Telephone Series, Box 8, DDE Library; and Ovendale, "Great Britain and the Anglo-American Invasion," p. 289.

14. Memo of Conversation, July 21, 1958, JFD Papers, Chronological Series, Box 16, DDE Library.

15. Legislative Leadership Meeting, Supplementary Notes, July 22, 1958, DDE Papers as President, AWF, DDE Diary Series, Box 38: Folder, Staff Memos, July 1958, DDE Library.

16. JFD telephone call to the President, July 19, 1958, JFD Papers, Telephone Call Series, Box 12, DDE Library.

17. Ashton, "Macmillan and the Middle East," pp. 52–53.

18. Memo for the Record, July 14, 1958, JFD Papers, Chronological Series, Box 16, DDE Library; Memo of Conference with the President, 11:25 A.M., July 15, 1958, DDE Papers as President, AWF, DDE Diary Series, Box 38: Folder, Staff Memos, July 1958, DDE Library; and Eisenhower, *The White House Years, Waging Peace, 1956–1961*, p. 273.

19. Horne, *Harold Macmillan*, Vol. II, p. 93.

20. See *Parliamentary Debates*, Common, 5th Series, vol. 589 (June 25, 1958), col. 399; vol. 589, (June 25, 1958), col. 414; and vol. 589 (July 2, 1958), col. 1309.

21. Caccia to Lloyd, Secret, 20 March 1958, FO 371/133789.

22. Andrew J. Goodpaster, Memorandum of Conference with the President, July 24, 1958, DDE Papers as President, AWF, DDE Diaries, Box 38: Folder, Staff Memos, July 1958, DDE Library.

23. Memo of Conversation, Subject: Lebanon and the Middle East, July 1, 1958, DDE Papers as President, AWF, DDE Diary Series, Box 38: Folder, Staff Memos, July 1958, DDE Library.

24. Eisenhower, *The White House Years, Waging Peace, 1956–1961*, pp. 274–275; and "Statement by the President Following the Landing of United States Marines at Beirut," July 15, 1958, *The Public Papers of the Presidents of the United States: Dwight D. Eisenhower, 1958*, pp. 553–557.

25. "Special Message to the Congress on the Sending of United States Forces to Lebanon, July 15, 1958," *The Public Papers of the Presidents of the United States: Dwight D. Eisenhower, 1958*, pp. 550–552.

26. Memo of Telephone Conversation, Macmillan to Dulles, July 16, 1958, 8 P.M. EDT, JFD Papers, Chronological Series, Box 16, DDE Library; and Eisenhower to Paul Hoffman, June 23, 1958, DDE Papers as President, AWF, DDE Diary Series, Box 33, DDE Library.

27. *Parliamentary Debates*, Commons, 5th Series, vol. 591 (July 17, 1958), col. 1559.

28. Memo of Conversation, July 21, 1958, JFD Papers, Chronological Series, Box 16, DDE Library.

29. Telegram 4890, Dept. of State to Beirut Embassy, International Series, Box 34, AWF, DDE Library.

30. Telephone call from Amb. Lodge, June 18, 1958, JFD Papers, Telephone Series, Box 8, DDE Library. Also see Memo of Conference with the President, July 14, 1958 (dated July 16, 1958), meeting with Congressional Leaders, DDE Papers as President, AWF, DDE Diary Series, Box 38: Folder, Staff Memos, July 1958, DDE Library.

31. Memo of Conversation, Subject: Lebanese Crisis, May 13, 1958, JFD Papers, White House Memo Series, Box 6, DDE Library; Memo for the Record, May 15, 1958, DDE Papers as President, AWF, DDE Diary Series, Box 32, DDE Library; and Eisenhower, *The White House Years, Waging Peace, 1956–1961*, p. 266.

32. Memo of Conference with the President, July 14, 1958 (dated July 16, 1958), meeting with Congressional Leaders, DDE Papers as President, AWF, DDE Diary Series, Box 38: Folder, Staff Memos, July 1958, DDE Library.

33. Telephone call from Nixon, July 15, 1958, JFD Papers, Telephone Series, Box 8, DDE Library. Eisenhower also saw an extremely small risk of a Soviet-American war over Lebanon. Andrew J. Goodpaster, Oral History 37, 2 of 3, Aug. 2, 1967, p. 90, DDE Library; Memo for the Record, May 15, 1958, DDE Papers as President, AWF, DDE Diary Series, Box 32, DDE Library; Synopsis—Intelligence and State Department Items Reported to the President, July 23, 1958, DDE, Papers as President, AWF, DDE Diary Series, Box 34, DDE Library; and Eisenhower, *The White House Years, Waging Peace, 1956–1961*, pp. 266, 282.

34. Memo of Conversation, Subject: Lebanon and the Middle East, July 1, 1958, DDE Papers as President, AWF, DDE Diary Series, Box 38: Folder, Staff Memos, July 1958, DDE Library.

35. This theory was discussed before 1958. For example, in 1951 Eisenhower talked about falling dominoes in Indo-China (see Olson, "Eisenhower and the Indo-China Problem," p. 97) and on April 7, 1954 Eisenhower related the "falling-domino" to Asia and Vietnam. See Lyon, *Eisenhower*, p. 601.

36. Memo of Conversation, Subject: Lebanese Crisis, May 13, 1958, JFD Papers, White House Memo Series, Box 6, DDE Library. Also see Memo for the Record, May 15, 1958, DDE Papers as President, AWF, DDE Diary Series, Box 32, DDE Library.

37. Telephone call from Amb. Lodge, June 18, 1958, JFD Papers, Telephone Series, Box 8, DDE Library.

38. Memo of Conversation, June 15, 1958, DDE Papers as President, AWF, DDE Diary Series, Box 33, DDE Library.

39. Memo for the Record, July 14, 1958, JFD Papers, Chronological Series, Box 16, DDE Library. Also see Eisenhower, *The White House Years, Waging Peace, 1956–1961*, p. 274.

40. Memo of Conference with the President, July 14, 1958, 10:50 A.M., DDE Papers as President, AWF, DDE Diary Series, Box 38: Folder, Staff Memos, July 1958, DDE Library.

41. Memo of Conference with the President, July 14, 1958 (dated July 16, 1958), meeting with Congressional Leaders, DDE Papers as President, AWF, DDE Diary Series, Box 38: Folder, Staff Memos, July 1958, DDE Library. Also see "Spe-

cial Message to the Congress on the Sending of United States Forces to Lebanon," July 15, 1958, *The Public Papers of the Presidents of the United States: Dwight D. Eisenhower, 1958*, p. 552.

42. Cabinet Conclusions, (58) 42, 13 May 1958, CAB 128/32, Part 1; Lamb, *The Macmillan Years*, p. 35; and Horne, *Harold Macmillan*, Vol. II, p. 93.

43. *Parliamentary Debates*, Commons, 5th Series, vol. 591 (July 17, 1958), col. 1559.

44. Ovendale, "Great Britain and the Anglo-American Invasion," pp. 295–296.

45. Fisher, *Harold Macmillan*, pp. 175–76.

46. Memo for the Record, May 15, 1958, DDE Papers as President, AWF, DDE Diary Series, Box 32, DDE Library.

47. Memo for the Record, May 15, 1958, DDE Papers as President, AWF, DDE Diary Series, Box 32, DDE Library; and Eisenhower, *The White House Years, Waging Peace, 1956–1961*, p. 267.

48. Memo of Conversation, June 15, 1958, DDE Papers as President, AWF, DDE Diaries, Box 33, DDE Library.

49. Memo for the Record, May 15, 1958, DDE Papers as President, AWF, DDE Diary Series, Box 32, DDE Library.

50. Memo for the Record, May 15, 1958, DDE Papers as President, AWF, DDE Diary Series, Box 32, DDE Library.

51. Qubain, *Crisis in Lebanon*, p. 113; and Eisenhower, *The White House Years, Waging Peace, 1956–1961*, p. 267.

52. Little discussed the different compositions of coalitions that support decisions to, or not to, intervene.

53. Memo of Conversation, June 15, 1958, DDE Papers as President, AWF, DDE Diary Series, Box 33, DDE Library; and Telephone call to Mr. Macomber, June 15, 1958, JFD Papers, Telephone Series, Box 8, DDE Library

54. Memo of Conference with the President, dated June 16, 1958 (held on June 15, 1958), DDE Papers as President, AWF, DDE Diary Series, Box 33, DDE Library.

55. Ibid.

56. Telephone call to Sec. Quarles, June 14, 1958, JFD Papers, Telephone Series, Box 8, DDE Library.

57. Telephone call to the President from Dulles, June 15, 1958, JFD Papers, Telephone Call Series, Box 12, DDE Library.

58. Memo of Conversation, June 15, 1958, DDE Papers as President, AWF, DDE Diary Series, Box 33, DDE Library.

59. Outgoing Telegram to Beirut Embassy from Dulles, June 19, 1958, DDE Papers as President, AWF, International Series, Box 37, DDE Library.

60. Eisenhower, *The White House Years, Waging Peace, 1956–1961*, p. 269.

61. Outgoing Telegram to Beirut Embassy from Dulles, June 19, 1958, DDE Papers as President, AWF, International Series, Box 37, DDE Library.

62. Memo of Conversation, June 15, 1958, DDE Papers as President, AWF, DDE Diary Series, Box 33, DDE Library.

63. Ibid.

64. Telephone call to the President, June 14, 1958, 5:36 P.M., JFD Papers, Telephone Call Series, Box 12, DDE Library.

65. Memo of Conversation, June 15, 1958, DDE Papers as President, AWF, DDE Diary Series, Box 33, DDE Library.

66. Allen Dulles, Briefing Notes, Meeting at the White House with Congressional Leaders, July 14, 1958, DDE Library.

67. Eisenhower, *The White House Years, Waging Peace, 1956–1961*, p. 270. Also see Memo of Conference with the President, July 14, 1958 (dated July 16, 1958), meeting with Congressional Leaders, DDE Papers as President, AWF, DDE Diary Series, Box 38: Folder, Staff Memos, July 1958, DDE Library.

68. Allen Dulles, Briefing Notes, Meeting at the White House with Congressional Leaders, July 14, 1958, DDE Library. Also see Memo of Conference with the President, July 14, 1958, 10:50 A.M., DDE Papers as President, AWF, DDE Diary Series, Box 38: Folder, Staff Memos, July 1958, DDE Library.

69. Eisenhower, *The White House Years, Waging Peace, 1956–1961*, p. 272.

70. Memo of Conference with the President, July 14, 1958 (dated July 15, 1958), DDE Papers as President, AWF, DDE Diary Series, Box 38: Folder, Staff Memos, July 1958, DDE Library; Andrew J. Goodpaster, Oral History 37, Interview 3 of 3, Sept. 8, 1967, p. 94, DDE Library; and Ambrose, *Eisenhower, The President*, p. 465.

71. Memo of Conversation, July 15, 1958, JFD Papers, Chronological Series, Box 16, DDE Library.

72. Ovendale, "Great Britain and the Anglo-American Invasion," p. 290.

73. Ibid., pp. 291, 295–296. At first Hussein wanted to send the Arab army into Iraq to reverse the coup, restore the Arab Union between Jordan and Iraq, and avenge Faisal. However, his advisors dissuaded him.

74. Allen Dulles, Briefing Notes, Meeting at the White House with Congressional Leaders, July 14, 1958, DDE Library; Telephone call from Amb. Lodge, July 14, 1958, JFD Papers, Telephone Series, Box 8, DDE Library; Eisenhower, *The White House Years, Waging Peace, 1956–1961*, p. 270; and Memo of Conference with the President, July 14, 1958, 10:50 A.M., DDE Papers as President, AWF, DDE Diary Series, Box 38: Folder, Staff Memos, July 1958, DDE Library.

75. Memo of Conference with the President, 11:25 A.M., July 15, 1958, DDE Papers as President, AWF, DDE Diary Series, Box 38: Folder, Staff Memos, July 1958, DDE Library.

76. Memo for the Record, Subject: Meeting in Secretary's Office re: Jordan, July 15, 1958, JFD Papers, Chronological Series, Box 16, DDE Library.

77. Minutes of 372nd NSC Meeting, July 24, 1958, DDE Papers as President, AWF, NSC Series, Box 10, DDE Library.

78. Memo of Conference with the President, July 16, 1958, DDE Papers as President, AWF, DDE Diary Series, Box 38: Folder, Staff Memos, July 1958, DDE Library,

79. Memo of Telephone Conversation, Macmillan to Dulles, July 16, 1958, 8 P.M. EDT, JFD Papers, Chronological Series, Box 16, DDE Library.

80. Eisenhower, *The White House Years, Waging Peace, 1956–1961*, p. 273.

81. Ovendale, "Britain and the Anglo-American Intervention," p. 292.

82. Telephone call from Macmillan, July 16, 1958, 6:20 P.M., JFD Papers, Telephone Series, Box 8, DDE Library.

83. Memo of Telephone Conversation, July 16, 1958, Macmillan to Dulles, 8

P.M. EDT, JFD Papers, Chronological Series, Box 16, DDE Library. Also see Eisenhower, *The White House Years, Waging Peace, 1956–1961*, p. 282.

84. For an account of the landing, see Thayer, *Diplomat*.

85. 372nd NSC Meeting Minutes, July 24, 1958, DDE Papers as President, AWF, NSC Series, Box 10: 372nd NSC Meeting, DDE Library; and Eisenhower, *The White House Years, Waging Peace, 1956–1961*, pp. 279–282.

86. Report from Allen Dulles to Dept. of State, July 17, 1958, JFD Papers, Telephone Series, Box 8, DDE Library; Macmillan to Dulles, July 16, 1958, JFD Papers, Chronological Series, Box 16: Memo of Telephone Conversation, DDE Library; and NSC Meeting Minutes, July 24, 1958, DDE Papers as President, AWF, NSC Series, Box 10: 372nd NSC Meeting, DDE Library.

87. Ambassador Lodge to JFD, July 14, 1958, JFD Papers, Telephone Series, Box 8, DDE Library.

88. Eisenhower, *The White House Years, Waging Peace, 1956–1961*, p. 275. Also see Andrew J. Goodpaster, Oral History 477, April 10, 1982, p. 22, DDE Library.

89. Memo of Conference with the President, July 14, 1958 (dated July 16, 1958), meeting with Congressional Leaders, DDE Papers as President, AWF, DDE Diary Series, Box 38: Folder, Staff Memos, July 1958, DDE Library.

90. Ibid.

91. Memo of Conference with the President, July 14, 1958 (dated July 15, 1958), DDE Papers as President, AWF, DDE Diary Series, Box 38: Folder, Staff Memos, July 1958, DDE Library.

92. JFD telephone call to Under-Secretary Quarles, June 14, 1958, JFD Papers, Telephone Series, Box 8, DDE Library. Also see Qubain, *Crisis in Lebanon*, p. 116.

93. Ovendale, "Great Britain and the Anglo-American Invasion," p. 291.

94. DDE, Oral History 11, July 20, 1967, pp. 60–61, DDE Library.

95. Andrew J. Goodpaster, Oral History 37, 2 of 3, Aug. 2, 1967, pp. 87–88, DDE Library.

96. 372nd NSC Meeting, July 24, 1958, DDE, Papers as President, AWF, NSC Series, Box 10, DDE Library.

97. Memo of Conference with the President, July 14, 1958, 10:50 A.M., DDE Papers as President, AWF, DDE Diary Series, Box 38: Folder, Staff Memos, July 1958, DDE Library; and Memo of Conference with the President, July 15, 1958, 11:25 A.M., DDE Papers as President, AWF, DDE Diary Series, Box 38: Folder, Staff Memos, July 1958, DDE Library.

98. Eisenhower, *The White House Years, Waging Peace, 1956–1961*, p. 276; and Memorandum of Conference with the President, July 15, 1958, 11:25 A.M., DDE Papers as President, AWF, DDE Diary Series, Box 38: Folder, Staff Memos, July 1958, DDE Library.

99. *Foreign Relations of the United States, 1958–1960, Vol. XI*, p. 138.

100. Lyon argued that this buildup was for possible intervention in Syria. Lyon, *Eisenhower*, pp. 775–776. There is no evidence in policy meetings at the time to suggest that Eisenhower ever seriously considered intervening from Lebanon into Iraq.

101. At first, only two battalions were available to intervene. Horne, *Harold Macmillan*, Vol. II, p. 94.

102. *Parliamentary Debates*, Commons, 5th Series, vol. 591 (July 17, 1958), col. 1557.

103. Horne, *Harold Macmillan*, Vol. I, pp. 33, 41.

104. Lyon, *Eisenhower*, p. 50.

105. For example, see Lloyd to Caccia, Secret, 23 June 1958, PREM 11/2387.

106. *Foreign Relations of the United States, Vol. XI*, pp. 207–208.

107. Ambrose, *Eisenhower, The President*, p. 465.

108. *Parliamentary Debates*, Commons, 5th Series, vol. 591 (July 17, 1958), col. 1559.

109. Memo of Telephone Conversation, Macmillan to Dulles, July 16, 1958, 8 P.M. EDT, JFD Papers, Chronological Series, Box 16, DDE Library.

110. Ann C. Whitman, Oral History 511, Feb. 15, 1991, pp. 11–12, DDE Library; and Andrew J. Goodpaster, Oral History 37, 2 of 3, Aug. 2, 1967, p. 88, DDE Library.

111. *Foreign Relations of the United States, Vol. XI*, pp. 207–208.

112. Cabinet Conclusions, (58) 42, May 13, 1958, CAB 128/32, Part 1. Also see Lamb, *The Macmillan Years*, p. 35; and Horne, *Harold Macmillan*, Vol. II, p. 93.

113. Brainstorming is a method of searching creatively for solutions to a problem by freely and in an unrestrained manner thinking of possible solutions.

114. Fisher, *Harold Macmillan*, p. 193; and Horne, *Harold Macmillan*, Vol. II, p. 43.

115. Horne, *Harold Macmillan*, Vol. I, pp. 370–371.

7

Conclusion

Policy makers often use historical analogies to draw lessons from history when they are faced with regional crises involving the potential use of military force. In many cases, historical information has a significant influence on perceptions of the adversary, the stakes, goals, risks, and policy options. Historical information also influences policy choices and how policy makers justify the policies that they select. This chapter reviews the influence of situational and individual variables on the use of analogical reasoning to retrieve information from history in comparison to the use of current information. Different characteristics of historical analogies are then discussed, as well as whether historical analogies are used for diagnosis and prescription or merely to justify policy chosen by other means. The process by which decision makers use historical information is then analyzed, followed by a discussion of the effects of historical analogies. The most commonly used historical analogy in the cases analyzed in this book, the 1930s, is then presented as an example of a master analogy. The relationship between analogical reasoning, history, and learning is then discussed, followed by analysis of the decision to use military force in regional contingencies. The last section surveys suggestions for further study.

SITUATIONAL AND INDIVIDUAL VARIABLES

A range of situational variables influence to what extent policy makers use analogies to retrieve historical information, as well as their perception of the value of historical information in comparison to current information. When faced by intense time pressures during dramatic, complex events, especially crises involving national security, such as an invasion of an ally, a coup in an allied or client state, or the nationalization of a strategically important industry in another state, policy makers use historical analogies as cognitive shortcuts to frame and diagnose international crises and to prescribe and legitimize policy. Current information is often lacking in pressure-filled crises, so policy makers rely on historical information as a cognitive framework to make sense out of the limited current information that is available. Historical analogies often provide missing information, especially about the intentions of an adversary and about what policies should be pursued. The finding that historical analogies are often used during foreign policy crises involving national security, especially when time is short, suggests that policy makers are more likely to accept the validity of a historical analogy when a perceived situation is more risky and involves greater commitment than in cases when a task involves little risk or commitment. The historical analogy acts as a cognitive shortcut to relieve time pressure by prescribing a single policy response. The analogy also frames the crisis and fills in missing information, which reduces anxiety about the unknown. Historical analogies are rarely used for routine, low-risk tasks that lack time pressure and involve little commitment, because in such situations there is ample time to analyze the issues using other, more time-consuming, means, such as cost-benefit analysis. Surprise, which is a component of drama, contributes to time pressures by eliminating time for planning and gathering current information, which reinforces the tendency to use historical analogies as a cognitive shortcut. If an issue is nonroutine and involves high-level decision making, then policy makers are likely to rely on historical information and analogies. A crisis is, by definition, nonroutine and involves high-level decision making. Policy makers use historical analogies, in part, because standard operating procedures do not exist for crises, which are novel and, therefore, not routine, and because cost-benefit analysis is difficult when current information is sparse, which is a common occurrence in crises.

Besides these situational variables, individual variables also influence the use of historical information. Throughout their careers, some policy makers use historical information more often than other policy makers. The broad differences between the British and American cultures and school systems do not explain differences in the use of historical analogies in this study. Some British policy makers, such as Macmillan, Churchill, and Eden, often used historical information and analogies, while others, such as Lloyd and Attlee, rarely used such information. Similarly, some U.S. policy makers, such as Truman, used historical analogies, while others, such as Dulles and Acheson, rarely used them.

This study suggests that the discipline that policy makers studied at university influences their future use of historical information and analogies in foreign policy crises. Those who studied law, such as Dulles, Acheson, Attlee, and Lloyd, were less likely to use historical analogies than those educated in other fields, such as Eden (Oriental languages) and Macmillan (a publisher). Legal training even overrode the tendency of Acheson and Dulles, who loved history, to use historical analogies. However, this finding is tempered by individual variation, especially in the case of Truman. Truman, who was a county judge and attended law school for two years, but did not graduate,[1] used historical analogies at least as often as Eden, who studied Oriental languages. The lack of a legal education, as opposed to working as a lawyer or judge, may explain the difference between Truman and the other lawyers, Dulles, Acheson, Lloyd, and Attlee.

The proposition that the wider scope of knowledge a leader possesses the less influence the most recent, major event will have on his decision making is not valid. Truman often read history, yet was dominated by the 1930's analogy during the Korean crisis. Macmillan, who possessed a vast knowledge of history, was influenced significantly by Suez during the Lebanon/Jordan crisis. Eden, who had some knowledge of history, was totally dominated by the 1930's analogy during the Suez crisis. Major recent events such as the 1930s and Suez, dominate both leaders who are knowledgeable about history and those who are not.

A policy maker's profession before he became a politician also influences his use of historical information and analogies. Policy makers who were reporters, writers, or publishers before they became national leaders are more likely to use historical analogies than those without newspaper, writing, or publishing backgrounds. Macmillan, a publisher who also wrote several books, used historical analogies more often than any other policy maker analyzed in this book. As a publisher, raised in a family that owned a publishing firm, Macmillan was more aware of language, rhetorical devices, and writing style than the other policy makers. Churchill, who was a war correspondent and prolific author, also used historical analogies more often than any policy maker except Macmillan. Although all of the policy makers analyzed in this study wrote books or memoirs and, therefore, were authors, some were, by background and inclination, far more interested in writing and rhetoric. Those interested in writing, such as Macmillan and Churchill, were more likely to use historical analogies than orators, such as Bevin, especially since Bevin tended to speak extemporaneously. Unfortunately, the sample size of policy makers in this study is too small to analyze rigorously individual variables and the use of historical information. Further research on these variables will help to explain why some leaders view events from a historical perspective, while others rely almost exclusively on current information.

Although differences between the American and British school systems do not explain differences in the use of historical analogies and historical information, differences between the British and American systems of government may contribute to differing uses of historical information. The British system appears to produce more orators, who are more interested in rhetoric and, therefore, more likely to use historical analogies. Because the British prime minister is drawn from Parliament, he must make speeches and answer questions as both an MP and as prime minister. Rhetoric and public speaking in the sometimes hostile environment of Parliament are important attributes in a prime minister. The U.S. president, although expected to make speeches, is not required to be the accomplished debater that the British prime minister often must be. Except for a few highly structured, quasi-debates during elections, the U.S. president never has to participate in the give and take of a parliamentary question period.

The British prime ministers and foreign secretaries studied in this book, however, were clustered in two groups: the first, including Macmillan, Churchill, and Eden, often used historical analogies; the second, including Attlee, Bevin, and Lloyd, used them rarely. Among the Americans, Eisenhower, Dulles, and Acheson fell toward the nonuse end of the spectrum. Truman is the outlier for the Americans, in that he tended to use historical information as much as some of the British leaders who often used such information. This finding suggests that the British system produces two types of politicians: the orator who uses historical analogies, such as Churchill and Macmillan, and the political organizer who rarely uses historical analogies. Two examples of the later were Bevin, who rose to power through organizing labor, and Attlee, who was a party organizer. With the exception of Truman, the U.S. political system produces men who rarely use historical information or analogies. This may be because the U.S. president tends to be more of a political organizer than an orator. It may also be because Britain is a far older state with a much longer history than the relatively young United States. The British may also culturally have more of tendency toward a historical view, although this would be a difficult hypothesis to test because of the difficulty of operationalizing culture.

The British cabinet, composed of elected members of Parliament (MPs), may also require the British prime minister to be more persuasive than an American president and, therefore, be more inclined to use historical analogies as a rhetorical device to persuade his colleagues. American cabinet members, by contrast, are not office holders in their own right. The U.S. president, therefore, may not need to use historical analogies to persuade his cabinet to support him as much as the British prime minister must do with his cabinet of independently elected ministers. This argument is supported by the prime ministers who used historical analogies, Macmillan, Churchill, and Eden, and the president, Eisenhower, who rarely used historical analogies. However, Attlee and Truman are outliers. Attlee rarely used historical analogies. He used other means of persuasion, especially consensus building, instead of historical analogies to maintain the support of his cabinet. Truman's personal interest in history may have overrode the usual nonuse of historical information and analogies by American presidents. Truman also had a strong belief that he was the final decision maker as evidenced by his famous phrase "the buck stops here." Therefore, he may have felt less of a need to persuade his cabinet than other presidents. Beyond the political system, the individual prime ministers and presidents, of course, significantly colored how their administrations used historical information and analogies. Eden's use of the 1930's analogy during Suez and the use of indirect aggression analogies by Eisenhower during the Lebanon/Jordan crises certainly dominated how the crises were framed and handled by their administrations. These, however, are suggestive findings and further research, based on a longitudinal study of a larger sample of decision makers would be required to determine which individual, cultural, and domestic political structure variables influence the use of historical information and analogies as compared to current information.

Situational and individual variables are the two ingredients that determine whether historical information is used during a foreign policy crisis. During the Korean crisis, situational variables dominated individual variables. Attlee, Bevin, Truman, and Acheson all relied on the 1930's analogy to frame the crisis, as well as to prescribe and justify policy, regardless of their individual inclinations to use historical analogies. This suggests that situational variables in the Korean crisis overrode individual tendencies in relation to the use of historical information. Time pressures, surprise, and the high stakes led to the use of historical analogies.

During the Iran crisis, the lack of any time pressure and forewarning about the Iranian nationalization contributed to the lack of use of historical information. Situational variables prevented any of the policy makers, with the partial exception of Eisenhower's use of the China analogy, from framing the crisis in terms of a historical analogy. The lack of time pressures and surprise allowed policy makers to take their time to analyze the Iran issue without resorting to cognitive shortcuts, such as historical analogies.

During the Suez crisis a more complex relationship between situational and individual variables emerged. The personal inclination of Eden to use historical information was reinforced by situational variables, especially time pressures, high stakes, and the fact that the nationalization of the canal was viewed as a national security issue. For the Americans, the individual tendencies of Eisenhower and Dulles to use historical information rarely, except in response to the use of historical analogies by others or to use them for a specific audience, was reinforced by the low stakes, lack of time pressures, and nonnational security nature of the crisis for the Americans.

In the Lebanon/Jordan case, the situational and individual variables contributed to a balance of current and historical information. Macmillan, Eisenhower, and Dulles all used historical information, but not nearly as much as Eden had during Suez. The time pressures, stakes, and national security nature of the crises in May, June, and July 1958 contributed to the use of historical information. However, as each crisis swiftly passed, individual tendencies took over. Macmillan continued to use historical analogies, while Eisenhower and Dulles shifted to focus more on the current situation. When Iraq's royal family was murdered in a coup, on July 14, 1958, however, time pressures, drama, and the stakes suddenly increased and the British and Americans then turned to historical analogies as a cognitive shortcut to frame the crisis, as well as to prescribe and justify policy.

Overall, situational and individual variables are independent of each other. If a situation has heightened time pressures, with high drama and stakes, as well as involving national security, then any leader will use historical analogies. Even leaders who rarely, if ever, use historical analogies, will use historical information in such a situation, if only because others raise an analogy, and they must respond to that analogy. If a situation lacks time pressure, high stakes, or national security issues, then individual variables will determine if a leader will use historical analogies. However, for a policy maker to use historical information for a low stakes, nonnational security issue that lacks time pressures his personal inclination to use such information must be extremely high.

CHARACTERISTICS OF HISTORICAL ANALOGIES

In none of the cases analyzed for this book did policy makers have to justify the use of analogical reasoning to retrieve historical information as a means of diagnosing a crisis, prescribing or legitimizing policy. This may be the result of a set of implicit rules that guide the use of analogies and historical information during foreign policy meetings. These common rules outline a set of characteristics that increases the probability that others will support the analogy itself, if the analogy fits these characteristics. For example, policy makers usually retrieve recent, personally experienced or observed, dramatic events that involve the policy maker's own state in a foreign policy failure, often involving national security. Historical analogies have to be familiar to fulfill their simplifying role, and recent events that fit the above characteristics are more likely to be familiar to the colleagues of a policy maker. Such historical analogies, therefore, are more likely to be deemed analogous and valid. Policy makers rarely use historical analogies based on obscure events or events from the distant past, let alone from antiquity, because they are not familiar to others and, therefore, do not simplify the current crisis. The fall of Babylon, the Scottish Highland Clearances, the warlord period in China, the Canadian Reil Rebellion, and other, obscure or ancient events are almost never drawn upon as analogies to current crises. If a policy maker retrieves an obscure or ancient historical analogy, he has to explain extensively the event to his colleagues. This explanation defeats the purpose of using a historical analogy: as a cognitive shortcut to simplify a current crisis. Those who use a historical analogy, as well as the audience, must believe that they are more familiar with the historical analogy than with the current case. Otherwise the analogy will not perform its simplifying role because the historical event or person will appear as complex as the current case. To take an extreme example, raising an analogy between the North Korean invasion of South Korea and the Hyskos invasion of ancient Egypt would fail utterly as an analogy for policy makers, save those with Egyptology as a hobby. The analogy sheds no light on the invasion of South Korea because most current policy makers probably do not even know who the Hyskos were. Anyone suggesting the Hyskos/Egypt analogy would have to explain extensively the historical case, thus negating the simplifying role of the analogy. Older historical events are only retrieved when a current event is unique. For example, when the British faced the Bolshevik Revolution, which involved a fundamental change in the political structure of a great power, they retrieved the French Revolution as an analogy. There appeared to be no analogy to the Russian Revolution in the living memory of the policy makers of the time.

Policy makers also tend to retrieve as analogies events that involve their own state, which increases the chance that other policy makers will be familiar with the event. They do not, however, focus on their own state's past successes. They instead usually recall cases where their state suffered a foreign policy failure. Humans tend to draw lessons from failures rather than from successes. A success requires no explanation. The policy was effective and events occurred as expected or, at least, as hoped. A failure requires explanation and analysis to explain the poor outcome and the unexpected course of events. This analysis leads to lessons that become familiar and well known, which can later be drawn upon for other crises. The lesson is often a negative one, in that policy makers avoid the policy that failed in the analogy and pursue a policy that has come to be accepted broadly as the policy that should have been followed in the historical case. For example, the British appeasement policy in the 1930s, at least to the British government at the time, unexpectedly failed. By the 1950s the lessons of the 1930s, which was seen as a period when Western diplomacy failed to avoid world war, were known broadly in the West. Leaders in the 1950s did not want to be Chamberlain and studiously avoided any hint of an appeasement policy.

How leaders frame a historical event is crucial to whether it is seen as a failure or a success. Today, for example, some scholars argue that appeasement was a success to the extent that British diplomacy and negotiation bought time for Britain to rearm and, ultimately, to prevail over Germany, Italy, and Japan. However, foreign policy makers in the 1950s framed the 1930s as a failure and, therefore, they were more likely to use it as a historical analogy.

Policy makers almost never use historical analogies from past successes. For example, lessons from the victory in World War II about the value of science (atomic research), technology (radar and sonar) and intelligence (the

British breaking of the German Ultra code and the American breaking of the Japanese Purple code), or the successful American pacification effort in the Philippines at the turn of the century, were much less commonly known and rarely, if ever, mentioned as lessons from history in the cases in this study. Lessons from the crises at the turn of the century that did not lead to world war—in a sense, successes—such as wars in the Balkans and disputes over control of Morocco, were also not mentioned.

The argument that the retrieval of historical events that have been experienced firsthand would be full of extraneous and dissimilar information, thus leading policy makers to reject the analogy as invalid for the current case, was not supported by the present study. Almost all of the historical analogies retrieved were personally experienced by the policy makers and were therefore full of extraneous, personal information. Such information did not lead policy makers to reject the analogy. This greater level of involvement increases the probability that the historical event will be retrieved as a historical analogy because it increases the chance that colleagues of a similar age as the policy maker who retrieved the analogy will also have experienced personally or observed the events in the analogy. Therefore, it is more likely that other policy makers also will be familiar with the analogy. Furthermore, traumatic, important events in the life of the leader, which are experienced personally, are of course more likely to come to mind and be retrieved as an analogy to the current crisis than cases that did not involve the policy maker or that were not traumatic or important.

Policy makers also tend to retrieve events or people that share surface similarities with the current crisis or adversary, which increases the perceived validity of the historical analogy to the current case. Any historical analogy will appear different if the causal variables are analyzed. In fact, no historical analogy is exactly the same as a current event, especially when deeper, causal variables are analyzed. Therefore, there are only degrees of surface similarity, given that causal variables can have vastly different effects even in cases that appear similar. However, policy makers use analogical reasoning to retrieve information from history because historical information adds a sense of stability and order to international relations, which usually is not present. Historical analogies that appear to be the same as a current case, even if the similarity is only superficial, provide a foundation of confidence for policy makers, as well as gaining support for a policy. In the cases analyzed in this book, policy makers used lessons that other policy makers and the public already knew and had accepted, especially master analogies, such as the 1930s. By doing so, the lessons helped garner support for current policies on the basis of those lessons and decreased anxiety about the chosen course because it appeared as if the chosen policy was based on past experience. Even better, because leaders who use analogies almost always base policies on past foreign policy failures, the leader appears to be smarter than a policy maker who merely copies a past success. In almost every case, the policy maker tries to learn from a past failure and to do better than the leader in the historical analogy, whose policy failed.

Current events that are dominated by an individual, such as Nasser's nationalization of the Suez Canal, usually lead policy makers to retrieve historical figures, such as Mussolini, as analogies. If a current event is not dominated by an individual, such as the North Korean invasion of South Korea, then a historical event is usually retrieved, such as the 1930s. Whether an event or an individual is retrieved from history influences how policy makers frame a crisis, as well as their policy choices. For example, because the British retrieved Mussolini as an analogy to Nasser, they were far more likely to pursue a policy that involved attempting to overthrow Nasser, than if the British had framed the crisis with less of an emphasis on Nasser. If the nationalization of the canal had been seen as a reflection of broader Egyptian, or even Arab, nationalism, then the British would have been less likely to retrieve Mussolini as an analogy. The British also would have been less likely to believe that by removing Nasser, the threat to the canal could be reduced. By framing the crisis in terms of Mussolini, Nasser was cast as the sole cause of the nationalization of the canal and the source of all the problems the British faced in Egypt. Of course, a historical analogy does not need to be used to focus attention on an individual. During the Iran crisis, even though no historical analogies were used, except for Eisenhower's use of China, the British and Americans focused on Mossadegh as the source of their troubles in Iran. In part, the belief that Nasser and Mossadegh were the prime forces behind the threats to British and American interests in the Suez and Iran crises, respectively, was based on the prominence and importance of the roles of the two leaders in the crises. However, the use of historical analogies, especially individuals from history, such as Mussolini, significantly reinforce the perception that the adversary is the source of the crisis and that his removal will solve the problem.

Policy makers tend to retrieve historical analogies that are recent, personally experienced, traumatic events, involving their own state in a foreign policy failure. They also tend to retrieve historical events as analogies for current events and leaders from history when a current crisis is dominated by a foreign leader. Policy makers also tend to retrieve historical analogies that provide general, macrolessons, which a range of decision makers can support. Historical analogies that prescribe narrow, microlessons are rarely used to frame a crisis or to prescribe or justify policy.

DIAGNOSIS AND PRESCRIPTION OR JUSTIFICATION

Many researchers have attempted to separate the diagnostic, prescriptive, and justification functions of historical analogies. Both those who argue that historical analogies are used for diagnosis and prescription, and those who argue that analogies are used solely to justify policies chosen by other means have made logical, convincing arguments supported by selective cases to support their positions. Both schools are able to make convincing cases because in most cases policy makers use historical analogies for all three functions, often at the same time. Attempts to separate the functions are an attempt to impose categories upon a process that does not have discrete categories. In general, decision making does not have distinct diagnosis, prescription, and justification phases, nor does the use of historical analogies. The phases overlap.[2] For example, when policy makers diagnose a crisis, they are already evaluating policy options (prescription) and intertwined with judging the effectiveness of policy options is their judgment of their ability to justify each policy to the public and to their colleagues. The key issue is to determine when policy makers use historical analogies to diagnose, prescribe, or justify a policy. Personality plays a crucial role. For example, Truman tended to use historical analogies after a decision was made to justify a policy, although he also relied on internalized lessons from history to prescribe policy. During Suez, Eden relied on the 1930s to diagnose the crisis, but also to prescribe and to justify policy. However, Eisenhower, during Suez, separated diagnosis from prescription, while during Lebanon/Jordan, he switched from policy prescription to policy prescription on the basis of different historical analogies, although all of them involved what he believed was indirect aggression. However, these functions of historical analogies are intertwined like the Gordian knot and cannot be separated in general, although in some specific cases, there is a clear delineation of functions by an individual policy maker.

THE PROCESS OF ANALOGICAL REASONING FROM HISTORY

This book presents a new model of the process of analogical reasoning by small groups of policy makers in foreign policy settings. The model that a policy maker mentions a historical analogy, whose validity is debated, and then accepted or rejected on the basis of mapping, was not supported and was, in many ways, too simplistic to describe what actually occurs in foreign policy meetings.

In meetings about the four crises analyzed in this study, historical analogies were often used in clusters. When one policy maker mentioned a historical analogy, it often, in a snowball effect, led to other policy makers raising other historical events or people as possible analogies to the current crisis. This suggests that one problem-solving technique, such as analogical reasoning, may spread within a decision-making group, in a form of groupthink. However, if someone pointed out one difference between the current case and the analogy, it was enough to cause policy makers to drop the analogy and not mention it again. This mode of policy making is common in crisis meetings, which tend to be free flowing, with issues and possible policies raised, put aside, and then raised again. Usually there was little, if any, debate about historical analogies during the decision-making process. There was never debate about the interpretation of the historical event or person, nor about the lessons drawn from history, although policy makers often narrowly criticized the implications of a particular lesson from a historical analogy for the current case. There was debate in Parliament about the lessons from Suez for Lebanon/Jordan. This is because Parliament had a greater diversity of beliefs and interpretations of history than the cabinet, which is usually composed of members with similar political beliefs. This diversity, therefore, led to more debate in Parliament than in the cabinet about the interpretation of history. In the cabinet, when a historical analogy was suggested, it was either accepted or invalidated by the mention of one difference. Furthermore, prime ministers, like presidents, wield a certain amount of authority over their cabinets. When a prime minister or president mentioned a historical analogy and used it to frame the crisis, it was immediately accepted by the other cabinet members. Therefore, who raises a historical analogy is crucially important.

The private use of lessons from history mirrored the public use of historical analogies in the cases analyzed for this book. This finding weakens Khong's argument that Vietnam was a hard case for analogical reasoning. He argued that Vietnam is a hard case to test whether policy makers use historical analogies to formulate foreign policy because so many historical analogies were mentioned both publicly and privately that it is unlikely that any single analogy determined policy. Furthermore, Khong argued that the use of so many historical analogies favors the conclusion that historical analogies were used for justification and not for diagnosis or for policy formulation. Even so, he found that historical analogies influenced policy selection even in this supposedly hard case. However, Vietnam was an easy case for testing whether policy makers used historical analogies to formulate policy because so many historical analogies were used. Analogical reasoning has a tendency to snowball in a group setting: If one policy maker mentions a historical analogy, other policy makers tend to think analogically and to mention other analogies, both to prescribe, and to justify, policy. More important for Khong's argument, the public use of historical analogies to justify policy tends to mirror the private use of historical analogies to diagnose a crisis and to prescribe policy. The profusion of historical analogies used in the Vietnam case, therefore, makes it an easy case for testing whether policy makers use historical analogies to formulate policy. A hard case would be where no historical analogies were mentioned publicly for justification, yet were used to frame a crisis and to prescribe policy. If the present study is correct, that public use mirrors private use, such cases should be rare. Furthermore, if diagnosis, prescription, and justification overlap, such cases should be even rarer, bordering on nonexistent.

Policy makers usually accept all or none of a historical analogy as valid.

Eisenhower was an exception in that during the Suez crisis he accepted part of the 1930's analogy, that Nasser was similar to Mussolini, while rejecting other aspects of the analogy, especially the policy prescriptions it raised. Eisenhower was, however, an exception. Every other policy maker in this study accepted all or none of an analogy. None of the policy makers derived new lessons from the historical analogies that they retrieved. The lessons policy makers relied on were already commonly held and widely known before they retrieved the analogies. This enabled the analogies to fulfill their simplifying functions, since other policy makers were already familiar with the analogy. Therefore, the familiar analogy shed light on the complex, unfamiliar current crisis.

EFFECT OF HISTORICAL INFORMATION ON DECISION MAKING

Policy makers often use historical analogies to diagnose crises, as well as to prescribe and justify policy, especially in crises involving the possible use of force. Therefore, analysis of a crisis, whether by mediators or researchers, must include the variable of the use of historical analogies by policy makers. In some cases historical analogies have little or no affect, but in many other cases they have a significant influence, such as in Korea and Lebanon/Jordan, and in other cases, such as the British during Suez, they are decisive. Analysts and researchers who ignore the role and influence of historical analogies on foreign policy making risk missing a significant variable in the policy making process because historical information and historical analogies can influence significantly foreign policy decision making. In the Suez case, the British relied on historical information far more than current information. Eden relied heavily on the 1930's analogy to diagnose the crisis, as well as to prescribe and justify his policy. Eisenhower also framed the Suez crisis in terms of the 1930s, although it had far less of an influence on his policy decisions. The Americans in the Korean case also used history to diagnose the crisis and to prescribe policy, as did the British, although current information also significantly influenced British policy in response to the Korean invasion. The British and the Americans framed the Korean crisis in terms of the 1930s and used the analogy to prescribe and to justify policy. In the Lebanon/Jordan case, the British and Americans balanced historical and current information. Eisenhower retrieved a cluster of analogies around the concept of indirect aggression, while the British framed the crisis in terms of Suez. In both cases, however, lessons from history were balanced against current information, although the historical information had a significant influence on both perceptions of the Lebanon/Jordan crisis and on policy choices. The Americans in the Suez case, as well as the British and the Americans in the Iran case, relied on current information almost to the point of excluding historical information.

Once a policy maker adopts a historical analogy to frame a crisis it forms a set of interlocking beliefs that are extremely resistant to change. The analogy affects perceptions of the stakes, risks, costs, the rationality of the adversary, time, and policy options, including the effectiveness of economic sanctions, the possibility of a negotiated settlement, and whether to use force. In the crises analyzed in this study, once a policy maker retrieved, and deemed valid, a historical analogy, he did not drop or significantly alter his beliefs based on that historical analogy. For example, if a retrieved analogy prescribed the use of force, policy makers did not change their minds about using force. This finding reinforces the argument that policy makers decide early in a crisis whether to use force. Policy makers also did not change their perceptions about time, stakes, costs, risks, an adversary, and policy options during a crisis that were based on a historical analogy after they decided that the analogy was valid.

This finding has significant implications for conflict resolution models and those who seek to negotiate peaceful solutions to international crises. If policy makers already have framed a crisis using a historical analogy and decided to use force, then it will be extremely difficult to dissuade the leader from that warlike course. Eden's early decision to use military force against Egypt in 1956 is an example of this phenomenon. Conversely, if policy makers have already decided not to use force on the basis of an analogy, then the negotiator faces a much easier task of avoiding armed conflict than it may appear from the level of drama and apparent risk inherent in a crisis. Military force will probably not be used. For example, during the Suez crisis, a substantial amount of time passed after the act—the nationalization of the canal—that apparently would have triggered a military intervention. In most cases, as time passes, the risk of military intervention in a crisis decreases, especially if the parties are negotiating actively, as the British and Egyptians did intermittently throughout the Suez crisis. Given Eden's early framing of the crisis in terms of the 1930s and his early decision to use military force, however, the risk of military intervention was much higher than it would have appeared if Eden's perceptions and beliefs had not been taken into account. In the Iran case, which appeared suited to a British intervention, Attlee decided at the start of the crisis not to use force. Therefore, the Iran crisis appeared to have a much greater risk of military intervention than actually existed.

If international mediators can determine, on the basis of the use of historical analogies, whether the participants in a crisis already have decided whether to use force it would be of great value in analyzing the potential for violence and the possible use of force in a crisis. It would also indicate the views of the participants of time, the stakes, and risks, which directly influence the time frame in which negotiations should be conducted. For example, if the lesson of a historical analogy is that the passage of time will make an adversary stronger, such as the beliefs of Truman and Attlee during the Korean crisis, Eden during the Suez crisis, and Macmillan during the Lebanon/Jordan crisis, then negotiations must be started promptly. In the Iran case, the British felt no time pressure, and there was ample time for negotiation and little risk of the use of force. Researchers and mediators should consider the effects of historical analogies on beliefs and perceptions when they analyze a crisis or they risk missing a sometimes crucial variable.

THE 1930s: HITLER'S SHADOW

Some events are so dominant, important and life-changing that they deeply influence anyone old enough to be aware of them. Such an event or series of events often become master analogies. A master analogy differs from an analogy that provides a macrolesson because the lessons based on a master analogy are also commonly known or accepted by a large group of people over a long period of time. The macrolessons based on a historical analogy that is not a master analogy are not commonly known or broadly accepted. For decades after the event, policy makers draw lessons from the master analogy and apply those lessons to a broad range of crises. The Korean, Suez, and Lebanon/Jordan cases illustrate the power and influence of a master analogy, the 1930s, over a long period and over several generations of policy makers who varied greatly by age, education, foreign policy experience, political beliefs, and use of historical information, including Truman, Acheson, Attlee, Churchill, Eden, Macmillan, Dulles, Lloyd, and most of their advisors. In fact the power of the 1930's analogy has lingered into the 1990s. During the Persian Gulf War in 1990–91, President George Bush and Prime Minister Margaret Thatcher framed the Iraqi invasion of Kuwait in terms of the 1930's analogy. The 1930's analogy also significantly influenced their choices of policy and was used as the justification for their policies. For example, in an August 8, 1990, speech Bush used World War II terms when he said that Iraq had "stormed in blitzkrieg fashion through Kuwait."[3] Bush also said,

We succeeded in the struggle for freedom in Europe because we and our allies remained stalwart. Keeping the peace in the Middle East will require no less. We're beginning a new era. This era can be full of promise. An age of freedom. A time of peace for all people. But if history teaches us anything, it is that we must resist aggression or it will destroy our freedoms. Appeasement does not work. As was the case in the 1930s, we see in Saddam Hussein an aggressive dictator threatening his neighbors.[4]

Bush told a Pentagon assembly on August 15, 1990, "A half century ago, our nation and the world paid dearly for appeasing an aggressor who should, and could, have been stopped. We are not going to make that mistake again."[5] Thatcher agreed with Bush and said: "First, aggressors must never be appeased. We learned that to our cost in the 1930s."[6] The influence of the 1930's analogy even continued after the war. In the postwar period, Thatcher drew parallels between the 1930s and 1990s,

I started to read more deeply about the ill-starred League of Nations [in May 1991]. . . . The rhetoric of that time struck me as uncannily like that which I was now hearing. Similarly, Smuts' [South African Jan Smuts, a principle architect of the League of Nations] own conclusion, when the League had failed to take action against the dictators and so prepared the way for the Second World War, struck me as equally damning of the kind of collective security upon which the future of post–Cold War stability and freedom was supposed to be based.[7]

President Bill Clinton also used rhetoric about the 1930s during the NATO air campaign against Yugoslavia in 1999. Hitler's shadow is indeed long. The 1930s, many believed, suggested that force should be used in concert with like-minded states promptly against aggressive dictators. The 1930s also suggested that time worked in favor of the aggressor; that the stakes were extremely high, even in an apparently unimportant, regional crisis; and that force should be used promptly or the aggressor would only grow stronger and aggression would be more costly and difficult to stop in the future.

The generation that personally experienced or observed the 1930s and World War II, however, is passing. For example, younger Americans were more likely to draw upon Vietnam than the 1930s when they analyzed the Iraqi invasion of Kuwait.[8] In the United States, Vietnam has taken the place of the 1930s as the overriding, master analogy that is applied to almost any international crisis that may involve the use of force in a regional contingency. For example, Bush and his advisors, as well as his critics, repeatedly mentioned the Vietnam War during the Gulf crisis.[9] Critics of military intervention in the Gulf warned that a war fought against Iraq might degenerate into a costly, drawn-out conflict that would end in defeat, just like the Vietnam War. Bush argued that, by using force promptly and overwhelmingly, Vietnam would not be repeated. For example, at a November 30, 1990, meeting with congressional leaders at the White House, Bush faced strong reservations about the military buildup in Saudi Arabia. He replied with an attack on the Vietnam analogy. He said, "We don't need another Vietnam War. World unity is there. No hands are going to be tied behind backs. This is not Vietnam. . . . I know whose backside's at stake and rightfully so. It will not be a long, drawn-out mess."[10] The American president also believed that President Saddam Hussein of Iraq was relying on the Vietnam analogy to buttress his belief that the United States would not fight, let alone win, a war in the Gulf. For example, Hussein told U.S. Ambassador April Glaspie, undoubtedly hoping to capitalize on the American beliefs about the Vietnam experience, "Yours is a society which cannot accept 10,000 dead in one battle."[11] Again replying with the Vietnam analogy, Bush said Hussein "was still living back in the Vietnam days. He didn't know we had a different ball game on here, different levels of technology, a different military force, a different president."[12] American participation in the Gulf War could, to a certain extent, be seen as a war to discredit the Vietnam-based lesson that the United States could not win a war in the Third World. At a January 3, 1991, White House meeting, Bush said, "There is no Vietnam parallel."[13] Just after the war, Bush said to reporters, "By God, we've kicked the Vietnam syndrome once and for all."[14]

Even after the fighting began, Bush and his advisors continued to frame the Gulf conflict in terms of Vietnam. For example, when Iraqi aircraft avoided combat and hid as best they could from coalition aircraft, U.S. planners worried about an "air Tet." They feared a surprise attack similar to the 1968 Viet Cong Tet offensive, when the Viet Cong seized the U.S. embassy in Saigon and many provincial capitals, gravely harming U.S. domestic support for the war.[15] However, even though Vietnam had become a master analogy, it is often juxtaposed to the 1930s. While the 1930's analogy prescribes the prompt use of military force, Vietnam cautions against the misapplication of force and prescribes the use of massive, overwhelming force. However, Vietnam also is used to warn against using any force at all in regional contingencies.

Although Suez was a master analogy for decades after 1956, it is unclear what analogy now dominates British decision making after the passing of leaders who lived through the 1930s. The successful response to the Argentine invasion of the Falkland Islands, however, may have decreased the influence of the Suez analogy, just as the Gulf War may decrease the influence of the Vietnam analogy. Further research on master analogies is needed to trace their origins, influence, and longevity.

As a master analogy, the 1930's analogy provides a puzzle. The lesson usually drawn from the 1930s is that military force should be used promptly against an aggressive dictator. However, if the British and French lacked the military forces to deter Hitler during the 1936 remilitarization of the Rhineland, the 1938 crisis over Czechoslovakia, or at the time of the Munich Conference, which it appears they lacked, given Hitler's continued aggressions, how could they have the military forces actually to use force successfully against Germany in the 1930s? Using military force usually requires more military capability than successful deterrence. This example highlights the paradox that the lessons drawn from a historical analogy do not have to agree with the facts of the situation on which it is based. The lesson that can be more accurately drawn from the 1930's crises is to have sufficient forces on hand to deal promptly with aggressive dictators.[16] However, if Hitler was irrational, he may have been undeterable since he did not make rational, cost-benefit analyses of situations based on the balance of forces between Germany and its adversaries. Deterrence relies on rational, cost-benefit analysis by the target of the deterrence attempt. If Hitler was irrational and undeterable, then the level of armed forces needed to deter him was extremely high, if he could be deterred at all. The level of armed force needed actually to rebuff German forces in the Rhineland in 1936, for example, or even to wage war against Germany in 1938, might have been far less than what would have been required to deter the irrational Hitler. In actuality, German forces reoccupying the Rhineland had orders to retreat if the French or British showed any kind of military response, regardless of how small.

A similar problem of determining the military forces necessary to deter a potential adversary from attacking compared to the level needed to compel a withdrawal from an occupied territory was faced during the Persian Gulf crisis. In the period before the Gulf War, during Operation Desert Shield, the coalition built up forces in Saudi Arabia, first to deter Hussein from attacking Saudi Arabia, which succeeded, but also in an attempt to compel Hussein to withdraw from Kuwait, which failed. The level of forces required to deter, compared to levels needed to compel and then, if needed, actually to use force successfully, vary greatly depending on the rationality and beliefs of the target of the attempt to deter or compel. This area also requires further study.

Policy makers retrieved from the 1930s a set of widely held and often internalized lessons that were frequently applied in foreign policy crises involving national security between 1945 and the 1990s, including the Gulf War and the conflict over Kosovo in 1999. Vietnam became a master analogy in the 1970s for the Americans, as did Suez for the British in the late 1950s. A master historical analogy precludes the use of other historical analogies that are more similar to the current case and blocks the influence of current information that contradicts the master analogy. Once retrieved and applied to a current crisis, lessons based on a master analogy form an interlocking set of beliefs that are powerful, resistant to change, and have a significant influence on perceptions of time, risks, stakes, and an adversary, as well as on policy decisions. Lessons on the basis of a master analogy, such as the 1930's analogy in the case of Eden during Suez, often form the foundation of a policy maker's entire foreign policy belief system.

HISTORICAL ANALOGIES AND LEARNING

Humans are cognitive misers who seek simple, easy to use heuristics, such as historical analogies. These heuristics lead to common errors and biases. The argument that greater rigor in the use of historical analogies by policy makers will lead to more valid and specific lessons that will improve the effectiveness of foreign policy is incorrect.[17] Even if policy makers used historical analogies with the precision and rigor of the most learned historians and social scientists they would still draw lessons from history that were invalid and that would not consistently or significantly improve the effectiveness of policy. It is extremely difficult to determine if a lesson based on a historical analogy is valid for a current crisis. Worse yet, even if the lesson is valid for the current case, it will not be valid consistently in future cases, even if the cases appear similar or even identical, because international relations is nonlinear and a small difference in causal variables can lead to vastly different outcomes. Therefore, good judgments are due, in large part, to intuition[18] or luck, in the sense that the policy maker cannot consistently repeat his success, even in situations that appear to be the same. There is evidence to support this model.

If an experienced policy maker can learn valid, specific lessons from history, then such a policy maker should be able to transfer such lessons from the past into the future and make predictions that are more accurate than those of a layman. However, if the model proposed here is valid there should be little difference in predictive ability between experts and novices. In asking foreign policy experts and novices to make specific, near-term predictions about international relations, Tetlock found no significant difference between experts and novices in the accuracy of their predictions.[19]

Policy makers appear instinctively to understand the difficulty of making specific, near-term predictions, since most of the lessons they retrieve from history by analogical reasoning are of a general, macrotype, rather than being narrow, micro, and specific. Leaders can learn broad, general lessons from history, such as to meet unprovoked aggression with the prompt use of force, or to ensure allied support before intervening, or that it is easier to intervene militarily in a civil war than to withdraw from such a conflict. Planning a military intervention, as well as maneuvering forces, communications, and logistics are all linear. Once fighting begins, however, or even if the parties agree to negotiate, then the crisis becomes nonlinear. Furthermore, the question of when to apply even the general lessons is extremely difficult to answer. Policy makers can also see simple patterns in complex events by focusing on underlying long-term geopolitical, economic, and technological trends and forces, such as predictions that China will surpass the United States in gross national product in a given year or that the military buildup in a state will reach a certain level in a certain year on the basis of extrapolating weapon acquisition trends. This is one method of focusing on linear aspects in nonlinear phenomena, thus increasing predictability and the potential for learning and retrieving valid lessons from history. However, even these general lessons, although usually valid, are not always so. Even broad trends change and vary.[20] For example, predictions about economic trends, such as national growth rates, can be disrupted by wars, crises, or policy changes, and weapon acquisition programs often hit bottlenecks. History does not repeat exactly, and historical analogies can only provide broad guidance and general lessons. History is just one pass

through the possibilities and foreign policy, like art, will never be standard-
ized or perfected.

The view of international relations as nonlinear explains the consistent
finding that the poor use of historical analogies often leads to ineffective
policy choices by policy makers. However, policy makers are not to blame.
The international relations environment is the cause of the poor use of historical analogies, which leads to invalid lessons and ineffective policies. Social
scientists and historians, more knowledgeable about history and more
schooled in logic than many politicians, would fare no better in learning
valid and specific lessons from history and prescribing effective policy than
policy makers. Before they entered government many policy makers, such
as Secretary of State Henry Kissinger and Churchill, were historians or political scientists, well aware of history and the rules of logic. When they drew
upon history for lessons for current crises, however, they also made common
errors that led to ineffective policies.

Improving the logic behind the use of historical analogies also will not
change the broadly accepted lessons, often invalidated by later research and
analysis, that policy makers retrieve from history. Such lessons are often
formed soon after an event and do not change even as revisionist historians
offer different, and often more valid, analysis of the events. For example,
during the Gulf War, Bush portrayed Iraqi leader Saddam Hussein as another Hitler and argued strongly in favor of a lesson based on the 1930s:
aggressive dictators must be dealt with promptly by force in coalition with
other, like-minded states. Bush and his advisors ignored the scholarship, if
any of them were even aware of it, on Chamberlain's appeasement policy
and the arguably valid geostrategic, economic, and political reasons for appeasement. Bush used the same lessons from the 1930s as Truman had used
forty years before during the North Korean invasion of South Korea. However, even if Bush had been aware of the questionable historical validity of
the lessons of the 1930s he espoused, he would have found far less political
support for a policy based on a new interpretation of the 1930s than he did
for a policy based on the more commonly accepted lessons. The key to
political support is not the validity of a lesson based on a historical analogy.
The key is instead how widely the lesson and the historical analogy are
accepted before the politician uses them. For example, when Bush used the
1930's analogy, the analogy and the lessons based on it were already widely
known and accepted by the policy-making elite, as well as by the public,
especially the generation that lived through the 1930s and early 1940s.[21]
Even though many Americans did not understand the intricacies of the situation in the Persian Gulf in 1990, they understood the general lessons of
the 1930's analogy, especially the lesson to respond to aggressive dictators
promptly with force. The general lessons based on the 1930's analogy were
accepted even though there were valid empirical and logical questions about
their validity. The historical analogy fulfilled its function of simplifying the

complex Gulf crisis. Therefore, most Americans supported Bush's policy. If Bush had used a more nuanced and, possibly, more accurate, but less commonly held lesson from the 1930s, he would have garnered less support. The historical analogy would not have fulfilled its simplifying function if others in his administration and the public were unfamiliar with the analogy or its lessons.

Even though international relations is nonlinear, policy makers will continue to use analogies to retrieve lessons from history because they are a security blanket for foreign policy decision makers. Without historical information, policy makers are left in an often bewildering world of multiple variables, goals, and actors, with cause and effect relationships unclear and time pressures, as well as constituents, demanding action in a stream of apparently unique foreign policy crises. There are benefits to using analogical reasoning to retrieve historical information. Historical analogies can provide information on similar, if not identical, past crises, especially when current information is difficult to obtain or is confusing, such as during a revolution, war, or on the brink of a military intervention. Past crises can supply a cognitive framework to simplify the current crisis. History can also suggest possible policy options, highlight potential risks, costs, and stakes, as well as contribute to justifying policy. Historical analogies can also suggest how similar adversaries behaved in the past, as well as the goals of an adversary and what goals might be achievable by a policy maker's own nation in the current crisis. Policy makers may never be sure which course to steer, but steer they must. Historical analogies are one means of setting a course and may even allow policy makers to trim the sails when the seas turn rough.

THE DECISION TO USE MILITARY FORCE

Decision makers decide early in a crisis, usually in the first twenty-four hours, whether to use force. The influence of historical information and analogies can lead to force being the preferred option in terms of time and of preference. The perceived rationality of an adversary, the stakes, and the type and degree of threat can also lead policy makers to select force as the preferred policy option to be tried before other means, such as diplomacy and economic measures. American and British policy makers chose military force as the preferred option early in the Korean and Lebanon/Jordan crises, while the British selected force as their first choice early in the Suez crisis. Even decisions not to use military force are made early in crises, usually within the first few hours. During the Iran crisis, the Americans and British decided early not to use force. Similarly, the decision to use force in the Gulf War, as well as in the conflict in Kosovo in 1999 was made very early in Washington and London. If policy makers perceive an adversary as irrational, they are more likely to use force. If a threat is a military threat, then policy makers usually respond with military force, especially if the stakes are perceived as being high, as happened with the British and Americans in Korea and in the Persian Gulf. Clandestine force may also be used, as the Americans and British did in Iran to avert a nonmilitary threat. This model is supported by the cases in this study that involved both decisions to use force and not use force.

The metaphor of a slippery slope was not supported by the cases in this book. The slippery slope metaphor portrays decision makers as losing control of a situation, as they may have done before World War I, and only deciding whether to use military force after diplomatic and economic means have failed and as events seemed to move out of control and preclude other options. In all the cases in this book, however, decision makers decided at the start of the crisis, well before events even had a chance to go out of control, whether the situation warranted the use of force. There was never any slippery slope. Even in the Lebanon/Jordan case, when the coup in Iraq appeared to force the hand of the British and Americans, the decision to use force had been made months before, in May, if the threat to Lebanon increased. During Suez, the British appeared to be sliding down a slippery slope. However, Eden decided at the start of the crisis to use force and never changed his mind. Even in the Iranian case policy makers decided at the start not to use force. They did, however, slowly escalate the diplomatic and economic means that they applied to Iran in an attempt to resolve the crisis, although they never did use military force. The British and Americans retained control of their policy by limiting it to the nonuse of military force, which is contrary to the slippery slope model.

This pattern of deciding early whether to use force has significant implications for conflict resolution and bargaining models that deal with crises involving the possible use of force in regional conflicts. If policy makers decide early in a crisis whether to use force, then conflict resolution attempts made later in the crisis may face a much more difficult problem than an escalation model would suggest. Policy makers who have already decided that force is the preferred option to settle a dispute, such as Eden during the Suez crisis, would be far less likely to be amenable to a peaceful settlement than if they had not yet made such a decision. Conversely, a crisis that appears to be on the brink of armed conflict may not be if policy makers have decided early in the crisis not to use force, such as Attlee decided about Iran.

Politicians tend to favor using limited, proportional force, while the military favors using massive, overwhelming force in military interventions. A historical analogy, such as Vietnam, that prescribes the use of overwhelming force, or a leader who was formerly a professional military officer, such as Eisenhower, can lead politicians to support the use of overwhelming force. For example, during the Suez crisis, the military plans created by the British military prescribed the use of overwhelming force against Egypt. The forces involved were downgraded at the behest of politicians. However, during the Persian Gulf conflict, with the Vietnam analogy prescribing the use of overwhelming force, the Americans assembled significant forces against Iraq. Politicians, who are often former businessmen or lawyers, apply business principles to war: Never pay more for something than is absolutely required. In warfare, however, using significantly more force than appears to be required for the operation often leads to fewer casualties than if proportional force is used.

Nations also vary in their willingness to use military force. Although almost all decisions to use military force are unanimous among the policy makers involved, there are variations in such decisions.[22] For example, Truman's decision to intervene in Korea was supported broadly. Similarly, Eisenhower's decision not to intervene in Suez was never questioned by his cabinet members or his advisors. However, there are also decisions to use military force that policy makers made reluctantly. For example, Attlee, at first, hoped to avoid intervention in Korea, and only intervened after the Americans did so. Similarly, the American decision to intervene in Lebanon in July 1958 was made reluctantly and only after all other means appeared to have been exhausted. Conversely, the British decision not to intervene in Iran divided the cabinet and was only made under intense American pressure to refrain from using force. The factions within a government as it decides whether to use military force is an understudied area with almost all the research in this area focusing on single-case studies. A comparative analysis of such decisions could contribute to our understanding of decisions to use military force, as well as cases where policy makers considered using force, but did not intervene militarily.

When policy makers decide to use force, the results are mixed, although military intervention usually stabilizes crises. The Anglo-American intervention in Korea was a success to the degree that the Republic of Korea was defended and its territorial integrity restored. However, the attempt to occupy North Korea failed at the cost of a war with China. In Iran, covert operations restored the shah and made Iran an ally of the West for more than twenty-five years until the 1979 revolution. The British military intervention in Suez was a total failure, while the American opposition to the invasion raised the stature of the United States throughout the Middle East. The British operation in Suez, alone of the interventions in this study, was an attempt to overthrow an established government without any domestic support. Such operations seem to be doomed to failure in the age of nationalism. In Lebanon, the American intervention contributed to stabilizing the country until the civil war of the 1970s and 1980s, while British support for King Hussein of Jordan in 1958 helped him to remain in control of a relatively stable Jordan until his death in 1999, albeit with some conflict in the 1970s. Overall, military intervention and the clandestine use of force buys time. The intervening force can usually stabilize the situation and restore order if it is supporting an established party or faction within the target state. Of course, the order brought about by military intervention never lasts forever. The underlying forces that led to the conflict and disorder are domestic and are always lurking beneath the surface. These forces erupted in Iran in 1979, in Lebanon and Jordan in the 1970s, and remain on the tense Korean peninsula, where American troops still face North Korean forces. Military force is not a solution to domestic political problems. Unless other mean are used during the time bought by military intervention to seek negotiated, long-term, political solutions to the domestic conflicts the intervention will have been in vain.

AREAS OF FURTHER STUDY

The study of the role of analogies and historical information in decisions to use military force still has many unanswered questions and unexplained issues. Areas for further study include master analogies, the selection and rejection of historical analogies, historical information in economic issues and in civil-military relations, and learning from history in a foreign policy environment.

Master analogies have a significant influence on foreign policy decisions over a period of decades and, in some cases, in several states, yet there has been no rigorous research on the concept. The process by which certain historical events, such as Vietnam or Suez, or clusters of events, such as the 1930s, become master analogies remains virgin territory for research. The fundamental perspectives and beliefs that policy makers hold throughout their careers about international relations are often based on master analogies. For example, Thatcher's foreign policy framework was based on lessons and principles she derived from the 1930s and World War II, and her memoirs are full of lessons from the 1930s she applied to issues during her tenure at Number 10 Downing Street. The lessons of the 1930s—stopping aggression with the prompt use of force in concert with like-minded states—significantly influenced the reactions of American, British, and other Western states to crises from the 1940s through 2000, including Korea, Suez, Lebanon/Jordan, Grenada, Panama, Vietnam, the Falklands, Afghanistan, the Gulf War, Kosovo, and many other regional contingencies and crises. Similarly, the lessons of Vietnam have cast a shadow over every American debate about military intervention in regional contingencies since the 1970s. Such historical analogies have rarely been analyzed. Researchers should study the evolution of the lessons of a master analogy as they solidify over time. To analyze the range of generalization of master analogies, researchers should conduct a study of a wide range of people over a broad range of cases to determine which policy makers apply the master analogy to which cases. Furthermore, the lifecycle of master analogies is also an area requiring further study. Other research questions include: Do the lessons drawn from a master analogy change over generations or during different crises? Why do some leaders, such as Eden, see the master analogy they retrieve as more valid and more generalizable than other policy makers analyzing the same crisis? Are master analogies international and/or bipartisan within a state? How does the success or failure of a more recent policy, conducted on the basis of an analogy, influence the future use of that analogy?

Because in such cases historical analogies are most often used, most of the research on analogies and the use of historical information has focused on crises involving national security. However, the role of historical analogies and information in economic issues, such as the General Agreement on Tariff and Trade (GATT) rounds or international trade disputes, is rarely studied. In laboratory studies, psychologists have not found any differences between the use of historical analogies by the type of issue. Therefore, why is there such a difference in international relations? Are analogies from law or business used in international economic crises instead of analogies from history as are commonly used during national security crises? It is hard to believe that economics is so lacking in drama, complexity, novelty, and time pressures that policy makers do not reason analogically, especially from historical cases, and, if they do, what is the influence of such reasoning on economic policy making?

A range of other issues and research questions remain to be addressed. There is little analysis of why some events, which may appear to be more similar and valid as analogies to a current crisis, are not used as historical analogies. The role of the media in creating commonly held interpretations of, and lessons from, historical events has been neglected, as has the role of academics and political memoirs in shaping commonly held lessons from history. Can politicians significantly influence how their policies are perceived in later years through their memoirs or speeches? How do revisionist studies influence lessons based on historical analogies, such as the 1930s, Suez, and Vietnam, that have been accepted broadly by both policy makers and the public? Research on how science evolves and progresses, such as the research by Thomas Kuhn and Imre Lakatos, may be a starting point to analyze how beliefs about historical events permeate governments and the public and may, over time, change. There has also been little study of the role of analogical reasoning in the processing of current information or about why certain lessons are derived from a historical analogy when other, equally valid lessons are ignored.

In the area of the use of military force, this study did not analyze civil-military relations. Do military leaders rely on historical information more, less, or to a similar extent as civilian leaders? Does the military draw more on different types of history, mainly military history, than civilians? Do military leaders usually favor the use of overwhelming force once the decision to intervene militarily has been made? Are there consistent differences between the services in their recommendations about the type and size of forces required to intervene? Little's excellent study of intervention in civil wars analyzed divisions within the government, but did not, nor did he intend to, focus on civil-military relations. Understanding the interplay between civilian and military officials is especially relevant today as the military argues that any intervention must meet specific guidelines, including the use of enough force to achieve the objective with minimal casualties, which is often assumed to mean overwhelming force. Do civilian leaders usually follow the military's recommendations on levels of force for an intervention? If so, the U.S. military's belief that only overwhelming force should be used will have a significant impact on future U.S. interventions and grants the military a veto if a president does not want to commit to a large-scale intervention for the goals involved. In some cases, a limited use of force may be more logical, especially if the goal is not one of major national interest. However, if civilian leaders follow their usual inclination to use proportional force, the impact of the recommendations of the military will be less than if civilian leaders follow the advice of their military leaders.

A significant area left open to future research is the issue of how most effectively to learn and draw lessons from history in the foreign policy environment. Researchers' expectations about whether policy makers can learn to improve the effectiveness of their policy choices on the basis of lessons from history must be revised drastically downward because of the difficulty of learning in a nonlinear environment. Determining the most effective strategies and tactics to employ in a nonlinear, chaotic environment, such as to focus on long-term trends to derive broad, general lessons, is a crucial area for research. This type of research would provide a more valid source of lessons to policy makers attempting to improve decision making than researchers who erroneously argue that greater rigor in the use of historical analogies will lead to more effective policies. International relations is not that simple.

CONCLUSION

The use of military force in regional contingencies shows no signs of declining in frequency in the post–Cold War world. Research, especially comparative, archival-based analysis, in this area should, therefore, be increased. The role of historical information and analogies on foreign policy decision making is a neglected, yet often significant, aspect of the decision-making process when leaders decide whether to intervene militarily, as well as in foreign policy in general. Without a better understanding of the influence of historical information and analogies on decisions to use force, attempts by mediators and international organizations to prevent or avert military conflict may be doomed to failure because they are based on invalid models. Suez, Vietnam, and Afghanistan remind us that without a better understanding of the use of historical information and analogies, policy makers may be doomed to repeat common errors in the use of historical analogies, which often leads to ineffective and sometimes disastrous military interventions in foreign lands. History offers an endless source of lessons. It is the responsibility of policy makers to retrieve the appropriate lessons to ensure that the young men and women of the armed forces only go in harm's way in support of the most effective national policies possible. Anything less is to waste the finest resource of a nation: its citizens.

NOTES

1. Ferrell, *Harry S. Truman: A Life*, pp. 70–71, 103.
2. See Stein and Tanter, *Rational Decision-Making*.
3. Kincade, "On the Brink," p. 295; and Woodward, *The Commanders*, p. 260.
4. Graubard, *Mr. Bush's War*, pp. 10–11.
5. Donaldson, *America at War Since 1945*, p. 143.
6. Thatcher, *Downing Street Years*, p. 817.
7. Thatcher, *Path to Power*, p. 510.
8. Spellman and Holyoak, "If Saddam Is Hitler Then Who Is George Bush?"
9. Vietnam is mentioned repeatedly in histories of the Gulf War. For example, Record, *Hollow Victory*, see Vietnam index heading; Dunigan and Bay, *From Shield to Storm*, p. 511; Woodward, *The Commanders*, p. 211; and Hallion, *Storm Over Iraq*, p. 242.
10. Woodward, *The Commanders*, p. 339. Also see Mervin, *George Bush and the Guardianship Presidency*, p. 197.
11. Donaldson, *America at War Since 1945*, p. 152. Hussein apparently had never heard of Gettysburg or Shiloh, and did not realize the British would intervene, with the experience of the Somme behind them.
12. Record, *Hollow Victory*, p. 92.
13. Woodward, *The Commanders*, p. 335.
14. Donaldson, *America at War Since 1945*, p. 141.
15. Hallion, *Storm Over Iraq*, p. 194.
16. I am indebted to Michael Fry for suggesting this argument.
17. For the difficulties of measuring policy effectiveness, see Breslauer and Tetlock, "Introduction," pp. 6, 13; Tetlock, "Learning in U.S. and Soviet Foreign Policy," pp. 22, 37–38; Etheredge, *Can Governments Learn?*, p. 66; Levy, "Learning and Foreign Policy," p.293; and Fearon, "Counterfactuals and Hypothesis Testing in Political Science," pp. 169–195.
18. Intuition is direct perception of truth independent of any reasoning process.
19. Except for long-term trends. Tetlock, "Is It a Bad Idea to Study Good Judgment?," pp. 429–434. Also see Tetlock, "Good Judgment in International Politics," pp. 517–539.
20. Tetlock, "Good Judgment in International Politics," pp. 518–19, 522–527, 532; and Pagels, *The Dreams of Reason*, p. 146.
21. Spellman and Holyoak, "If Saddam Hussein Is Hitler Then Who Is George Bush?"
22. Little, *Intervention: External Involvement in Civil Wars*, p. 94.

Bibliography

The main subjects of the book's introduction are military intervention in regional contingencies and the role of historical analogies in decisions to intervene militarily. Therefore, the first section of the bibliography focuses on works about the use of military force in regional contingencies and the second section deals with the role of historical analogies in foreign policy decision making, in general, and in military intervention decisions, in particular. The next four sections of the bibliography contain the works used for the four historical case studies: Korea, Iran, Suez, and Lebanon/Jordan. Works on the leaders are cited in the first case in which they were involved. For example, although Truman was involved in Korea and Iran, books and articles on him are only in the Korea section of the bibliography. The final section of the bibliography focuses on learning in foreign policy, which is the subject of part of the conclusion. Although much of the conclusion deals with the role of historical information and analogies in decisions to use force in regional contingencies, works on these subjects, however, are in the first two sections of the bibliography.

The bibliography is further divided into primary and secondary sources. Primary sources include original documents from the Truman and Eisenhower Libraries, the Public Records Office, and books and articles written by participants involved in the historical cases. Secondary sources are articles and books written by individuals who did not participate in the cases. Each section of the bibliography is also divided between articles and books, with book chapters included in the book sections.

Abbreviations: Ann Whitman File (AWF); Cabinet Minutes (C.M.); Cabinet Office (CAB); Dwight D. Eisenhower (DDE); Foreign Office Papers (FO); John Foster Dulles (JFD); National Security Council (NSC); Office of the Special Assistant for National Security Affairs (OSANSA); President's Secretary's File (PSF); Prime Minister's Office (PREM); and White Hosue Central File (WHCF).

THE USE OF MILITARY FORCE IN REGIONAL CONTINGENCIES

Articles

Eckhardt, William, and Edward Azar. "Major World Conflicts and Interventions, 1945 to 1975." *International Interactions* 5, no. 1 (1978): 75–110.

Gochman, Charles, and Russell Leng. "Militarized Disputes, Incidents, and Crises: Identification and Classification." *International Interactions* 14, no. 2, (1988): 157–163.

Pearson, Frederic S., and Robert A. Baumann. "International Military Interventions: Identification and Classification." *International Interactions* 14, no. 2 (1988): 173–180.

Truver, Scott. "The U.S. Navy in Review." *U.S. Naval Institute Proceedings* 125, no. 5 (May 1999): 76–82.

Books

Blainey, Geoffrey. *The Causes of War*, 3rd ed. New York: The Free Press, 1988.

Blechman, Barry, and Stephen Kaplan. *Force Without War*. Washington, D.C.: Brookings Institution, 1978.

Bull, Hedley. "Introduction." In *Intervention in World Politics*, edited by Hedley Bull, pp. 1–35. Oxford: Clarendon Press, 1984.

Carpenter, Ted. "Direct Military Intervention." In *Intervention in the 1980s: U.S. Foreign Policy in the Third World*, edited by Peter J. Schraeder, pp. 131–144. Boulder: Lynne Rienner Publishers, 1989.

Connaughton, Richard. *Military Intervention in the 1990s*. London: Routledge, 1992.

Donaldson, Gary A. *America at War Since 1945: Politics and Diplomacy in Korea, Vietnam and the Gulf War*. Westport, Conn.: Praeger, 1996.

Doyle, Michael. "Grenada: An International Crisis in Multilateral Security." In *Escalation and Intervention: Multilateral Security and Its Alternatives*, edited by Arthur R. Day and Michael W. Doyle, pp. 123–151. Boulder: Westview Press, 1986.

Duner, Bertil. *Military Intervention in Civil Wars: The 1970s*. New York: St. Martin's Press, 1985.

Dunigan, James F., and Austin Bay. *From Shield to Storm*. New York: William Morrow & Co., 1992.

Feste, Karen A. "Introduction." In *American and Soviet Intervention: Effects on World Stability*, edited by Karen A. Feste, pp. 1–8. New York: Crane Russak, 1990.

Foreign Affairs Division, Legislative Reference Service, Library of Congress. *Background Information on the Use of United States Armed Forces in Foreign Countries*. Washington, D.C.: U.S. Government Printing Office, 1970.

Fuller, J.F.C. *The Conduct of War*. New York: Da Capo Press, 1992.

Gaddis, John Lewis. *The Long Peace: Inquiries into the History of the Cold War*. Oxford: Oxford University Press, 1987.

Girling, John L. S. *America and the Third World*. London: Routledge & Kegan Paul, 1980.

Graubard, Stephen R. *Mr. Bush's War: Adventures in the Politics of Illusion*. New York: Hill and Wang, 1992.

Hallion, Richard P. *Storm Over Iraq: Air Power and the Gulf War*. Washington, D.C.: Smithsonian Institution Press, 1992.

Hart, B. H. Liddell. *Strategy*. New York: Meridian Books, 1991.

Hosmer, Stephen T. *Constraints on U.S. Strategy in Third World Conflicts*. New York: Crane Russak & Co., 1987.

Jentleson, Bruce W., and Ariel E. Levite. "The Analysis of Protracted Foreign Military Intervention." In *Foreign Military Intervention: The Dynamics of Protracted Conflict*, edited by Ariel E. Levite, Bruce W. Jentleson, and Larry Berman, pp. 3–22. New York: Columbia University Press, 1992.

Jentleson, Bruce W., Ariel E. Levite, and Larry Berman. "Foreign Military Intervention in Perspective." In *Foreign Military Intervention: The Dynamics of Protracted Conflict*, edited by Ariel E. Levite, Bruce W. Jentleson, and Larry Berman, pp. 303–325. New York: Columbia University Press, 1992.

Kincade, William H. "On the Brink in the Gulf Part 2: The Route to War." *Security Studies* 3, no. 3 (winter 1993/94): 295–329.

Kupchan, Charles A. "Getting In: The Initial Stage of Military Intervention." In *Foreign Military Intervention: The Dynamics of Protracted Conflict*, edited by Ariel E. Levite, Bruce W. Jentleson, and Larry Berman, pp. 241–260. New York: Columbia University Press, 1992.

Levy, Jack S. "The Causes of War: A Review of Theories and Evidence." In *Behavior, Society, and Nuclear War*, Vol. I, edited by Philip E. Tetlock, Jo L. Husbands, Robert Jervis, Paul Stern, and Charles Tilly, pp. 209–333. New York: Oxford University Press, 1989.

Little, Richard. *Intervention: External Involvement in Civil Wars*. Totowa, N.J.: Rowman and Littlefield, 1975.

Mervin, David. *George Bush and the Guardianship Presidency*. New York: St. Martin's Press, 1996.

Moisi, Dominique. "Intervention in French Foreign Policy." In *Intervention in World Politics*, edited by Hedley Bull, pp. 67–77. Oxford: Clarendon Press, 1984.

Odell, John S. "Correlates of U.S. Military Assistance and Military Intervention." In *Testing Theories of Imperialism*, edited by Steven J. Rosen and James R. Kurth, pp. 143–161. Lexington, Mass.: Lexington Books, 1973.

Record, Jeffrey. *Hollow Victory: A Contrary View of the Gulf War*. Washington, D.C.: Brassey's, 1993.

Rosenau, James. "Internal War as an International Event." In *The International Aspects of Civil Strife*, edited by James Rosenau, pp. 45–91. Princeton: Princeton University Press, 1964.

Schoonmaker, Herbert G. *Military Crisis Management: U.S. Intervention in the Dominican Republic, 1965*. New York: Greenwood Press, 1990.

Schraeder, Peter J. "Concepts, Relevance, Themes, and Overview." In *Intervention in the 1980s: U.S. Foreign Policy in the Third World*, edited by Peter J. Schraeder, pp. 1–14. Boulder: Lynne Rienner Publishers, 1989.

Schwarz, Urs. *Confrontation and Intervention in the Modern World.* New York: Oceana, 1970.

Smoke, Richard. "Analytic Dimensions of Intervention Decisions." In *The Limits of Military Intervention*, edited by Ellen P. Stern, pp. 25–44. Beverly Hills: Sage Publications, 1977.

Steel, Ronald. *Pax Americana.* New York: Viking Press, 1967.

Steigman, Andrew. *The Iranian Hostage Negotiations, November 1979–January 1981.* PEW case 348–88–0. Washington, D.C.: Georgetown University PEW Case Study Center, 1988.

Stern, Ellen P. "Prologue." In *The Limits of Military Intervention*, edited by Ellen P. Stern, pp. 9–24. Beverly Hills: Sage Publications, 1977.

Thatcher, Margaret. *The Downing Street Years.* New York: HarperCollins, 1993.

———. *The Path to Power.* New York: HarperCollins, 1995.

Thorndike, Tony. "Grenada." In *Intervention in the 1980s: U.S. Foreign Policy in the Third World*, edited by Peter J. Schraeder, pp. 249–263. Boulder: Lynne Rienner Publishers, 1989.

Tillema, Herbert K. *Appeal to Force.* New York: Thomas Y. Crowell Company, 1973.

———. *International Armed Conflict Since 1945: A Bibliographic Handbook of Wars and Military Interventions.* Boulder: Westview Press, 1991.

Van Creveld, Martin. *The Transformation of War.* New York: The Free Press, 1991.

Woodward, Bob. *The Commanders.* New York: Pocket Star Books, 1991.

Wright, Quincy. "A Study of War." In *International Encyclopedia of the Social Sciences*, edited by David L. Sills. New York: Crowell Collier and Macmillan Inc., 1968. p. 453.

Zartman, William I. "Conflict in Chad." In *Escalation and Intervention: Multilateral Security and Its Alternatives*, edited by Arthur R. Day and Michael W. Doyle, pp. 13–30. Boulder: Westview Press, 1986.

ANALOGICAL REASONING

Articles

Anderson, Paul. "Justifications and Precedents as Constraints in Foreign Policy Decision-Making." *American Journal of Political Science* 25 (1981): 738–761.

Beyerchen, Alan. "Clausewitz, Nonlinearity, and the Unpredictability of War." *International Security* 17, no. 3 (winter 1992/93): 59–90.

Fearon, J. "Counterfactuals and Hypothesis Testing in Political Science." *World Politics* 43 (1991): 169–195.

Gick, Mary L., and Keith J. Holyoak. "Analogical Problem Solving." *Cognitive Psychology* 12 (1980): 306–355.

Gick, Mary L., and Keith J. Holyoak. "Schema Induction and Analogical Transfer." *Cognitive Psychology* 15 (1983): 1–38.

Gilovich, Thomas. "Seeing the Past in the Present: The Effect of Associations to Familiar Events on Judgments and Decisions." *Journal of Personality and Social Psychology* 40, no. 5 (1981): 797–808.

Janis, Irving L. "Groupthink." *Psychology Today* (November 1971): 43–76.

March, James. "Bounded Rationality, Ambiguity, and Engineering Choice." *The Bell Journal of Economics* 9, no. 2 (autumn 1978): 590–592.

Read, Stephen J., and Ian L. Cesa. "This Reminds Me of the Time When . . . : Expectation Failures in Reminding and Explaining." *Journal of Experimental Social Psychology* 27 (1991): 1–25.

Schuman, Howard, and Cheryl Rieger. "Historical Analogies, Generational Effects, and Attitudes Toward War." *American Sociological Review* 57 (June 1992): 315–326.

Spellman, Barbara A., and Keith J. Holyoak. "If Saddam Is Hitler Then Who Is George Bush? Analogical Mapping Between Systems of Social Roles." *Journal of Personality and Social Psychology* 62, no. 6 (1992): 913–933.

Zashin, Elliot, and Phillip C. Chapman. "The Uses of Metaphor and Analogy: Toward a Renewal of Political Language." *Journal of Politics* 36, no. 2 (May 1974): 290–326.

Books

Baron, Jonathan. *Thinking and Deciding.* Cambridge: Cambridge University Press, 1988.

Bartlett, John. *Familiar Quotations.* Boston: Little, Brown and Co., 1980.

Bobrow, Daniel G. "Dimensions of Representation." In *Representation and Understanding: Studies in Cognitive Science,* edited by Daniel G. Bobrow and Allan Collins, pp. 1–34. New York: Academic Press, Inc., 1975.

Bonham, G. Mathew, and Michael J. Shapiro. "Thought and Action in Foreign Policy." In *Thought and Action in Foreign Policy,* edited by G. Mathew Bonham and Michael J. Shapiro, pp. 1–9. Stanford: Center for Advanced Studies in the Behavioral Sciences, 1977.

Cohen, Eliot A., and John Gooch. *Military Misfortunes: The Military Anatomy of Failure in War.* New York: Vintage Books, 1991.

Cook, Karen S., and Margaret Levi, eds. *The Limits of Rationality.* Chicago: University of Chicago Press, 1990.

Dallin, Alexander. "Learning in U.S. Policy Toward the Soviet Union in the 1980s." In *Learning in U.S. and Soviet Foreign Policy,* edited by George W. Breslauer and Philip E. Tetlock, pp. 400–428. Boulder: Westview Press, 1991.

Einhorn, Hillel J., and Hogarth, Robin M. "Decision Making under Ambiguity." In *Rational Choice: The Contrast Between Economics and Psychology,* edited by Robin M. Hogarth and Melvin W. Reder, pp. 41–66. Chicago: University of Chicago Press, 1987.

Fry, Michael G. "Introduction." In *History, The White House and the Kremlin: Statesmen as Historians,* edited by Michael G. Fry, pp. 1–19. London: Pinter Publishers, 1991.

Green, Donald P., and Ian Shapiro. *Pathologies of Rational Choice Theory: A Critique of Applications in Political Science.* New Haven: Yale University Press, 1994.

Haslam, Jonathan. "The Boundaries of Rational Calculation in Soviet Policy Towards Japan." In *History, The White House and the Kremlin: Statesmen as Historians,* edited by Michael G. Fry, pp. 38–50. London: Pinter Publishers, 1991.

Heclo, H. *A Government of Strangers: Executive Politics in Washington.* Washington, D.C.: Brookings Institution, 1977.

Henrikson, Alan. "Conclusion." In *History, The White House and the Kremlin: States-men as Historians*, edited by Michael G. Fry, pp. 239–266. London: Pinter Publishers, 1991.

Hoffman, Stanley. *Gulliver's Troubles, or the Setting of American Foreign Policy*. New York: McGraw-Hill, 1968.

Hogarth, Robin M., and Melvin W. Reder, eds. *Rational Choice: The Contrast Between Economics and Psychology*. Chicago: University in Chicago Press, 1987.

Holsti, Ole. "Foreign Policy Decision-makers Viewed Psychologically: Cognitive Processes Approaches." In *Thought and Action in Foreign Policy*, edited by G. Matthew Bonham and Michael J. Shapiro, pp. 10–74. Stanford: Center for Advanced Studies in the Behavioral Sciences, 1977.

Hybel, Alex R. *How Leaders Reason: U.S. Intervention in the Caribbean Basin and Latin America*. Cambridge: Basil Blackwell Inc., 1990.

———. "Learning and Reasoning by Analogy." In *History, The White House and the Kremlin: Statesmen as Historians*, edited by Michael G. Fry, pp. 215–238. London: Pinter Publishers, 1991.

Inoguichi, Takashi. "Wars as International Learning: Chinese, British and Japanese in East Asia." Ph.D. diss., Massachusetts Institute of Technology, Dept. of Political Science, 1974.

Jervis, Robert. *Perception and Misperception in International Politics*. Princeton: Princeton University Press, 1976.

Khong, Yuen Foong. *Analogies at War: Korea, Munich, Dien Bien Phu, and the Vietnam Decisions of 1965*. Princeton: Princeton University Press, 1992.

Kindleberger, Charles P. *The World in Depression 1919–1939*. Berkeley: University of California Press, 1973.

Kuhn, Thomas. *The Structure of Scientific Revolutions*. Chicago: University of Chicago Press, 1962.

Kunz, Diane B. "Being a Borrower: The Re-emergence of the United States as a Debtor Nation." In *History, The White House and the Kremlin: Statesmen as Historians*, edited by Michael G. Fry, pp. 123–136. London: Pinter Publishers, 1991.

Lakatos, Imre. "Falsification and the Methodology of Scientific Research Programmes." In *Criticism and the Growth of Knowledge*, edited by Imre Lakatos and Alan Musgrave, pp. 81–196. Cambridge: Cambridge University Press, 1970.

Larson, Deborah W. *The Origins of Containment: A Psychological Explanation*. Princeton: Princeton University Press, 1985.

Lewis, Lloyd. *Sherman: Fighting Prophet*. New York: Harcourt, Brace and Co., Inc., 1932.

McClellan, David S. *Dean Acheson: The State Department Years*. New York: Dodd, Mead and Co., 1976.

May, Ernest R. *"Lessons" of the Past: The Use and Misuse of History in American Foreign Policy*. New York: Oxford University Press, 1973.

Mefford, Dwain. "The Power of Historical Analogies: Soviet Interventions in Eastern Europe and US Interventions in Central America." In *History, The White House and the Kremlin: Statesmen as Historians*, edited by Michael G. Fry, pp. 185–214. London: Pinter Publishers, 1991.

Mercer, Jonathan. *Reputation and International Politics*. Discussion Paper #37. Los

Angeles: Center for International Studies, University of Southern California, 1993.

Neustadt, Richard E., and Ernest R. May. *Thinking in Time: The Uses of History for Decision-Makers.* New York: Free Press, 1986.

Odell, John S. *United States International Monetary Policy.* Princeton: Princeton University Press, 1982.

Schank, Roger C. *Dynamic Memory: A Theory of Reminding and Learning in Computers and People.* Cambridge: Cambridge University Press, 1982.

Schrodt, Philip A. "Adaptive Precedent-Based Logic and Rational Choice: A Comparison of Two Approaches to the Modelling of International Behavior." In *Dynamic Models of International Conflict,* edited by Urs Luterbacher and Michael D. Ward, pp. 373–400. Boulder: Lynne Reinner Publishers, 1985.

Simon, Herbert A. "Rationality in Psychology and Economics." In *Rational Choice: The Contrast Between Economics and Psychology,* edited by Robin M. Hogarth and Melvin W. Reder, pp. 25–40. Chicago: University of Chicago Press, 1987.

Stein, Janice Gross, and Raymond Tanter. *Rational Decision-Making: Israel's Security Choices, 1967.* Columbus: Ohio State University Press, 1980.

Sternberg, Robert J. *Intelligence, Information Processing, and Analogical Reasoning: The Componential Analysis of Human Abilities.* New York: Lawrence Erlbaum Association, 1977.

Tversky, Amos, and Daniel Kahneman. "Rational Choice and the Framing of Decisions." In *Rational Choice: The Contrast Between Economics and Psychology,* edited by Robin M. Hogarth and Melvin W. Reder, pp. 67–94. Chicago: University of Chicago Press, 1987.

Vertzberger, Yaacov Y. I. *The World in Their Minds: Information Processing, Cognition, and Perception in Foreign Policy Decisionmaking.* Stanford: Stanford University Press, 1990.

KOREA

Primary Sources

Harry S. Truman Library, Independence, Missouri

> Dean Acheson Papers
> Matthew J. Connelly Papers
> George M. Elsey Papers
> John B. Moullette Papers
> Frank Pace Jr. Papers
> Harry S. Truman Papers
> James E. Webb Papers
> President's Secretary's File (PSF)
>
> > Intelligence Files
> > Korean War File
> > Miscellaneous (1948)
> > NSC Meetings (Korea)

　　　　　Subject File, Cabinet, Secretary of State
　　　　　Subject File, Foreign Affairs
　　Naval Aide to the President Files
　　　　　Korea
　　Student Research File, B file, Korean War
White House Central Files
　　　　　Confidental File
　　　　　General File
　　　　　Official File
　　　　　President's Personal File
Karl R. Bendetsen Oral History
Robert L. Dennison Oral History
John J. Muccio Oral History
Richard G. Nixon Oral History
Frank Pace Jr. Oral History
Public Records Office, Kew, England
　　　　　Cabinet Conclusions (CAB)

Department of State Bulletin, 23, no. 576, (July 17, 1950). Washington, D.C.: Department of State, 1950.

Foreign and Commonwealth Office, *Documents on British Policy Overseas*, edited by H. J. Yasamee and K. A. Hamilton, Series II, Vol. IV. London: Her Majesty's Stationery Office, 1991.

Foreign Relations of the United States, 1950, Korea. Vol. III. Washington, D.C.: U.S. Government Printing Office, 1976.

Parliamentary Debates, Commons, 5th Series, vols. 476, 477. London: His Majesty's Stationery Office, 1950.

The Public Papers of the Presidents of the United States: Harry S. Truman, 1950. Washington, D.C.: U.S. Government Printing Office, 1965.

Books

Acheson, Dean. *Morning and Noon*. Boston: Houghton Mifflin Co., 1965.

———. *Present at the Creation: My Years in the State Department*. New York: Norton, 1969.

———. *Fragments of My Fleece*. New York: W. W. Norton, 1971.

Bohlen, Charles E. *Witness to History, 1929–1969*. New York: W. W. Norton and Co., 1973.

Farrar-Hockley, Anthony. *The British Part in the Korean War, Vol. I, A Distant Obligation*. London: Her Majesty's Stationery Office, 1990.

Ferrell, Robert. *Off the Record: The Private Papers of Harry S. Truman*. New York: Harper & Row, 1980.

McClellan, David S., and David C. Acheson. *Among Friends: Personal Letters of Dean Acheson*. New York: Dodd, Mead and Co., 1980.

Macmillan, Harold. *Tides of Fortune, 1945–1955*. New York: Harper & Row, 1969.

Truman, Harry S. *Memoirs*. Vols. I and II. Garden City, N.Y.: Doubleday, 1956.

Truman, Margaret. *Margaret Truman's Own Story: Souvenir.* New York: McGraw-Hill, 1956.
Williams, Francis. *A Prime Minister Remembers.* London: Heinemann, 1961.

Secondary Sources

Books

Baldwin, Frank. *Without Parallel: The American-Korean Relationship Since 1945.* New York: Pantheon Books, 1974.
Boyle, Peter G. "Oliver Franks and the Washington Embassy, 1945–1952." In *Officials and British Foreign Policy, 1945–1950,* edited by John Zametica, pp. 189–211. Leicester: Leicester University Press, 1990.
Brookshire, Jerry H. *Clement Attlee.* Manchester: Manchester University Press, 1995.
Bullock, Alan. *The Life and Times of Ernest Bevin, Vol. I, Trade Union Leader 1881–1940.* London: Heinemann, 1960.
———. *The Life and Times of Ernest Bevin, Vol. II, Minister of Labour, 1940–1945.* London: Heinemann, 1967.
———. *The Life and Times of Ernest Bevin, Vol. III, Foreign Secretary, 1945–1951.* London: Heinemann, 1983.
Burridge, Trevor. *Clement Attlee: A Political Biography.* London: Jonathan Cape, 1985.
Cochran, Bert. *Harry Truman and the Crisis Presidency.* New York: Funk and Wagnalls, 1973.
Cumings, Bruce. *The Origins of the Korean War, Vol. II, The Roaring of the Cataract 1947–1950.* Princeton: Princeton University Press, 1990.
Ferrell, Robert H. *Harry S. Truman: A Life.* Columbia: University of Missouri Press, 1994.
Foot, Rosemary. *The Wrong War: American Policy and the Dimensions of the Korean Conflict 1950–1953.* Ithaca, N.Y.: Cornell University Press, 1985.
Hamby, Alonzo L. *Man of the People: A Life of Harry S. Truman.* New York: Oxford University Press, 1995.
Harper, John Lamberton. *American Visions of Europe: Franklin D. Roosevelt, George F. Kennan, and Dean G. Acheson.* Cambridge: Cambridge University Press, 1994.
Harris, Kenneth. *Attlee.* London: Weidenfeld and Nicolson, 1982.
Hastings, Max. *The Korean War.* New York: Simon and Schuster, 1987.
Kaufman, Burton I. *The Korean War: Challenge in Crisis, Credibility, and Command.* Philadelphia: Temple University Press, 1986.
Lowe, Peter. *The Origins of the Korean War.* London: Longman, 1986.
———. "The Frustrations of Alliance: Britain, the United States, and the Korean War, 1950–1951." In *The Korean War in History,* edited by James Cotton and Ian Neary, pp. 80–99. Atlantic Highlands, N.J.: Humanities Press International, 1989.
———. "The Significance of the Korean War in Anglo-American Relations, 1950–1953." In *British Foreign Policy, 1945–1956,* edited by Michael Dockrill and John Young, pp. 126–148. London: Macmillan, 1989.
McClullough, David. *Truman.* New York: Simon and Schuster, 1992.

Macdonald, Callum. *Korea: The War Before Vietnam*. New York: Free Press, 1986.
————. *Britain and the Korean War*. Oxford: Basil Blackwell, 1989.
McGibbon, Ian C. *New Zealand and the Korean War, Vol. I, Politics and Diplomacy*. Aukland: Oxford University Press, 1992.
McGlothlen, Ronald L. *Controlling the Waves: Dean Acheson and U.S. Foreign Policy in Asia*. New York: Norton and Co., 1993.
Morgan, Kenneth O. *Labour in Power 1945–1951*. Oxford: Clarendon Press, 1984.
————. *The People's Peace: British History 1945–1989*. Oxford: Oxford University Press, 1990.
Ovendale, Ritchie. "Britain and the Cold War in Asia." In *The Foreign Policy of the British Labour Governments, 1945–1951*, edited by Ritchie Ovendale, pp. 121–148. Leicester: Leicester University Press, 1984.
Paige, Glenn D. *The Korean Decision: June 24–30, 1950*. New York: Free Press, 1968.
Pearce, Robert. *Attlee's Labour Governments 1945–1951*. London: Routledge, 1994.
Pelling, Henry. *The Labour Governments, 1945–1951*. New York: St. Martin's Press, 1984.
Pelz, Stephen. "U.S. Decisions on Korean Policy." In *Child of Conflict The Korean-American Relationship, 1943–1953*, edited by Bruce Cumings, pp. 93–132. Seattle: University of Washington Press, 1983.
Pruessen, Ronald W. *John Foster Dulles: The Road to Power*. New York: Free Press, 1982.
Rees, David. *Korea: The Limited War*. Baltimore: Penguin, 1970.
Sanders, David. *Losing an Empire, Finding a Role: An Introduction to British Foreign Policy Since 1945*. New York: St. Martin's Press, 1989.
Stueck, William. *The Korean War: An International History*. Princeton: Princeton University Press, 1995.
Sunoo, Harold H. *America's Dilemma in Asia: The Case of South Korea*. Chicago: Nelson-Hall, 1979.
Weiler, Peter. *Ernest Bevin*. Manchester: Manchester University Press, 1993.
Williams, Francis. *Twilight of Empire: Memoirs of Prime Minister Clement Attlee*. Westport, Conn.: Greenwood Press, 1978.

IRAN

For a discussion of the U.S. government's failure to release key documents relating to Iran for 1951–53, see James F. Goode, *The United States and Iran, 1946–1951* (New York: St. Martin's Press, 1989), pp. 145–155; Moyara De Moraes Ruehsen, "Operation 'Ajax' Revisited: Iran, 1953," *Middle Eastern Studies* 29, no. 3 (July 1993): 467; and William Roger Louis, "Musaddiq and the Dilemmas of British Imperialism," *Mussaddiq, Iranian Nationalism and Oil*, edited by James A. Bill and William Roger Louis (Austin: University of Texas Press, 1988), pp. 248–249. Declassification of materials since 1949 has been slowed since the 1979 Iranian revolution. Many boxes of documents at the Truman and Eisenhower Libraries on Iran between 1950–53 contain only a few, thin files, or have been so censored that only a few lines remain. Some of the holes can be filled from memoirs and British archives.

Primary Sources

Dwight David Eisenhower Library, Abilene, Kansas

Dwight D. Eisenhower Papers as President

Ann Whitman File (AWF)

Diary Series
Dulles-Herter Series
International Series
NSC Series

Dwight D. Eisenhower Records as President, White House Central Files

Confidential File
General File
Official File

John F. Dulles (JFD) Papers

Chronological Series
General Correspondence and Memoranda Series
Special Assistants Chronological Series
Subject Series
Telephone Conversations Series
White House Memoranda Series

White House Office, Office of the Special Assistant for National Security
Affairs (OSANSA), Records

NSC Series, Briefing Notes Subseries
NSC Series, Policy Papers Subseries
NSC Series, Status of Projects Subseries

White House Office, Office of the Staff Secretary, Records

International Series
Subject Series, Alphabetical Subseries

Dwight D. Eisenhower Oral History
Andrew J. Goodpaster Oral History
Bryce N. Harlow Oral History
Ann C. Whitman Oral History

Harry S. Truman Library, Independence, Missouri

NSC Files
Dean Acheson Papers

Memos of Conversations

George M. Elsey Papers
Henry F. Grady Papers
Charles S. Murphy Papers
Charles W. Thayer Papers

James E. Webb Papers
President's Secretary's Papers (PSF)

    Intelligence Files
    Subject File, Box 180, Iran
    Subject File, Cabinet, Secretary of State
    Subject File, Foreign Affairs
Records of the NSC, CIA Intelligence Memos, 1948–51
Staff Member and Office Files
State Department Correspondence, re: Mossadegh
White House Central Files

    Confidential File
    General File
    Official File
    President's Personal File

Lucius Battle Oral History
Henry Bryoade Oral History
Matthew J. Connelly Oral History
Robert L. Dennison Oral History
Loy Henderson Oral History
George C. McGhee Oral History
John H. Muccio Oral History
John B. Moullette Oral History
Charles S. Murphy Oral History
Robert G. Nixon Oral History
John E. O'Gara Oral History
Frank Pace Jr. Oral History

Books

Eden, Anthony. *Full Circle*. Boston: Houghton Mifflin, 1960.
Eisenhower, Dwight D. *The White House Years, Mandate for Change: 1953–1956*. Garden City, N.Y.: Doubleday and Co., 1963.
Eisenhower, Dwight D. *At Ease: Stories I Tell My Friends*. 1967; reprint Blue Ridge Summit, Pa.: TAB Books, 1988.
Ferrell, Robert H. *The Eisenhower Diaries*. New York: W. W. Norton, 1981.
Parliamentary Debates, Commons, 5th series, vols. 486, 489, 491, 494. London: His Majesty's Stationery Office, 1951, 1952, 1953.
The Public Papers of the Presidents of the United States: Dwight D. Eisenhower, 1953. Washington, D.C.: U.S. Government Printing Office, 1960.
The Public Papers of the Presidents of the United States: Harry S. Truman, 1951. Washington, D.C.: U.S. Government Printing Office, 1965.
The Public Papers of the Presidents of the United States: Harry S. Truman, 1952–3. Washington, D.C.: U.S. Government Printing Office, 1966.
Roosevelt, Kermit. *Countercoup: The Struggle for Control of Iran*. New York: McGraw-Hill, 1979.
Woodhouse, C. M. *Something Ventured*. London: Granada Books, 1982.

Secondary Sources

Articles

Ruehsen, Moyara De Moraes. "Operation 'Ajax' Revisited: Iran, 1953." *Middle Eastern Studies* 29, no. 3 (July 1993): 467–486.

Books

Abrahamian, Ervand. *Iran Between Two Revolutions.* Princeton: Princeton University Press, 1982.

Ambrose, Stephen E. *Ike's Spies: Eisenhower and the Espionage Establishment.* Garden City, N.Y.: Doubleday and Co., 1981.

————. *Eisenhower: The President.* New York: Simon and Schuster, 1984.

Ashley, Maurice. *Churchill as Historian.* New York: Charles Scribner's Sons, 1969.

Bill, James A. *The Eagle and the Lion: The Tragedy of American-Iranian Relations.* New Haven, Conn.: Yale University Press, 1988.

Bill, James A., and William Roger Louis. "Introduction." In *Mussaddiq, Iranian Nationalism and Oil,* edited by James A. Bill and William Roger Louis, pp. 1–19. Austin: University of Texas Press, 1988.

Cable, James. *Intervention at Abadan, Plan Buccaneer.* New York: St. Martin's Press, 1991.

Diba, Farhad. *Mohammad Mossadegh: A Political Biography.* London: Croom Helm, 1986.

Ferrier, Ronald W. "The Anglo-Iranian Oil Dispute: A Triangular Relationship." In *Mussaddiq, Iranian Nationalism and Oil,* edited by James A. Bill and William Roger Louis, pp. 164–199. Austin: University of Texas Press, 1988.

Gasiorowski, Mark J. *U.S. Foreign Policy and the Shah: Building a Client State in Iran.* Ithaca, N.Y.: Cornell University Press, 1991.

Gilbert, Martin. *Churchill: A Life.* New York: Henry Holt and Co., 1991.

Goode, James F. *The United States and Iran, 1946–1951: The Diplomacy of Neglect.* New York: St. Martin's Press, 1989.

Griffin, Charles J. G. "New Light on Eisenhower's Farewell Address." In *Eisenhower's War of Words: Rhetoric and Leadership,* edited by Martin J. Medhurst, pp. 273–284. East Lansing: Michigan State University Press, 1994.

Heikal, Mohamed Hassanein. *The Return of the Ayatollah: The Iranian Revolution from Mossadeq to Khomeini.* London: Andre Deutsch, 1981.

Hersh, Burton. *The Old Boys: The American Elite and the Origins of the CIA.* New York: Charles Scribner's Sons, 1992.

Hogan, J. Michael. "Eisenhower and Open Skies: A Case in 'Psychological Warfare' ". In *Eisenhower's War of Words: Rhetoric and Leadership,* edited by Martin J. Medhurst, pp. 137–155. East Lansing: Michigan State University Press, 1994.

Hourani, Albert. "Conclusion." In *Mussaddiq, Iranian Nationalism and Oil,* edited by James A. Bill and William Roger Louis, pp. 329–340. Austin: University of Texas Press, 1988.

Katouzian, Homa. *Musaddiq and the Struggle for Power in Iran.* London: I. B. Tauris and Co., 1990.

Louis, William Roger. "Mussaddiq and the Dilemmas of British Imperialism." In

Mussaddiq, Iranian Nationalism and Oil, edited by James A. Bill and William Roger Louis, pp. 228–260. Austin: University of Texas Press, 1988.

Lyon, Peter. *Eisenhower: Portrait of a Hero*. Boston: Little, Brown & Co., 1974.

Lytle, Mark Hamilton. *The Origins of the Iranian-American Alliance 1941–1953*. New York: Holmes & Meier, 1987.

Medhurst, Martin J. "Eisenhower's Rhetorical Leadership: An Interpretation." In *Eisenhower's War of Words: Rhetoric and Leadership*, edited by Martin J. Medhurst, pp. 287–297. East Lansing: Michigan State University Press, 1994.

———. *Eisenhower's War of Words: Rhetoric and Leadership*. East Lansing: Michigan State University Press, 1994.

Miyasato, Seigen. "John F. Dulles and the Peace Settlement with Japan." In *John Foster Dulles and the Diplomacy of the Cold War*, edited by Richard Immerman, pp. 189–212. Princeton, NJ: Princeton University Press, 1990.

Mosley, Leonard. *Power Play: Oil in the Middle East*. Baltimore: Penguin Books, 1974.

Northedge, F. S. "Britain and the Middle East." In *The Foreign Policy of the British Labour Governments, 1945–1951*, edited by Ritchie Ovendale, pp. 149–180. Leicester: Leicester University Press, 1984.

Olson, Gregory. "Eisenhower and the Indochina Problem." In *Eisenhower's War of Words: Rhetoric and Leadership*, edited by Martin J. Medhurst, pp. 97–135. East Lansing: Michigan State University Press, 1994.

Painter, David S. *The United States, Great Britain, and Mossadegh*, PEW Case Study 332A and 332B. Washington, D.C.: Georgetown University, PEW Case Study Center, 1993.

Ramazani, Rouhallah. *Iran's Foreign Policy, 1941–1973: A Study of Foreign Policy in Modernizing Nations*. Charlottesville: University of Virginia Press, 1975.

Rubin, Barry. *Paved with Good Intentions: The American Experience in Iran*. New York: Penguin Books, 1981.

Sampson, Anthony. *The Seven Sisters: The Great Oil Companies and the World They Shaped*. New York: Viking, 1975.

Schaefermeyer, Mark J. "Dulles and Eisenhower on 'Massive Retaliation.' " In *Eisenhower's War of Words: Rhetoric and Leadership*, edited by Martin J. Medhurst, pp. 27–45. East Lansing: Michigan State University Press, 1994.

Toulouse, Mark G. *The Transformation of John Foster Dulles from Prophet of Realism to Priest of Nationalism*. Macon, Ga.: Mercer University Press, 1985.

SUEZ

American and British government documents relating to the Suez crisis between July 26 and November 7, 1956, were analyzed. To analyze the public use of analogies, *The Department of State Bulletin* from July 26, 1956 (vol. 35, no. 892) to December 17, 1956 (vol. 35, no. 912) was also analyzed, as were Eisenhower's *The Public Papers of the Presidents of the United States* for the year 1956. The major debates in the House of Commons were also analyzed.

PRIMARY SOURCES

Dwight David Eisenhower Library, Abilene, Kansas

John F. Dulles Papers

Chronological Series
General Correspondence and Memoranda Series
White House Memoranda Series, Subject Series

Dwight D. Eisenhower Papers as President

Ann C. Whitman File

Diary Series
Dulles-Herter Series
International Series
Legislative Meeting Series
NSC Series

Office of the Special Assistant for National Security Affairs

Chronological Subject Series
Special Assistant Series

Dillon Anderson Oral History
Eugene Black Oral History
Andrew J. Goodpaster Oral History
James Haggerty Oral History

Public Records Office, Kew, U.K.

Cabinet Meeting Minutes, Prime Minister's Office (PREM 11/1094, 11/1100, 11/1103)

Books

Eisenhower, Dwight D. *The White House Years, Waging Peace, 1956–1961*. Garden City, N.Y.: Doubleday, 1965.

Macmillan, Harold. *Riding the Storm, 1956–1959*. London: Macmillan, 1971.

Nutting, Anthony. *Nasser*. New York: E. P. Dutton and Co., 1972.

The Public Papers of the Presidents of the United States: Dwight D. Eisenhower, 1956. Washington, D.C.: U.S. Government Printing Office, 1958.

United Nations. *Official Records of the General Assembly*, 11th Session, Plenary Meetings, vol. I, 1956–57. New York: United Nations, 1956, 1957.

———. *Security Council Official Records*, 11th Year, Supplement for October, November and December, 1956. New York: United Nations, 1956.

Secondary Sources

Articles

Ashton, Nigel. "Macmillan and the Middle East." In *Harold Macmillan and Britain's World Role*, edited by Richard Aldous and Sabine Lee, pp. 37–65. London: Macmillan Press, 1996.

Orbovich, Cynthia Biddle. "The Influence of Cognitive Style on National Security Decision Making: A Look at the Eisenhower Administration." Paper Presented at the 27th Annual Meeting of the International Studies Association, March 25–29, 1986, Orange County, Calif.

Thorton, A. P. "The Trouble with Cousins." *International Journal* 34, no. 2 (spring 1979): 281–286.

Books

Aldous, Richard. " 'A Family Affair': Macmillan and the Art of Personal Diplomacy." In *Harold Macmillan and Britain's World Role*, edited by Richard Aldous and Sabine Lee, pp. 9–35. London: Macmillan Press, 1996.

Aster, Sidney. *Anthony Eden*. New York: St. Martin's Press, 1976.

Calvocoressi, Peter. "Egyptian Outlook." In *Suez: Ten Years Later*, edited by Anthony Moncrieff, pp. 34–58. New York: Pantheon Books, 1967.

Heikal, Mohamed Hassanein. *The Cairo Documents*. Garden City, N.Y.: Doubleday and Co., 1973.

James, Robert R. "Harold Macmillan: An Introduction." In *Harold Macmillan and Britain's World Role*, edited by Richard Aldous and Sabine Lee, pp. 1–7. London: Macmillan Press, 1996.

Kyle, Keith. *Suez*. New York: St. Martin's Press, 1991.

Rothwell, Victor. *Anthony Eden: A Political Biography 1931–1957*. Manchester: Manchester University Press, 1992.

Taylor, A.J.P. "Introduction." In *Anthony Eden*, edited by Sydney Aster. New York: St. Martin's Press, 1976.

Wyllie, James H. *The Influence of British Arms: An Analysis of British Military Intervention Since 1956*. Boston: Allen & Unwin, 1984.

LEBANON/JORDAN

Some of the key documents are blacked out and notes were not taken at a crucial meeting on July 14, 1958. For example, see NSC Meeting, June 19, 1958, DDE Papers as President, AWF, NSC Series, Box 10; Memo, Discussion at the 370th Meeting of the NSC, June 27, 1958, DDE Papers as President, AWF, NSC Series, Box 10: 370th NSC Meeting; and Special NSC Meeting, July 14, 1958, "No Memorandum," DDE Papers as President, AWF, NSC Series, Box 10.

Primary Sources

Dwight David Eisenhower Library, Abilene, Kansas

John F. Dulles Papers

Chronological Series
General Correspondence and Memoranda Series
Telephone Series
White House Memoramda Series

Dwight D. Eisenhower Papers as President

Ann C. Whitman File
   Diary Series
   International Series
   NSC Series
Dwight D. Eisenhower Oral History
Andrew J. Goodpaster Oral History
Ann C. Whitman Oral History

Books

Eisenhower, Dwight D. *The White House Years, Waging Peace, 1956–1961*. Garden City, N.Y.: Doubleday & Co., 1965.
Foreign Relations of the United States, 1958–1960, Lebanon and Jordan. Vol. XI. Washington, D.C.: U.S. Government Printing Office, 1992.
Hughes, Emmet John. *The Ordeal of Power: A Political Memoir of the Eisenhower Years*. New York: Atheneum, 1963.
Murphy, Robert. *Diplomat Among Warriors*. New York: Pyramid Books, 1965.
Parliamentary Debates, Commons, 5th Series, vols. 587 to 592. London: His Majesty's Stationery Office, 1958.
The Public Papers of the Presidents of the United States: Dwight D. Eisenhower, 1958. Washington, D.C.: U.S. Government Printing Office, 1959.
Thayer, Charles W. *Diplomat*. New York: Harper, 1959.

Secondary Sources

Articles

Fry, Michael G. "The Uses of Intelligence: The United Nations Confronts the United States in the Lebanon Crisis, 1958." *Intelligence and National Security* 10, no.1 (January 1995): 59–95.
Ovendale, Ritchie. "Great Britain and the Anglo-American Invasion of Jordan and Lebanon in 1958." In *The International History Review* 16, no. 2 (May 1994): 284–303.

Books

Aldous, Richard, and Sabine Lee, eds. *Harold Macmillan and Britain's World Role*. London: Macmillan Press, 1996.
Alin, Erika G. "*The 1958 United States Intervention in Lebanon*." Ph.D. Diss., Washington: American University, 1990.
Ashton, Nigel. "Macmillan and the Middle East." In *Harold Macmillan and Britain's World Role*, edited by Richard Aldous and Sabine Lee, pp. 37–65. London: Macmillan Press, 1996.
Fisher, Nigel. *Harold Macmillan*. New York: St. Martin's Press, 1982.
Goria, Wade R. *Sovereignty and Leadership in Lebanon 1943–1976*. London: Ithaca Press, 1985.
Horne, Alistair. *Harold Macmillan, Vol. I, 1894–1956*. New York: Viking, 1989.
———. *Harold Macmillan, Vol. II, 1957–1986*. New York: Viking, 1989.

Korbani, Agnes G. *U.S. Intervention in Lebanon, 1958 and 1982: Presidential Deci-sionmaking.* New York: Praeger, 1991.

Lamb, Richard. *The Macmillan Years, 1957–1963.* London: John Murray, 1995.

Meo, Leila M. T. *Lebanon: Improbable Nation, A Study in Political Development.* Bloomington: Indiana University Press, 1965.

Qubain, Fahim I. *Crisis in Lebanon.* Washington, D.C.: The Middle East Institute, 1961.

Thorpe, D. R. *Selwyn Lloyd.* London: Jonathan Cape, 1989.

LEARNING

Articles

Levy, Jack S. "Learning and Foreign Policy: Sweeping a Conceptual Minefield." *International Organization* 48, no. 2 (spring 1994): 279–312.

Roncolato, Gerard D. "Chance Dominates in War." *U.S. Naval Institute Proceedings* 121, no. 2 (Feb. 1995): 36–39.

Tetlock, Philip E. "Is It a Bad Idea to Study Good Judgment?" *Political Psychology* 13, no. 3 (September 1992): 429–434.

———. "Good Judgment in International Politics: Three Psychological Perspec-tives." *Political Psychology* 13, no. 3 (September 1992): 517–539.

Books

Breslauer, George W. "What Have We Learned About Learning?" In *Learning in U.S. and Soviet Foreign Policy*, edited by George W. Breslauer and Philip E. Tetlock, pp. 825–856. Boulder: Westview Press, 1991.

Breslauer, George W., and Philip E. Tetlock. "Introduction." In *Learning in U.S. and Soviet Foreign Policy*, edited by George W. Breslauer and Philip E. Tet-lock, pp. 3–19. Boulder: Westview Press, 1991.

Etheredge, Lloyd S. *Can Governments Learn? American Foreign Policy and Central American Revolutions.* New York: Pergamon Press, 1985.

Gleick, James. *Chaos, Making a New Science.* New York: Viking, 1987.

Kaplan, Fred. *The Wizards of Armageddon.* New York: Simon and Schuster, 1983.

Larson, Deborah W. "Learning in U.S.–Soviet Relations: The Nixon-Kissinger Struc-ture of Peace." In *Learning in U.S. and Soviet Foreign Policy*, edited by George W. Breslauer and Philip E. Tetlock, pp. 350–399. Boulder: Westview Press, 1991.

Pagels, Heinz R. *The Dreams of Reason: The Computer and the Rise of the Sciences of Complexity.* New York: Simon and Schuster, 1988.

Ravenal, Earl C. *Never Again: Learning from America's Foreign Policy Failures.* Phil-adelphia: Temple University Press, 1978.

Snyder, Jack. *Myths of Empire: Domestic Politics and International Ambition.* Ithaca, N.Y.: Cornell University Press, 1991.

Tetlock, Philip E. "Learning in U.S. and Soviet Foreign Policy: In Search of an Elusive Concept." In *Learning in U.S. and Soviet Foreign Policy*, edited by

George W. Breslauer and Philip E. Tetlock, pp. 20–61. Boulder: Westview Press, 1991.

Woodcock, Alexander, and Monte Davis. *Catastrophe Theory*. New York: E. P. Dutton, 1978.

Index

Subentries are in chronological rather than alphabetical order.

About the Author

SCOT MACDONALD has taught at the University of Southern California and Occidental College and has guest lectured at the University of Nevada and at California State University, San Bernardino. His articles have appeared in the U.S. Naval Institute *Proceedings*, the U.S. Marine Corps *Gazette*, and the *Fletcher Forum of International Affairs*. His research has focused on the use of military force in regional contingencies.

ISBN 0-313-31421-7

EAN

9 780313 314216

HARDCOVER BAR CODE